CISTERCIAN STUDIES SERIES: NUMBER ONE HUNDRED FIFTY-TWO

Stones Laid Before the Lord
A History of Monastic Architecture

by

Anselme Dimier

CISTERCIAN STUDIES SERIES: NUMBER ONE HUNDRED FIFTY-TWO

Stones Laid Before the Lord

A History of Monastic Architecture

by

Anselme Dimier, OCSO

Translated from the French by

Gilchrist Lavigne, OCSO

Cistercian Publications
Kalamazoo, Michigan — Spencer, Massachusetts

© Copyright, Translation, Cistercian Publications Inc. 1999
Translated from *Les Moines Batisseurs*
Paris: Librairie Arthème Fayard, 1964
with revisions supplied by the author.

Available from

Cistercian Publications (Distribution)
Saint Joseph's Abbey
167 North Spencer Road
Spencer MA 01562–1233

Cistercian Publications (UK)
Mount Saint Bernard Abbey
Coalville, Leicester LE67 5UL

Cistercian Publications (Editorial Offices)
The Institute of Cistercian Studies
Western Michigan University
Kalamazoo 49008

The work of Cistercian Publications is made possible in part
by support from Western Michigan University to
The Institute of Cistercian Studies

Library of Congress Cataloguing in
Publication data available on request.

Typeset by Bookcomp, Grand Rapids, Michigan
Printed in the United States of America

TABLE OF CONTENTS

FOREWORD

AMONG THE MANY MONUMENTS which witness eloquently to the past, which we are fond of recalling and re-animating, those belonging to monastic architecture have generally been neglected. Perhaps the reason for this lies in the fact that, aside from the few well-known monasteries which have been high-spots of Christianity or places of celebrated pilgrimage—and are for this reason easily accessible—most monasteries are located in places which, until the advent of the automobile, only professional archaeologists had the courage to explore. Aside from the great monasteries everyone knows at least by name—Mont Saint-Michel, the Grande Chartreuse, Westminster Abbey, Our Lady of Einsiedeln, the Charterhouse of Pavia, Mount Athos, the Escorial, and Montserrat—there exists a sizeable number of monasteries, both large and small, which are ignored by the general public because of their isolation from main roads.

In the first centuries of Christianity—and even before the coming of Christ, if we take into consideration the desert community at Qumran excavations—there were men who chose to withdraw from the world's noise to devote themselves more easily to prayer and seeking God, men soon to be followed by women who often outstripped them in their austerity, mortification, and the fervor of their lives.

The often impressive remains of these monastic buildings bear witness to this timeless and ubiquitous quest for God. Europe was dotted with so many monasteries that in spite of the wars and revolutions which destroyed many of them, a good number still escaped destruction. At every turn and on every road we discover abbeys, sometimes perched on high rocks, sometimes buried at the bottom of a deserted valley, and other times hidden away in dense thick forests. The most interesting of these buildings date back to the Middle Ages, the richest monastic epoch. The Cluniac monk Raoul Glaber tells us in his *Histories* that in the early years of the eleventh century churches were being rebuilt over most of the world, but principally in Italy and Gaul. And he adds, 'It was as if the entire world had shaken off its rags to clothe itself with a new white mantle of churches. The faithful rebuilt nearly all the cathedrals as well as monasteries and even small village churches.' To appreciate this movement and people's enthusiasm for building new churches, we need to read a letter written in 1145 by Abbot Aimon of Saint-Pierre-sur-Dives—not far from Séez in Normandy—to the religious of Tutbury Priory in Staffordshire, England, a dependent house of his abbey. He recounts the reconstruction of his church:

> Try to imagine kings, princes and nobles, submitting themselves like beasts of burden to pull wagons and drag loads of wine, wheat, oil, limestone, rocks, wood, and all else necessary to the building of churches for Christ. And although there were a thousand men and women harnessed to each cart—so large and heavy was the load they were bearing—all walked in such silence that we heard no voice, not even a whisper, to a point that if we had not seen it with our own eyes, we would never have believed that the crowd was so large.

Of all these monasteries, a few have remained almost intact and are still occupied by monks. Others are inhabited by new owners and are so perfectly maintained that the monks could resume the common life overnight without being in the least disoriented, taking up once again the life of prayer and the quest for God interrupted for centuries. Other monasteries are inhabited by solitaries of a different sort. Clairvaux, for example, has been transformed into a prison and Prémontré to an insane asylum. Many monasteries are no more than ruins and yet their misshapen and lamentable stumps are imposing as they tower against the sky. Restored ruins are maintained and kept up for tourists who come in droves because these are one of those sights which 'must be seen'. Many visitors feel obliged to inscribe their names on these venerable stones to leave some trace of their visit. To these 'monomaniacs of graffiti' (as André Hallays stigmatized them) Victor Hugo addressed an avenging verse sketched on the walls of the Abbey of Villers-en-Brabant near Brussels, when he visited it in 1862 during his exile. True to his style, he took the three words by which Caesar announced his rapid victory at the Rubicon and wrote:

I HAVE COME, I HAVE SEEN, I HAVE CONQUERED
Oh fops! Stupid upstarts! Oh paltry brood,
Why bring you here your foolish ignorance and your vanity,
Cease spurning this admirable ruin,
Slobbering it with your names, which like vermine, defile
    its majesty.

At some monasteries, only a few stones remain, hidden in lush envelopping vegetation, unknown except to rare archaeologists who sometimes find finely sculptured capitals from the hand of some anonymous monk who put his whole heart into it purely for the love of God.

Finally, there are sites which retain no trace of their former use. Abandoned for centuries, the buildings have gradually fallen into ruin. Nature has reclaimed them. People have treated them as quarries of stones for their own buildings. To cite the words Lucan in the *Pharsalis* gave to Caesar beholding the site of Troy: *Etiam periere ruinae*, 'Even the ruins have perished'. This has been the fate of a large number of monasteries, not to mention those which have—incredibly—been moved far from their place of origin. Many monasteries have been dismantled and sold this way. Henri-Paul Eydoux in his tragically stirring book on the dead cities and desolate places in France, recalls how the benedictine cloisters of Saint-Guilhelm-du-Desert in Languedoc, Saint-Michel de Cuxa in Roussillon, and Trie in Gascony were shipped to America, as was the cloister of Bonnefont in Comminges and the chapter room of Pontaut in Gascony—both cistercian abbeys—to be reassembled in the famous Cloisters Museum in New York. An entire monastery, except for the church, was crated and shipped across the ocean. The cistercian abbey of Sacramenia, founded in the twelfth century in Old Castile not far from Segovia, was bought by American wealth in 1920 and the buildings were taken apart stone by stone. The 35,874 stones—carefully numbered and classified by category—were wrapped in straw. No less than 10, 751 crates were needed and these were moved by truck to the closest port, where they were loaded for America. On their arrival—and here the story becomes incredible—after inspection by the department of agriculture, the cases were put into quarantine for fear the straw used in the packing was contaminated. An order was given to unpack the cases on the spot and to burn all the straw. Imagine what the operation required and the number of workmen needed to carry it off. That's not all. It all had to be repacked then. This took three years. To make matters worse, the owner died. Finally, after great difficulty, a buyer was found who shipped the cases to Miami. But there it was discovered that all the stones—originally so carefully numbered and classified—had been repacked pell-mell in New York and were now in complete disorder. The identification of the 35,874 stones posed a dreadful gigantic puzzle. After more than ten months, the buildings were somehow reassembled. Now one has to travel as far as Florida to visit the castilian monastery of Sacramenia.[1]

Even if the last stones of a monastery have disappeared and no trace reveals its site, place names have remained through the centuries as a memorial to the monks who once lived there. These are found in every country. In France alone, Moûtier, Mostier, Monasatier, Monêtier and the various other forms are derived from the latin *monasterium*, monastery. Sometimes these are combined with other names like Vimoutier, Noirmoutier, Faremoutiers, Marmoutier, Montiéramey. Names like Montreuil, Montreux, Montereau, Menestrol, Menetou, are derived from the diminutive, *monasteriolum*, small monastery. The same is true of places like la Celle, la Cellette, la Celle-Saint-Cloud, Celle-Dunoise, Cellefrouin, which indicate a small monastery or *cella*. Abbie, Abadie, les Abadies, Abiette, the Abeyette, the Biette, or le Prieuré, le Priorat reveal the former existence of an abbey or priory. The list of names is endless. Even in cities where the municipality has had the good taste to retain the names of streets and places of historic interest, we often find names recalling some vanished convent or a lodging used for business purposes by a large abbey. The Boulevard Port-Royal in Paris is named after the famous abbey whose church is still used as a chapel for a maternity hospital there.

Rue de Cîteaux, which runs alongside Saint Anthony's Hospital, recalls the large abbey of cistercian nuns. The rue des Bernardines in the Saint Bernard district runs by the last existing building of the fourteenth-century College of Saint Bernard, built for cistercian students, and later transformed into a firehouse. Rue du Clairvaux, which overlooks rue Saint-Martin not far from the famous Quincampoixs, marks the site of a house owned by the great abbey in Champagne. There is the rue Blanc-Manteaux, once the site of the convent of the Servants of Mary, who dressed in white. Nonnains d'Yerres street recalls the Benedictines of Yerres Abbey, near Corbeil, who had a house in the area. There are also other streets: Filles-du-Calvaire Street, Mathurins (or Trinitaires) Street, Capuchin Boulevard, Feuillantines Street (where Victor Hugo lived), Ursuline Street not far away, Temple Street, Chartreux Street, and many others.

Both in time and space monastic architecture is an huge topic requiring a series of volumes. Within the limits of this small book we can give only a simple fragmentary sketch attempting to show how monastic architecture occupies a very special and unique place distinct from all other branches of architecture. Buildings erected for secular, religious, or military purposes shelter people for only a part of their lives. Monastic buildings, on the other hand, constituted the monk's permanent home for his entire life. The monk's whole day and his entire life flow into the monastery as into a sort of mold. Everything jells together. This is so true that we can say that a monk outside his monastery is an exception. This is what the old spiritual writers meant when they likened a monk outside his monastery to a fish out of water. The monastery, wrote Saint Benedict, the patriarch of Western Monks, is the workshop where the monk learns the spiritual craft. He is bound to his monastery to such a degree that Benedict, in designating cenobites used an expression which is hard to translate: These monks are the *genus monasteriale*—the monastery-kind—and Benedict considered them the strongest kind of monk. This is the main reason monasteries have a peculiar characteristic we find nowhere else. Everything necessary to the life of body and soul is brought together into a compact whole, arranged according to a fixed order, the fruit of long experience.

The spirituality of each religious order imprints its own mark on the stone. The monk—as well as the nun, whose enclosure is much stricter—is bound to his or her monastery, which becomes the whole horizon. If buildings bear the imprint of the order's spirituality, then the stone monastery, and consequently its architecture, cannot fail to exercise an influence on those living there. Imperceptible as it may seem, this influence is profound. The following pages will develop and expand all this.

NOTE

1. [Father Dimier neglects to mention the parallel case of the monastery of La Oliva, also imported by William Randolph Hearst. Its uncrated stones lie scattered in Golden Gate Park in San Francisco, although some of the decorated stones will be incorporated on permanent loan into the chapter house of Our Lady of New Clairvaux Abbey in Vina, California—ed.]

TABLE OF ILLUSTRATIONS

Credits

Most photographs were provided by the late Anselme Dimier. For additional photographs the editors are grateful to Alinari/Art Resources, N.Y., David N. Bell, James France, Carole Hutchison, Maureen M. O'Brien, Saint John's Abbey-Collegeville, the Abbey of New Clairvaux, Our Lady of Gedono Monastery, New Melleray Abbey, Our Lady of Guadalupe Abbey.

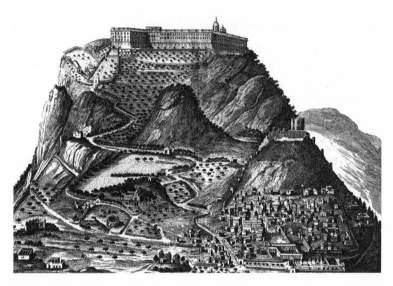

Figure 1.0. Monte Cassino Abbey, Italy.

1

AN OVERVIEW OF MONASTIC ORDERS

ALL RELIGIOUS ORDERS have as their aim the sanctification of their members by the practice of the evangelical counsels. These are summed up in three vows—poverty, chastity, and obedience—which constitute the religious state. The first of these vows frees the religious from temporal goods, the second from human affections, and the third from self-will. To this primary aim, some religious orders add a secondary goal, such as pastoral work, preaching, teaching, care of the sick or other works of charity. The monastic orders are unique in that they add no secondary goal. This is why we call them 'contemplative' in distinction to orders which are called 'active'.

THE ORIGIN OF MONASTICISM IN THE EAST

Very early in the Church, Christians wanted to reach perfection by practising the counsels contained in the Gospel. People whom we call the ascetics (from the Greek *ascètès*, someone who exercises self-restraint) distinguished themselves by the renunciation of temporal goods, by meditation on eternal truths, and by prayer, as well as by the practice of chastity and mortification. To escape the persecutions, these Desert Fathers withdrew to the wilderness. As we would say today: they made for the woods. There, far from temptation, they lived as hermits (from the Greek *érèmos*, wilderness). Others began to form into groups to share a common life. These were the cenobites (from the Greek *koinos bios*, common life).

The first great representatives of these ascetics are Saint Anthony—considered the Father of Monks—and Saint Paul of Thebes. The former has become very famous, not least on account of the famous *Temptations of Saint Anthony* which became a favorite theme of painters in the Middle Ages and the Renaissance. The saint is portrayed in his hermitage surrounded by demons in bizarre and monstrous forms personifying the seven deadly sins, and by women partially or totally nude, tormenting the solitary with physical temptation. There are those who would have us believe that the purpose of the innocent little pig—which iconography almost always depicts with Saint Anthony—is to remind us of the sensual temptations which plagued the poor hermit. In reality, it means something quite different. The Order of Antonites, founded in the eleventh century, ran hospitals and in order to maintain their hospitals, these religious raised pigs. They were granted the privilege of letting their swine wander the streets in search of food as long as they wore a bell around their necks. The pig in paintings of Saint Anthony is a reminder of this privilege.

We are also familiar with the legends of the Desert Fathers who supposedly tamed wild beasts and practised extraordinary fasts and penances', some of which became contests among the solitaries to see who could go the longest without food or sleep. The large movement characterized by the flight from the world into solitude dates back to the fourth century. The Nitrian and Scetan deserts of Egypt, southwest of Alexandria, the desert of the Thebaid in the region of

Thebes, and the Nile Valley to the south, may be considered the birthplace of monasticism. From there monasticism spread to Syria, to Cappadocia, then to Greece, Italy, and then Gaul.

Saint Pachomius and Saint Basil were the first in the east to organize the common life in large monasteries according to a rule and observances. Thanks to these great reformers, and particularly to Saint Basil, monasticism became a durable institution where the excesses and the extravagances of the Desert Fathers were banned.

FROM EGYPT TO LEBANON

In lower Egypt, in the vast sand deserts of Nitria, Scete, and Tabennesis (in the region of Thebes) the monks settled close to water. Some of these ancient monasteries are still in use, inhabited by the Greek Melkite (imperial) and Coptic (from the Greek *aiguptos*, Egyptians) monks.

Of primary interest is Saint Anthony's Monastery, founded in the fifth century south of Cairo not far from the Red Sea. An enormous quadrangle surrounded by walls ten yards high, it is guarded by turrets and watchtowers and is accessible by a single door, always kept closed. Inside, a network of buildings, arranged in no particular order, resembles a large village. In the center is the many-domed main church, as well as the community room and refectory. All these buildings date back to the eleventh century. From the thirteenth to the fifteenth century, monasteries were known for their great intellectual activity. Monks copied large numbers of manuscripts and the small cells where the copyists worked can still be seen. In fact, these monks lived as hermits, coming together twice a day in chapel, morning and evening, to chant the Office and celebrate the Divine Liturgy.

Further to the south is the monastery of Saint Paul-in-the-Desert. It is less significant and was formerly dependent on Saint Anthony's. At Wâdi Natrûn, near Cairo, four

Figures 1.1 and 1.2. The coptic monastery at Saint Anthony (above) and Saint Catherine Sinai (below). The buildings of Saint Catherine's, crouched at the foot of the Mount of the Decalogue, are surrounded by powerful ramparts attributed to the Emperor Justinian. Orthodox monks occupy this monastery, whose library is famous.

monasteries resembling fortresses date back to the fourth and fifth centuries. Greek and Syriac manuscripts have been found in their libraries, and a good number of them sent to the libraries at the British Museum, Paris, Milan, and the Vatican.

At the close of the third and fourth centuries some hermits established themselves on the Sinai Peninsula, but in large part they were massacred by Arabs raiding the country-side. An important sixth-century monastery built for the cenobitic life, this monastery was well protected from Arab attacks by strong high ramparts six kilometers in length. Originally called Saint Mary's, it later came to be known as Saint Catherine of Alexandria's because legend had it that the martyr-saint's remains were carried to Mount Sinai by angels. It is there that the *hegumen* (*higouménos*; the verb is *higoumai*, to lead, guide) was the famous John Climacus (*klimax*, degree). He was given this surname because of his well-known work, *The Ladder of Paradise*.

The monastery church, still occupied by Orthodox monks, is built like a basilica. Its apse is adorned by a magnificent sixth-century mosaic representing the Transfiguration. The library, very rich in manuscripts, possesses among other documents the oldest complete Greek manuscript of the Bible, dating to the fourth century. Until it was discovered by Tischendorf in 1859, the monks were unaware of its value. The manuscript was then given by the monks to the Czar and became the famous property of the Russian Imperial Library. There, it became known as the *Codex Sinaiticus*. In 1933, the Soviet governor, who needed money, sold the manuscript to the British Museum for the sum of £100,000.

At the end of the third century, the first christian monks of Palestine made their appearance in the Judaean desert, not far from the place where the Essenes had once lived, as we have only fairly recently discovered through the sensational Dead Sea Scrolls at Qumran. The christian monks originally lived in caves but soon built more than one hundred thirty monasteries. They lived as hermits in their cells and came together to celebrate the Office in common in church only on Saturday evenings and Sundays.

In the Jordan only three monasteries remain: Mar ('Lord') Saba, just outside Jerusalem, and Choziba (Saint George's) near Jericho. The first and most important of the three was founded by Sabas in 478. Built in layers, suspended somehow on narrow platforms, the buildings are supported by enormous buttresses projecting the length of the vertical side of the rock, and overshadowed by the blue dome of the church. This small basilica, dedicated to the Annunciation, is thirty yards long and twelve yards wide with stalls along the sides. The walls are covered with frescoes and icons. About thirty Greek Orthodox monks live there as hermits. They rise during the night to recite the Office together and they gather again in the evening to sing Vespers. The rest of their time is spent in their cells or caves.

In the eighth century the monks of Mar Saba displayed great intellectual activity. The most celebrated among them was Saint John Damascene (†c. 760)—an important doctor of the Church. Among his many works, particularly famous were three treatises on *Images* written against the Iconoclasts.

In Lebanon monasteries abound. The most important christian community, the Maronites, are named after Saint Maroun, a Syrian ascetic who founded monasteries in the fifth century in Apamea on the edge of the Oronte. The Maronite Church, in communion with Rome, has always remained firmly anchored in its faith despite numerous bloody persecutions. Many of the Maronite monasteries are still being used. At the end of the seventeenth century they came into closer contact with Rome through the influence of Latin missionaries in Lebanon and because young Lebanese monks were sent to the Eternal City to do their theological studies in the universities. Important modifications in the organization of the life of these monasteries followed as they began to take on some of the works of a more active life. Besides the houses of monks, there are also a few convents of nuns in Lebanon. All have experienced a great renewal recently in artistic and intellectual activity.

THE MONASTIC REPUBLIC OF MOUNT ATHOS

For over a thousand years, Mount Athos—also called the Holy Mountain—has been one of the main centers of monastic life in the East and one of the high-spots of Christianity. It is the most eastern of the three Khalkidhiki peninsulas, projecting into the Aegean Sea.

In the ninth century, a large number of hermits began to seek solitude in these mountains which have peaks over a mile high. The first permanent monastery or *laura* (from the Greek *lavra*, monastery) was founded by Saint Athanasius towards the end of the ninth century. Eventually, other monasteries were begun, until there were nineteen main monasteries, seventeen of them occupied by Greek monks, one by Serbian monks, and one by Bulgarian monks. In the eighteenth century, a twentieth was added, founded by Russian monks. Besides these main monasteries, there are twelve sketes (*skete*, apparently an abbreviation of the word *askètèrion*, a group of ascetics; skete corresponds to the word priory) and two hundred four kellias (*kelleia*, cells). Almost all these monks—whom we call Caloyers or Cologers (*kalogéroi*, from *kalos*, good, and *gérôn*, old fellow)—live a cenobitic life under the direction of an hegumen.

Another group of monks keep some personal property and live in family groupings under the authority of a president. We call this lifestyle idiorrhythmic (*idioorythmos*, a personal way of acting). All these monasteries own libraries rich in manuscripts and countless art treasures.

Mount Athos is part of the Republic of Greece but it forms an autonomous republic governed by a council of twenty monks elected by the monasteries. The council resides in Karyes, the capital. A police force stands ready to maintain

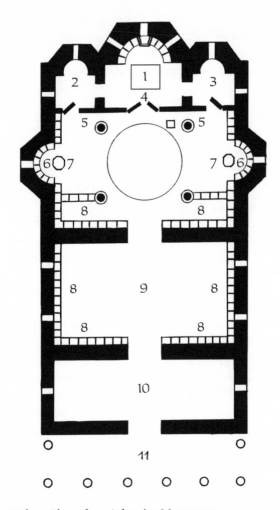

Figure 1.3. Floor Plan of an Athonite Monastery.

1.	Hagia Trapeza	Altar or sanctuary area generally
2.	Proskomydiae	'Chapel' for preparing bread and wine
3.	Diakonikon	Deacons' area; vestment and book cup-boards
4.	Bema	Sanctuary; area behind the iconostasis
5.	Templon	Iconostasis
6.	Choros	Choir
7.	Analoghla	Lecterns for service books
8.	Stasidia	Stalls
9.	Exonarthex	Inner Narthex
10.	Esonarthex	Outer Narthex
11.	Pronaos	Porch

order. For its spiritual needs, Mount Athos depends on the greek Patriarch of Constantinople. The Holy Mountain is inhabited exclusively by some four thousand monks. Entrance to the mountain is forbidden to all women as well as to female animals including cows, ewes, and hens. This small monastic republic has survived centuries of wars and revolutions, a fact so unique to world history that a millennium commemoration was especially celebrated on the Holy Mountain in 1963.

An Athonite monastery is surrounded by an enclosure wall. All of the monks' cells are grouped around a large square. The church, called the *katholicon*, is always in the center. It resembles all byzantine churches, topped by a central dome around which other smaller domes are sometimes added. The apse always faces the east, and the sole entry is at the west end.

The apse, generally semi-circular and bounded by a three-panelled wall, is furnished with stalls along the walls and the abbot's chair in the middle. The altar is in the center with two smaller semi-circular apses to the right and to the left. The northern apse is reserved for the *protheses* (*prothèsis*, proposition). There the preparation for the liturgy takes place and the chalice, paten, and sacrificial wine are found. On the other side, the *diakonikon* is used, as the name indicates, by deacons and contains the books for the divine service. The sanctuary is adorned with a profusion of crosses and icons embellished with gold-leaf and precious stones. In front is the iconostasis (*eikoostasi*=standing images) a wall of icons which separates the sanctuary from the nave. Before the many icons painted on wood hang vigil lamps. Three doors serve as passageways between the sanctuary and the nave. The center or Royal Door is provided with a curtain which hides the altar. It is opened only at certain times during the liturgy.

On both the right and the left side of the nave are the choirs with two large richly decorated lecterns holding the liturgical books and a row of stalls against the wall. In the center of the nave is suspended a very large richly decorated candelabrum, holding a great number of candles. The walls are covered with mosaics and paintings, giving the impression that the monks are surrounded with the whole heavenly choir as they chant the Office or celebrate the Liturgy. This makes a striking contrast with the poverty and starkness of the other parts of the monastery. This model was used by the monks of Chevtogne, Belgium, when they built their church as an ecumenical center dedicated to christian unity.

RUSSIAN MONASTERIES

In Slavic nations, Christianity and monasticism appeared simultaneously. As elsewhere, there were first hermits living in isolated places. Only in the second half of the eleventh century was the first monastery founded in Kiev by Saint Anthony and Saint Theodore the Studite, abbot of the monastery of the Studion in Constantinople. This monastery was called the Laura of Kiev Petcherski, or Monastery of the Caves. Soon other foundations were made in the same area, and by the twelfth century there were already seventeen monasteries. At many of them the monks lived under an idiorrhythmic regime introduced by Greek monks.

Princes were soon moved to found monasteries, which therefore sprang up everywhere to the point that by 1240 there were over seventy of them. The rule of Theodore the Studite was established in the monastery of Kiev Petcherski. This rule, in opposition to the idiorrhymic system, encouraged poverty and the common life. The monks lived in strict enclosure, devoting themselves to prayer, study, and manual labor.

Little by little monasticism spread; monasteries of monks and of nuns were founded at Novgorod. There were also double monasteries where adjoining buildings within the same enclosure gave rise to abuses and scandals. There were even recluses and gyrovagues—the worst kind of monk according to Saint Benedict—who lived by exploiting others. In the wake of the mongolian invasions many monasteries were destroyed. Reconstruction got under way during the reign of the Grand Duke of Kiev, Alexander Nevski (1247–1263). In the fourteenth and fifteenth centuries an immense flowering of new monasteries brought the number to one hundred twenty.

During the fifteenth and sixteenth century, three hundred monasteries came into existence. But while their numbers grew, in many places the Studite rule was no longer observed. Common life was abandoned. In idiorrhythmic monasteries, the Office was celebrated in common only on Sundays and feast days. As late as the seventeenth century, a strong expansion gave birth to two hundred twenty new monasteries. Among these the most famous were the laura of Saint Alexander Nevski, founded by Czar Peter the Great in 1710 at Saint Petersburg; and the Optina Poustynis, or the Desert of Opna, between Moscow and Kiev, a foundation which began in the fifteenth century but did not really flourish until the eighteenth and nineteenth centuries.

Although these monks never engaged in any outside activity, they nevertheless made a profound social impact on the people simply by the examples of their disciplined lives and by their land-clearance and colonization, not to mention their writings, especially their chronicles, the manuscripts they copied and the magnificent illuminations they produced. Most of the buildings of these monasteries date back to the sixteenth, seventeenth, and eighteenth centuries. The churches are topped with cupolas culminating in an onion dome. Around the central dome are often four small towers also crowned with bulbous bell-turrets.

THE GREAT PIONEER MONKS OF THE WEST

Meanwhile, in the West at Ligugé (where Dom Jean Coguet led some important excavations after 1952, reconstructing the primitive fourth century chancel), at Trier, and at Verceil, religious began grouping to live in common. In Gaul, near Tours, Saint Martin founded the monastery of Marmoutier (*Majus Monasterium*) which became a haven of prayer and study. In Marseille, the monks of the Abbey of Saint Victor preserved the writings of Cassian who, as we can read in his *Institutes and Conferences*, formed monks in humility, obedience, and the other great christian virtues. In Provence, on the islands which border the coastline of Fréjus, the abbey of Lérins became a school for such bishops as Saint Honoratus and Saint Caesarius. Nor can we forget Cassiodorus, who in the middle of the sixth century made his monastery, Vivarium, an intellectual center endowed with one of the most important libraries of the century.

But it was Benedict of Nursia who was destined to become the founder of western monasticism. His rule, known for its

Figure 1.4. Aerial view of Lérins Abbey. On a small island off Cannes, Lérins was founded by Saint Honoratus at the beginning of the fifth century and is therefore one of the oldest abbeys in France. Only the fortified buildings in the foreground are ancient. The rest of the buildings date from the nineteenth century, and are now occupied by a cistercian community.

wisdom and discretion, organized the Divine Office, spiritual reading, and manual work with an order and a balance that so assured its success that in the West it supplanted all other rules.

In the sixth and seventh centuries, Irish monks spread the Gospel to Wales, Scotland, Britain, the Low Countries, Germany, and even Italy. The most famous of the Irish monks was Saint Columban, who founded the abbey of Luxeuil in the wilderness of the Vosges in 590, Bregenz Abbey on Lake Constance, and Bobbio near Milan. These rugged pioneers were great preachers of the Gospel and untiring workers who cleared the forests and tilled the land. Among their ranks we find Philibert, the founder of the abbeys of Jumièges in Normandy and Noirmoûtier in Vendée, and Saint Gall, the founder of the famous Swiss monastery which bears his name.

In the eighth century, the Rule of Saint Benedict began to supplant Columban's much stricter rule, full of fasts and mortifications of all kinds, not to mention a penal code in which a whole gamut of corporal punishments were inflicted on delinquents. Less rigid, yet still based on strict discipline, the Rule of Benedict was eventually adopted by all the monasteries of the West. These monasteries soon became centers of religious studies. The monks worked at copying Holy Scriptures, the Church Fathers, and the great classical writers. To them we owe the preservation of many historical and scientific works. Pope Gregory the Great, who has left us a *Life of Saint Benedict*, sent a group of Bene-dictines to England to preach the Gospel under the direc-tion of Saint Augustine. Soon monasteries were founded there, among them Malmesbury, Wearmouth, and Jarrow. Monks like Aldhelm, Benedict Biscop, and the Venerable Bede distinguished themselves by their literary works. These Anglo-Saxon monks went in turn to Frisia and Germany. Among the most famous of them were Saint Willibrord, the apostle of the Frisians, and Saint Boniface, who evangelized

Germany, founded the famous Abbey of Fulda, became bishop of Mainz, and died as a martyr in 755. The large Picardian abbey of Corbie founded Corbey Abbey in Saxony, where the monks preached the Gospel, bringing peace and civilization to a pagan country. In Sweden and Denmark, another monk of Corbie, Saint Ansgar, led the evangelization of the north and became Archbishop of Hamburg.

Then came the Viking invasions which ravaged the coasts of England, Ireland, and Germany. France was not spared as the hoards of barbarians made their way along the Seine Valley, arriving in Paris which they besieged, winning the region of the Loire. The work of the missionary monks was interrupted to a large degree, and, carrying their sacred vessels and relics, they fled the invaders. Nonetheless, still other monks took the Gospel to Central Europe and to the Slavic nations, to Poland, Moravia, and Bohemia, led in this apostolate by two Greek monks from Salonika, Cyril and Methodius.

As soon as the Viking invasions ended and peace and calm returned, the monasteries joined the great movement known as the Carolingian Renaissance. Within the cloisters, even on the darkest days, intellectual activity never ceased. Monks like Alcuin of York, Theodulph the Spaniard, the Lombard Paul the Deacon and Paulinus of Aquileia, led the movement under the strong impetus of Charlemagne. This renaissance of arts and letters was a monastic movement. Everywhere, abbey schools set it in motion: Saint Martin of Tours, Corbie, Saint Denis, Saint Gaul, and Fulda, which boasted such scholars as Hincmar of Reims, Walafrid Strabo, Einhard, and Rabanus Maurus.

In the ninth century, Saint Benedict of Aniane, counselor to the Emperor Louis the Pious, worked at a reform which bears his name to group monasteries together and to unify them in their rule and observances. At the beginning of the tenth century, in the year 910, the abbey of Cluny was founded in Burgundy by William of Aquitaine.

This foundation marked an important step in the history of monasticism, for the spirit of reform inspired its founding. The reform's principal characteristics were order, discipline, poverty, and submission to the authority of the abbot. Soon, older abbeys asked to join Cluny while other abbeys began to adopt its customs. The new order spread rapidly and exercised a considerable influence on monasticism.

THE REFORMS OF THE ELEVENTH AND TWELFTH CENTURIES

The eleventh century gave rise to many reforms and the birth of new monasteries. Saint Romuald, in founding Camaldoli in 1010, reintroduced the eremitical life. Saint John Gualbert began Vallombrosa in 1022. Saint Stephen of Muret withdrew to the depths of the forest and founded the order of Grandmont in 1080. In 1084 Saint Bruno and a few companions arrived at the mountains of the Dauphiné to lead the eremitical life at the Grande Chartreuse. In 1098, a new monastery was established in the forest of Cîteaux, in Burgundy, not far from Dijon. It was a monastery marked by a return to the poverty of the early monks, an esteem for manual labor, and a return to the observance of the benedictine rule in its original purity and integrity. Later foundations included Tiron in the Perche and Savigny in Normandy. In 1120 Saint Norbert, a native of Xanten, in Prussia, founded his abbey of Canons Regular at Prémontré, Picardy. Other new abbeys were Fleury-sur-Loire, Brogne (near Namur), Gorze not far from Metz, Saint—Èvre de Toul, Ghent, Stavelot, and Malmedy deep in the forest of the Ardennes, Einsiedeln in Switzerland, Hirsau in Württemburg, Glastonbury in Somerset, Ripoll in Catalonia, Silos in Castile—not to mention the abbeys of Cluny and Cîteaux which outstripped them all. These two great Orders, both begun in Burgundy, spread rapidly either by making new foundations or by affiliating with other monasteries all over Europe and even in the East.

MONKS AS SETTLERS AND COPYISTS

Do we really need to discuss the important role of monks in european civilization? It is so well known that one hesitates to broach it. Yet it would seem inappropriate not to say at least a few words on the various monastic contributions, among which architecture holds an important place.

The monks accomplished a genuine colonization of Europe as early as the eighth century, as they were clearing the forests and draining up the marshes of Gaul and Germany. They began agricultural centers, planted grains, fruit trees and vines, introduced fisheries, and transformed every aspect of the countryside. In times of famine, abbeys became the granaries of the poor. In many places there were hospitals for the sick and hostels for travelers, and everywhere, monks contributed to the survival of the population. Besides this, they played a large role in the development of crafts, teaching various trades, creating industries, and training craftsmen.

In the realm of the arts, monks were above all great builders, as the following pages will show. But they also successfully devoted themselves to sculpting, painting, illuminating, goldsmithing, and carving. They were also masters in music and until the end of the twelfth century, first in the art of making stained-glass.

As we have seen, monks preserved the treasures of ancient literature. They copied the Holy Scriptures and the works of the Church Fathers. They themselves wrote all kinds of books, excelling in philosophy, theology, and biblical exegesis. Among them were great historians and chroniclers. They shone in mathematics and geometry, as their architectural work testifies, and also in astronomy. It would be useless and time-consuming to mention names. We need only say that throughout the centuries we find monks who have excelled in most areas of learning.

To say this is not to plead one's own case. The facts are well known and no one would dream of contesting them. We must, however, remember that clearing the forests, draining up the marshes, copying manuscripts, promoting the fine arts, and even converting the pagans and barbarians was not the goal of monachism. Its unique and sole aim is to seek God in solitude and silence. All the rest is secondary. The late Marc Bloch in his work, *The Feudal Society*, wrote that:

> In this christian society, no function of collective interest seemed more indispensable than that of the spiritual organism. Let us make no mistake: they were founded as spiritual enterprises. The great chapter cathedrals and monasteries may have played a considerable charitable, cultural, and economic role, but to the eyes of its contemporaries, all this was simply a by-product.

We often tend to forget this. And so, when a hostile government in France prepared early in this century to expel religious, the only argument put forth to defend the monks was that they had settled Europe and saved its civilization by preserving its ancient, classical masterpieces. To which Clemenceau, president of the Commission of Inquiry, did not hesitate to respond that all of Europe was now settled and that the printing press had advantageously replaced the copyists of the Middle Ages, and that therefore the monks had no further purpose. What could anyone say?

But truth has a power so mysterious that it was another kind of argument that won the case. Dom Chautard, the Cistercian abbot of Sept-Fons, when he appeared before the Commission of Inquiry was not afraid to argue solely on the issue of religion. The abbot spoke not of monks plowing the fields or working in scriptoriums but of men who believed in God and had left the world to worship him in spirit and in truth. The Cistercians were not expelled.

MONASTERIES OF NUNS

In the early centuries of Christianity, while men were withdrawing to the wilderness to pray to God far from the noise of the world and were forming communities of hermits and cenobites, women also yearned to withdraw by themselves while still living at home. They prayed, studied the sacred Scriptures and did manual work. Clothed very simply, their heads covered by a veil in order to avoid attention, they consecrated their virginity to God, leading lives of poverty and mortification. They were called the holy virgins, (*virgines sanctae*, or *sanctimoniales*). Soon these virgins met to live in monasteries or parthenons (*parthenos*, virgin). Around 330, Saint Pachomius founded a monastery of virgins close to his monastery of Tabennesis in Egypt. At Bethlehem Saint Jerome brought together some roman virgins and holy widows who lived under his guidance. At Hippo, Saint Augustine also founded a monastery of nuns; it was to them that he addressed his famous Letter 221, which we now call the *Rule of Saint Augustine*. In Rome, too, monasteries were raised in the shadow of the basilicas of Saint Lawrence and Saint Agnes.

The movement spread to Gaul. Saint Martin founded monasteries of virgins in Touraine and in Normandy while Cassian built a nuns' house near his own monastery, Saint Victor of Marseille. From the fifth century onwards, the abbey of Lérins had under its care nuns established on Saint Margaret Island. In the sixth century, a monk of Lérins become bishop of Arles, Saint Caesarius, built a monastery for nuns at Alyscamps (*Elyssei campi* = *Champs-Élysées*). To them he gave a rule later adopted by Saint Radegunde when, in 547, she founded Holy Cross Monastery at Poitiers. Also worth mentioning is the Abbey of Chelles, located close to Lagny in Brie, founded by Queen Saint Clotilde in 538. Nearby Faremoutiers Abbey began in 617, taking its name from its first abbess, Saint Fare. From Faremoutiers the foundation of the equally well-known abbey of Jouarre sprang up around 628. A group of sisters from this abbey were then asked to repopulate the Abbey of Chelles, rebuilt by the Queen, Saint Bathilde, around 646. Many of these monasteries of nuns followed the *Rule of Saint Columban* in the beginning, but later adopted the *Rule of Benedict* as did the mens' monasteries.

In northern Gaul, the abbeys of Nivelles and Brabant, of Marchiennes near Douai, and Andenne not far from Namur, date back to the same period. There was a double abbey at Whitby in York, England. In the Germanic countries, there were monasteries of nuns dating back to the seventh century near Trier, at Cologne, and at the famous Alsatian abbey at Hohenburg. This last abbey eventually later took the name of Saint Odile in honor of its most celebrated abbess. Soon monasteries of women spread to Bavaria and central Germany, many of them founded by Saint Boniface. Recruitment was done primarily among the noble families. During the same period, numerous convents were founded in Italy, particularly in Brescia, Pavia, Milan, Venice, Ferrara, Lucca, Capua, and Benevento. Eventually, the *Rule of Benedict* was adopted almost everywhere, yet more slowly in the womens' monasteries than in the mens'.

THE DOUBLE MONASTERIES: FONTEVRAULT ABBEY

We have already mentioned several examples of double monasteries, that is, monasteries which contained both a community of men and a community of women. In the early centuries, Saint Pachomius in Egypt and Saint Basil in Asia Minor had built monasteries for women near their mens' monasteries, placing both groups under the direction of the same abbot. In the West, things were not done the same way. Monasteries of nuns called on monks to be their chaplains and to help them in business affairs. Because of this, these monks came under the authority of the abbess. Many examples of this existed in Gaul, England, and Spain. The cloister buildings of the two communities were completely separated, and, although they sometimes shared a common church, they were strictly forbidden to celebrate the Office together.

Fontevrault was the most famous of these double monasteries, built in 1101 by Robert d'Arbrissel. He located it in the middle of Fontevrault Forest in Anjou, near Saumur. The monastery contained three distinct communities of women: Grand Moutier for nuns, Saint Madeline for delinquent girls, and Saint Lazarus for lepers. Added to these was the monastery of Saint John for the monks who served as chaplains and took care of business matters. The monks there made profession before the abbess, to whom they vowed obedience. This was a unique case in the history of monasticism. Although the monks repeatedly tried to free themselves from the yoke of the abbess—even applying to Rome—it was in vain, and this state of affairs continued until the French Revolution.

Endowed and protected by the Plantagenets, who were the counts of Anjou, Fontevrault Abbey soon became rich and powerful. From the beginning, the foundation held as many as three hundred sisters, and it soon ruled over a large number of priories in France, Spain, and England, all of them under the immediate jurisdiction of the abbess of Fontevrault.

The church of Fontevrault, still in existence, was built in the twelfth century to grandiose proportions yet without any ornamented sculptures. It consists of a single-aisled nave of four bays, each covered with a cupola. Opening from the huge transept which rests on soaring columns, is the choir and ambulatory, which gives access to three radiating chapels. The Plantagenets chose this church as their final resting place. At the upper end of the nave, the tombs of Henry II, Eleanor of Aquitaine, Richard the Lion-Hearted, and Isabelle d'Angoulême, the wife of John the Landless, can still be admired. We also find an elaborate octagonal kitchen with eight small projecting apses, three of which have been destroyed. Surrounding the central fireplace is a whole series of smaller ones, in all twenty-five fireplaces arranged in two rows. This is the only kitchen of its kind that has been preserved. There were similar ones in the abbeys of Vendôme, Marmoutiers in Tourraine and Saint Peter of

Chartres which have been destroyed. At Fontevrault, an immense new monastery built in the seventeenth and eighteenth centuries was transformed into a central detention camp during the Revolution. Recently it has been restored as a museum of fine arts.

THE NUNS OF CLUNY AND CÎTEAUX

In the Cluniac Order there were no double monasteries but once the abbot Hugh had founded Marcigny Abbey, not far from Paray-le-Monial, for nuns dependent on Cluny, monasteries of Cluniac nuns were soon founded in France, Spain, Italy, and England. In the beginning, the Cistercians refused to oversee monasteries of nuns, but faced with ever more pressing demands, they finally gave in. Around 1125 the abbey of Tart was founded near Dijon by a group of nuns from the benedictine abbey of Jully. Other abbeys were soon begun in France, Spain, Belgium, England, Denmark, and Germany. In the thirteenth century, not only were a number of abbeys founded, but, again, many existing abbeys asked to join the Cistercian Order, so many, in fact, that in 1220 the General Chapter voted to refuse all new requests. Many abbeys therefore, adopted the cistercian habit and customs without becoming, strictly speaking, members of the Order. Abbeys of cistercian nuns became extremely numerous in France, Spain, Britain, Germany, Italy, Portugal, the Low Countries, and as far afield as Cyprus and Palestine. Each of these abbeys was dependent on a cistercian abbot responsible for finding it a chaplain and for making a canonical visitation once a year.

For a while the cistercian abbesses met together annually at Tart to hold a general chapter, as did the cistercian abbots. Some twenty abbeys dependent on Tart took part in the chapter, whose sessions continued until the beginning of the fourteenth century. After that we find no further trace of them. The same kind of chapter was held in Spain at the royal abbey of Las Huelgas at Burgos. Alphonse VIII, the king of Castile who founded the abbey in 1187, wanted it to be the mother-house of all the other cistercian abbeys of the kingdom. At Las Huelgas, under the presidency of the abbess, the Spanish Cistercians held their general chapters for many years. Unfortunately, the sweeping authority given the abbess of Las Huelgas soon led to serious abuses. The third abbess, Doña Sanchia Garcia (1207–1230), assumed abbatial power, including certain sacerdotal functions. In 1210 she invested and blessed the novices, gave homilies from the pulpit, and heard the sisters' confessions. Following her example, other abbesses in the dioceses of Burgos and Palencia did the same. As soon as Pope Innocent III was informed of this, he quickly sent a letter, dated 11 December 1210, delegating the bishops of those dioceses to put an end to these abuses. At the end of his letter, the Pope wrote:

> Even if the Holy Virgin Mary is more worthy and deserving than the apostles, it was to them, and not to her, that Our Lord confided the keys of the kingdom.

Also worth mentioning is the abbey of the Paraclete, founded by Abelard for Heloise. This abbey prospered rapidly and became the head of a congregation with numerous priories in Brittany, Anjou, Poitou, Touraine, and even England.

The most famous abbeys of cistercian nuns in France are Lys, Saint Antoine, Flines, Port Royal, and Maubuisson. Port Royal was made famous both by its young abbess, Angelique Arnauld, who reformed the monastery, and by Jansenism, which cast a long shadow over the French Church. Maubuisson, near Pontoise, was founded by Blanche of Castile, the mother of Saint Louis (IX). In February of 1618, the abbess of this famous monastery, Angelique d'Estrées, was seized from her bed by the royal archers at the order of King Louis XIII, whom she had annoyed with her criticisms. While still in her nightgown, rolled up on a blanket, she was carried off on her mattress to a home for delinquent girls.

The abbey of Lys, near Melun, was another foundation of Blanche of Castile, and the foundress' heart was preserved in the abbey church. The remains of this monastery are slowly falling to ruin. Saint Antoine, for which an area in Paris is named, and Flines, near Lille, founded by Margaret of Constantinople, Countess of Flanders, both deserve mention.

Figure 2.0. New Melleray Abbey, Dubuque, Iowa.

2

MONASTIC ARCHITECTURE AS A REFLECTION OF THE LIFE OF THE MONKS

I N HIS BOOK, *The Christian Churches of Syria,* Jean Lassus makes this pertinent remark:

> To the archeologist, a monument serves a purpose; a plan is the reflection of a program. Archeology—an auxiliary discipline to history—gives us information on the life of the men in various buildings.[Jean Lassus, *Sanctuaires chrétiens de Syrie*]

Yet we can also say that people's life-style conditions the architecture, and this is particularly true of monks, whose entire lives unfold within the walls of the monastery to which they are bound by their vow of stability. To give a better understanding of monastic architecture, we need to give some details on the life of those who live in these cloisters. We noted earlier that the cenobitic or communal life is the most widespread form of monasticism. It was for cenobites that Saint Benedict drew up his Rule, a rule which eventually prevailed over all others and to which we owe the organization of all the monasteries in the West.

WHAT IS A MONK?

The monk (Greek, *monos*, alone) is someone who leaves the world to live in solitude and silence for God alone. A person who feels called by God to be a monk must undergo a period of novitiate training which usually lasts one year, or in some orders, two years. During this time, the novice examines his vocation under the direction of a novice master who instructs him in all that the life entails, without hiding any of its difficulties from him. The life that the novice leads is the same one he will live for the rest of his life: Office in choir, study, prayer, and manual work. He begins by studying the Rule and by learning the psalms which form the basis of the Divine Office. Before admitting them to profession, the ancient monks would require that a novice be able to recite the hundred-fifty psalms by heart. And surprisingly enough, there were very few incapable of doing it. Mother Agnes Arnauld, who was named abbess of Saint Cyr when she was five years old, knew the entire psalter by the time she was nine. Nowadays our memories are more obstinate and we find few monks, even the older ones, who know the psalter by heart. Needless to say, this requirement no longer exists. If it did, the number of monks might be small indeed!

If, at the end of one or two years, as the case may be, the novice has shown by his conduct that he is fit to embrace the monastic life, and if the community votes him in, he pronounces his vows. Like other religious, he takes the three vows of poverty, chastity, obedience, but he also vows stability, which binds him to his monastery.

A monastery also included, along with the monks, lay-brothers or *conversi*. The latin *conversus*, meaning 'converted', is the antonym of *nutritus* (nursed), which was used to designate those who had been promised to the religious life as infants. During the Middle Ages nearly all monks were recruited from among the young people who were taught in clergy-staffed schools. There they learned the liberal arts; we could say, they were fed both the human and divine alphabet. They formed the group called the *nutriti*. On the other hand, those who entered at a later age after having followed another way of life were called *conversi* because they were completely changing their lives. Because they were usually uneducated or illiterate, the term *conversus* (or in French *convers*) came, in time, to designate the illiterate.

The *conversi* led a life that was a bit different from that of the monks. Their Office—composed of the Lord's Prayer, the Hail Mary, and the Creed—was much shorter than that of the monks. While the monks were singing their long Office, the laybrothers busied themselves at manual labor, especially farm labor, cattle-raising, and diverse occupations. The Cistercians put their laybrothers in charge of the granges (farms) where they worked on weekdays, only returning to the abbey on Sundays and feast days. Yet these laybrothers were also full religious making perpetual vows recognized by the Church. In the Middle Ages, as we will see, the cistercian laybrothers formed a separate group within the community, and had their own chapter room, refectory, dormitory, and their own choir in the church, separated from the monks' choir.

Nowadays this separation between monks and laybrothers no longer exists. For a long time now, the chapter room, refectory and dormitory have been used in common. Moreover, the laybrothers are no longer illiterate, far from it. Today there are only monks; some of them are ordained to the priesthood and some are laymen.

THE ABBOT AND HIS OFFICERS

At the head of the monastery is the abbot, the father of the community, representing Christ. In most communities and congregations, the abbot is elected for life. He is completely responsible for the monastery, for its spiritual as well as its temporal needs. He receives the vows of the monks and laybrothers and they promise obedience to him until death. His powers are limited in certain areas specified by the constitutions of the Order—for example, for purchases or sales over a certain amount, and for the admission of novices to profession, where a majority vote of the community is required. The abbot appoints the prior, the cellarer (the name Benedict gave to the treasurer), and all the other officers of the monastery. He is responsible before God and his Order for how the affairs of his monastery are conducted.

The prior (Latin: *prior*, first)—also called a provost (*praepositus*)—helps the abbot and takes his place in his absence. Then comes the subprior, the third superior. The cellarer is in charge of monastery administration. He must be sure that each person has what he needs, particularly the sick. The sacristan takes care of everything having to do with the church and the altars. The cantor or choirmaster, as his name indicates, directs the chanting and is responsible for seeing that the Office is carefully and correctly performed. In earlier days, the choir master was also responsible for the *armarium* where manuscripts were kept. Nowadays the number of books has increased so much that a librarian now has charge of that. The novice master is responsible for the spiritual formation of candidates to the monastic life and teaches them the observances of the cloister. The guestmaster receives guests—who are never lacking in a monastery, according to Benedict—and sees to their accomodations. The infirmarian is there to nurse the sick and elderly monks who can no longer follow community exercises.

In large abbeys, there were a number of officers. At Cluny, for example, a first prior and a second prior came after the abbot. The cellarer had a whole army of monks under his direction: the kitchen cellarer, the wine cellarer, the refectorian, the butcher, the gardener, the pittancer—in charge of distributing 'extras' on certain feasts—and the constable (*comes stabularum*) or master of stables. There was also a chamberlain, in charge of finances, and someone who took care of the monks' clothing. There was also a precentor and succentor, a notary or chancellor, a treasurer in charge of sacred vessels and relics, an infirmarian who, besides caring for the sick, took care of a garden of medicinal plants and herbs. A chaplain helped the poor who came to the door. A master of works oversaw the maintenance of the buildings. Other officers included the master of students and the porter. In brief, the community formed a small hierarchically organized world of its own. Each person had his job. Order reigned in the house and everyone lived in peace.

This is why the monks could face any unforeseen event. A case in point is Pope Innocent IV's visit to Cluny in 1245. After the Council of Lyons, the pope wanted a meeting with King Louis IX of France to negotiate a peace settlement regarding Italy. The meeting took place the second week of November. The chronicler, William of Nangis, a thirteenth-century monk of Saint Denis, described the arrival of the king accompanied by his three brothers, Queen Blanche of Castile, and a whole armed troop:

> In front were one hundred sergeants, well mounted and liveried, and armed with bows; another hundred followed them, dressed in coats of armor with gorgets, bucklers, and shields. After these two hundred men, another hundred marched directly in front of the king, armed with all kinds of weapons, and having dracow gleaming swords in hand; and finally, the king arrived.

The pope was also accompanied by a large entourage. On the feast of Saint Andrew (30 November), when he celebrated a pontifical Mass in the immense abbey church, he was assisted by twelve cardinals and a large number of bishops and abbots, including the abbot of Cîteaux. The church was full with people from everywhere, but in spite of these crowds, the chronicler does not neglect to add:

> The pope with his chaplains and his entire court as well as the bishops of Senlis, Soissons, and Langres all received hospitality within the enclosure, and yet the monks were not

disturbed from their dormitories, chapter room, refectory, or from any of their conventual places.

This demonstrates the magnificent monastic organization.

The monk's day begins at two or three o'clock in the morning with the Office of Vigils (or Matins) which lasts an hour or an hour and a half, depending on the day. The Office of Lauds is said at dawn. Around seven o'clock, the community celebrates the Eucharist (in the Middle Ages the priest-monks said private masses and younger monks acted as servers). The office of Prime followed (until it was eliminated in recent reforms). Then, in the chapter room, the martyrology is read aloud with the proclamation of the next day's feast. This reading is followed by various prayers calling upon God's blessing for the work of the day. A chapter from the Rule of Saint Benedict is read. After this, the abbot gives an instruction and briefly outlines the work needing to be done that day. Finally he announces the deaths of members of the various houses of the Order. This practice dates back to the early years of monastic life when a courier was responsible for visiting all the monasteries carrying a necrology, or death roll. Some couriers had to visit more than five hundred monasteries and their tour lasted over a year. Each house inscribed the names of its deceased brethren on the parchment and attached a biographical note. When the parchment came to its end, a new piece was sewn on, and the list continued. Some of the necrologies which have survived measure more than thirty yards in length.

After chapter, the monk spends an hour or two in spiritual reading (called *lectio divina*) until the hour of Terce, (the third hour—*tertia hora*— of the roman day). Each monk then works at the job assigned him. During this period, young monks preparing for Holy Orders take courses in philosophy, theology, Scripture, canon law, and church history, taught by certified professors. At the end of this work period, around noon, the monks go to the church for the Office of Sext (the sixth roman hour) which marks midday.

At the end of Sext, the community gathers in the refectory for its noon meal. After grace, the monks sit at table in complete silence and listen to someone read aloud. First a scripture passage is read. This is followed at the discretion of the abbot, by a reading from some historical work, from the lives of the saints or from some other spiritual work. At the end of the meal there is a thanksgiving, and everyone leaves the refectory, processing to the church singing the *Miserere* (psalm 51). After this, the monks are free to pray or to read.

Around two o'clock in the afternoon the Office of None (the ninth hour of the day) brings the monks back into choir before the afternoon work is assigned, as in the morning. This work takes about two and a half hours, depending on the season.

Around five o'clock Vespers (Evening Prayer) is followed by the evening meal which is usually a simple collation without reading during the season of the monastic fast (from the fourteenth of September until Easter). A short interval follows the meal after which the Office of Compline (the last Office of the day) brings the community to the cloister gallery alongside the church. A short reading begins the Office, which is then continued in church. After the Office, the monks file out past the abbot who blesses them with holy water and they then go up to the dormitory.

This is, in outline, the monk's day—not mentioning the differences we find among the various Orders and monasteries, or the changes in horarium occasioned by the changing seasons of the year.

THE SITE OF A MONASTERY

First of all, a monastery must be situated far from the affairs of men. The monk, as his name indicates, should live in solitude. This is why monasteries have almost always

been founded far from cities, towns, or highways. Imagine
what would happen if monks lived in a large city and rang
their bells full-force for the Office of Vigils at two o'clock in
the morning!

People like to say that monks knew how to choose beautiful sites for their monasteries. In the introduction to *The
Monks of the West*, Montalembert mentions that monks had
'a deep understanding of the beauties of nature' and that
'they proved this especially in their choice of sites for their
monasteries, so remarkable in their innate suitability and
the indelible charm of the site'. Indeed many abbeys were
founded on incomparable sites which provoke our admi-
ration. And yet, could it be that what we see now was
unforeseeable to the founding monks? In actuality, most
often the monks had to content themselves with what was
given to them, and we may believe that these gifts were not
the best available land. Not to mention the possibility that

Figure 2.1. An aerial view of Mont Saint Michel

in earlier times, when Europe was dotted with monasteries, people were much less sensitive to beautiful scenery.

At most of these sites, what attracts us now is the result of the work monks did over the centuries as they drained marshes, straightened watercourses, cleaned up the area, farmed the land and cleared pasture-land. On the whole, the monks transformed into beautiful gardens sites which, on their arrival, they did not hesitate to describe as 'barren and frightful deserts', the same terms used by Moses in the book of Deuteronomy to describe the country where God found the Hebrews and adopted them as his own people. The founding monks paid little attention to aesthetics when they chose places for their establishments. What they were primarily looking for was solitude and good water sources.

In the same way, most writers on the monastic life seem to feel obliged to repeat the Latin verses:

> *Bernardus valles, colles Benedictus amabat,*
> *Franciscus vicos, celebres Ignatius urbes.*

This means: 'Bernard loved valleys, Benedict hills, Francis villages, and Ignatius crowded cities', or, something along these lines. The variations are infinite, not to mention the completely false versions. Each mimics another without bothering to investigate the origin of these verses. After a long search, I believe that these verses echo a passage in the *Chronologia monasteriorum germaniae illustrium (Chronology of the Illustrious Monasteries of Germany)* from the german poet, Gasper Brusch (in the first half of the sixteenth century) who wrote about the cistercian monastery of Königsbrunn in Wurttemberg:

> *Semper enim balles sylvestribus undique cinctas*
> *Arboribus, divus Bernardus amoenaque prata*
> *Et fluvios; juga sed Benedictus amabat et arces*
> *Caelo surgentes e quarum vertice late*
> *Prospectus petitur; secessum plebia uterque.*

Holy Bernard always liked valleys completely surrounded by forests, flowing prairies, and rivers,

> while Benedict preferred hills and heights reach-
> ing to the heavens as far as one could see. But
> both of them searched for secluded places.

To be sure, many benedictine monasteries are perched on
the heights, beginning with Monte Cassino and Saint Martin
of Canigou. But this is not a general rule and we find many
monasteries established on the plains, and at the bottoms of
valleys, like Cluny, Fleury-sur-Loire, Bonneval, Morienval
and many others.

In any case, Bernard's monasteries and those of the Cistercians show a definite preference for valleys. It has been
said that this preference was due to humility and to a need
to remain hidden. The real reason is much simpler and more
prosaic: the Cistercians established themselves by rivers in
order to have water for their domestic needs and to power
their mills, forges, and fulling-boards. Through a whole
system of underground canals, they were able to distribute
water to all the buildings of the monastery, last but not least,
to latrines.

The Cistercians, even more than other monks, liked to
give their monasteries names which expressed a love of life.
Orderic Vitalis, a twelfth century benedictine chronicler of
Saint Evroult, remarked at the time—the founding years of
the Order of Cîteaux—that:

> The Cistercians like to give their monasteries such sacred
> names as Domus Dei (House of God), Claravallis (Clear Val-
> ley or Clairvaux), Bonus Mons (Good Mount), Eleemosyna
> (Almsgiving), in order to draw people to come and taste the
> happiness expressed by such a chosen name.

The Cistercians loved the place to which they were bound
until death, and the joy and peace they knew was re-
flected in the monsatery name. A few other names are
Clairmont (Bright Mount), La Clarté-Dieu (Light of God),
Beaulieu (Beautiful Place), Bellecomb (Beautiful Vale),
Bellevaux (Beautiful Dale), Bonnevaux (Good Dale), Claire-
fontaine (Clear Fountain), Bonne-fontaine (Good Foun-

Figures 2.2 and 2.3. Aerial views showing the situations of Fontenay Abbey in Burgundy (above) and la Thoronet Abbey (below). Fontenay, erected in the solitude of a wooded dale and irrigated by a small stream, is one of the most beautiful and most complete still available to us. To the left is the steepleless church, and in the center are the various buildings ranged around the cloister.

tain), Benôitevaux (Benedict's Dale), Laval-Bénite (Blessed Valley), Merci-Dieu (Thank God), L'Amour-Dieu (Love of God), La Benisson-Dieu (God's Blessing), La Charité (Charity), Bonrepos (Good Rest). The list could go on endlessly.

CÎTEAUX: A DECENTRALIZED ORDER

The organization of the Order of Cîteaux was not comparable to that of Cluny. Cluny's government was extremely centralized and the abbey had direct control over its dependent priories and abbeys. The abbot of Cluny, the prince of abbots, had immediate jurisdiction over all the houses and all the monks of his order. This was not the case with Cîteaux. Nor did the Order of Cîteaux group its monasteries into provinces or regions like other Orders.

At Cîteaux, the Charter of Charity of Saint Stephen Harding—the basis of the Order's government—managed to preserve the autonomy of each abbey while at the same time establishing a strong central authority represented by a general chapter which brought all the cistercian abbots together each year at Cîteaux. This chapter's purpose was to promote the salvation of souls and to see to the maintenance of discipline and the observance of the Rule, as well as assuring an indispensable unity among the abbeys of the Order. This bond between Cîteaux and its daughter abbeys did not include the annual subsidy to the mother house demanded by the Order of Cluny. In the Cistercian Order, the bond among the houses was one of charity, whence came the name Saint Stephen gave to the charter of the new Order.

Therefore, each abbey was established as an autonomous house with an independent abbot who watched over spiritual and temporal affairs. Each house also had its own novitiate, allowing for the recruitment and formation of its members. And if the house grew too large to receive new recruits, it could eventually found its own daughter houses.

NEW FOUNDATIONS: A SWARM LEAVING THE HIVE

We can easily compare a monastery preparing to make a new foundation to a hive of swarming bees. This is an apt comparison and an old one. Dating to the end of the fifth century, it comes to us in all probability from the anonymous biographer of Saint Romaine, who later became the founder and first abbot of Condat Abbey, which later became Saint Claude in honor of its most illustrious abbot.

The new foundation, headed by an abbot, became autonomous and, in time, when the number of monks allowed, it founded daughter houses. We might say that the mother abbey and daughter abbeys made up a family. The Father Abbot had to make a canonical visitation to all the daughter abbeys once a year to maintain the regularity and uniformity of the observances. When a vacancy occurred in the abbatial seat of one of the daughter houses, the Father Abbot supervised this monastery until the election of a new abbot. All the abbeys were subject to the decisions of the general chapter.

From the beginning, Cîteaux's first three daughter houses, La Ferté, Pontigny, and Clairvaux, and very soon a fourth house, Morimond, held a special place at the head of the order. The abbots of these four abbeys were considered as the founding fathers. Each year they made the canonical visitation of Cîteaux and would take over its direction in the case of a vacancy in the abbatial see. These filiations formed families within the larger cistercian family. Clairvaux, because of Saint Bernard, rapidly became and always remained the largest of the four. Morimond was the second largest. After these first four daughter houses, Cîteaux continued to found houses belonging to her own filiation. Soon these abbeys formed a network which blanketed Europe and

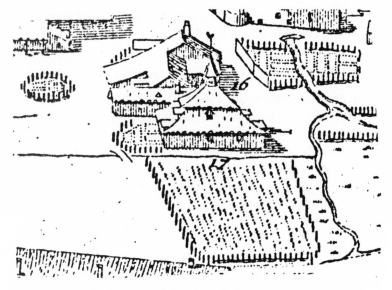

Figure 2.4. Early drawing of the plan of Clairvaux.

beyond: from Lisbon to Syria and from Norway as far south as Sicily.

LIFE IN THE SOLITUDE OF A CELL: THE CARTHUSIANS

The organization of the monasteries of the Carthusian Order resembles that of monasteries following the Rule of Benedict, but there are some differences. The superior has the title, not of abbot, but rather of prior. No outward sign identifies him. He is simply first among his peers (*primus inter pares*). The second in command in the house is the Father Vicar who assists the Prior in watching over the spiritual welfare of the monks, while the Father Procurator takes care of temporal affairs. The Prior General of the order is the prior of the *Grande Chartreuse* and bears the title, Reverend Father. The procurator may have a coadjutor to help him in his work. There are choir monks and monks called Brothers in charge of various departments such as the forests, cattle-raising, and a few industries. A Father Scribe acts as secretary to the Father General. The life of the Carthusians, who are hermits, is very different from that of the Benedictines and Cistercians. Choir monks spend almost all their time in the silence and solitude of the cell while the Brothers also work in their workshops. At about 11:30 each night, the Carthusian is awakened by the bell for Matins. He rises, and while still in his cell, recites Matins of the Office of the Blessed Virgin. Then he remains in quiet prayer until the bell rings again about midnight calling him to the church to chant in common Matins and Lauds of the canonical Office. This Office normally lasts two or three hours, depending on the feast.

The Carthusian returns to his cell around two or three o'clock in the morning. He recites Lauds of the Blessed Virgin and then retires. The bell awakens him around six-thirty in the morning, and he recites Prime of the Office of the Blessed Virgin and of the canonical hours in his small oratory. After that, he spends some time in prayer in his cell and then goes to the church for the High Mass sung by the community. The choir monk then says his own Mass, after which he returns to his cell where he says Terce of Our Lady and the day, and prays and reads, while the Brothers go to their workshops. Before dinner, around noon he says Sext in his oratory. He then eats his meal which a brother slips through a little hatch in the cell. After the meal, he says None, and may study, work in his garden, or do some carpentry in his workshop. In the winter, he cuts and saws wood to heat himself. The brother, meanwhile, returns to his workshop. In the afternoon, the choir monk will recite Vespers of Our Lady in his cell, and there go to chapel for Vespers of the day. After he returns, he takes a light collation, recites the Office of Compline, and retires, around eight o'clock.

The Carthusian choir-monk leaves his cell only three times a day—the Brother somewhat oftener—except on Sundays and major feasts when he chants the Little Hours

Figure 2.5. A view of the cloister at Mont Saint Michel

with the community in the church and takes his noon meal in the refectory with all his brothers. On these days, too, there is an afternoon period of recreation. Each week, the choir monks take a long walk together, and are allowed to converse among themselves.

This life, a happy balance of the eremitic and cenobitic life, gives the Carthusians the advantages of the hermit life while avoiding its dangers.

THE MENDICANT ORDERS

Properly speaking, the mendicant orders founded in the beginning of the thirteenth century—in particular, the Friars Minor (Franciscans) and the Friars Preachers (Dominicans)—are not monastic orders, for they are engaged in caring for souls and in preaching. Their members should not be called 'monks', reserved to contemplative religious who have no exterior ministry. The Friars Minor and the Friars Preachers belong to the canonical order, the Order of Canons Regular. That is, they belong to the group of religious who profess the three vows of poverty, chastity, and obedience, live in common under a superior, and are responsible for celebrating the Diving Office in a public church. The name 'mendicants' means that, ideally, they have no possessions or fixed revenue, but live from day to day, depending on the charity of others, begging from door to door for their daily bread.

We mention these mendicant orders because they live in community. The lives of these religious are ordered by customs and observances, borrowed for the most part from existing monastic customs, which have conditioned, as in the case of the monks, the arrangement of their 'convents'. The rules governing the simplicity and poverty of their buildings would be another reason to mention them. We will see that many of the customs and rules of the Dominicans simply repeat what we found with the Cistercians.

The life of the mendicants differs greatly from that of the monks, as mendicants are intended to have an apostolate which may include teaching, preaching, and publishing. But one part of their lives resembles that of the monks, the life they lead within their convents with Office in choir, a chapter, and common meals in the refectory, all regulated by custom and observances.

Under the name Franciscan there are three different Orders, all having Francis of Assisi as their patron: The Friars Minor, the Friars Minor Conventual, and the Friars Minor Capuchin. A Minister General heads each order. The friaries are divided into provinces, each governed by a Provincial Minister, and each friary has a 'guardian' as superior. The Minister General is elected for six years by the general chapter which gathers every six years during the season of Pentecost. The same chapter also elects the Procurator General and the six Deputy Generals. The Provincial Minister and his four deputies are elected for three years by the provincial chapter. The Guardian is chosen by the Provincial Minister and his deputy. The Provincial Minister is assisted by a vicar and two religious who form his council. The Minister General and the Provincial Minister exercise control over the convents through canonical visitations.

The Dominicans, or Friars Preachers, are governed by a Master General. Their convents are grouped into provinces, each headed by a Provincial Prior. Each convent is governed by a conventual prior elected by the religious of that house. The Master General is elected by the Provincial Priors and two delegates from each province. The Provincial Priors are elected by the conventual priors and by delegates from each house.

THE RULE OF SILENCE

All religious communities have a rule of silence, but with monks, silence is stricter. All monastic codes consider it as an important observance. The rule of Saint Pachomius early drew attention to this point, and to avoid conversations that may degenerate into useless talking, sign language has been developed to aid communication. In tenth-century Cluny, a whole series of signs was composed to express what was most necessary. The abbey of Hirsau in Germany soon adopted these signs and little by little the list of signs lengthened according to need.

In the Cistercian Order, where silence has been strictest, sign language was also adopted. Very detailed regulations determined which of the monks were authorized to speak because of the needs of their work. And it was also stressed that the use of sign language should not be abused. Signs were only to be used in necessity and not to carry on conversations.

This pantomine among monks naturally surprised outsiders, and no less new recruits on their entry into the cloister. The anonymous author of *Our Lady's Juggler*—which inspired one of Anatole France's famous tales—depicts his hero astonished at his arrival at Clairvaux, seeing the monks communicating by sign language, deducing that they must all be deaf and dumb:

> *Quant en cel ordre fu rendus*
> *Si vit cess gens si haut tondus*
> *Qui par signe s'entreraisnoient*
> *Et des bouches mot ne sonoient;*
> *Et quida bien certainement*
> *Qu'il ne parlaissent altrement.*

> When he had entered this haven
> And seen the monks close-shaven
> Chatting amiably with signs
> Their mouths seemingly in bind
> You can imagine his dismay
> That they spoke no other way.

The Camoldolese and the Carthusians also keep silence. The customs of the latter contain rules regarding the use of language: silence can only be broken in cases of grave necessity—serious danger, sudden illness, fire, or something on that order. Unlike the cenobites, however, Carthusians did not want to adopt sign language. Their rules expressly state that, as the tongue is the natural organ of communication, the simplest practice is to use it in cases of necessity, saying what is needed in as few words as possible. The orders which have an active apostolate also have a rule of silence but it is not as strict as in the monastic orders.

ABSTINENCE

Abstinence from animal flesh has also always been considered an important observance in monastic orders. Following the example of the Desert Fathers, the first monks contented themselves with fruit, herbs, and roots for all their food. Saint Benedict, in his rule, calls for abstinence but permits meat for sick brethren. Since he forbade the meat of four-footed animals, commentators have long engaged in unending discussions on whether the meat of two-footed animals—birds—would be permitted the monks. Most monastic orders held to a total abstinence from meat. The Cluniacs modified this rule little by little and finally in the twelfth century, Abbot Peter the Venerable wrote to all the priors of the Order informing them that he was not in sympathy with the meat-eaters. His letter took on the appearance of a pamphlet written in the style of Bernard. An excerpt from it reads:

> Roasted or boiled pork, heifer, rabbit hare, choice goose, chicken—in short, all quadrupeds and domestic birds—fill the tables of these holy monks . . .. In our day, a monk cannot be satisfied except with squirrel meat, deer, bear, and wild boar.

The abbot of Cluny soon put things in order. We read in the statutes he drew up that from then on, no one was to eat meat except the sick and the weak, according to the Rule of Saint Benedict.

The Cistercians also adopted abstinence, according to the Rule which they affirmed in every aspect. They applied this law of abstinence to everyone, including strangers who passed through the guesthouse, whether they were princes or bishops. They were censured for their severity in this regard. The English poet, Walter Map, a canon of Saint Paul's in London who had little regard for Cistercians, scoffed at them, writing:

> Charlemagne permitted monks to eat meat but the Cistercians refuse to benefit from this allowance. They keep to the original discipline. And yet, like all the others, they raise thousands of pigs and sell hams, maybe not all of them. . . . However, the heads and feet of the pork they neither sell, give, nor throw away. God alone knows what becomes of them! And what they do with the poultry that they have in abundance is also between God and them.

Figure 2.6. The monks' refectory at Maulbronn Abbey (Wurtemberg).

Figure 2.7. The lavabo of the cloister at Maulbronn Abbey.

The Carthusians made no exception to this rule of abstinence. Even the sick were given no meat. Only fish was allowed them. In our day, almost everywhere, the rule of abstinence has been mitigated. In many orders, meat is permitted a number of days a week. Nevertheless, abstinence, whether total or mitigated, is always included within monastic observances. Its meaning is always the same and can be encapsulated in these words of Saint Bernard: 'I abstain from eating meat for fear that in nourishing my flesh too well, I will also nourish the vices of the flesh'.

We will now investigate the framework within which the lives of the silent and solitary monks unfolded.

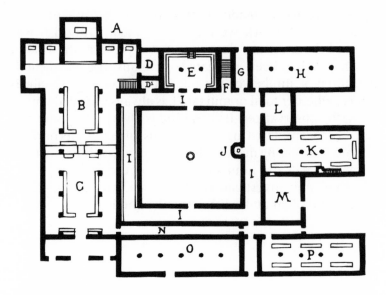

Figure 3.1. This typical plan of a cistercian monastery shows the distribution of various buildings constituting the 'monks' area' which forms the ordinary framework within which the monk's life unfolds. This basic arrangement is found in all monasteries regardless of Order.

A.	Church	I.	Cloister
B.	Monks' Choir	J.	Fountain
C.	Laybrothers' Choir	K.	Monks' Refectory
D.	Sacristy	L.	Calefactory
D¹.	Armarium for books	M.	Kitchen
E.	Chapter	N.	Laybrothers' Lane
F.	Dormitory Stairs	O.	Storeroom/
G.	Auditorium (Parlor and Passageway		Laybrothers' Dormitory (2nd level)
H.	Community Room/Monks' Dormitory (2nd level)	P.	Laybrothers' Refectory

3

THE BUILDINGS
OF A MONASTERY

THE OLDEST MONASTIC RULES never mentioned the building arrangements of the monastery and allusions to them are too vague to provide any precise idea of the ground plan. Nor does the *Rule of Saint Benedict* mention the building plan. The only information it gives is that the monastery should be built in such a way that monks can find within the enclosure all that is necessary to live the common life. This was designed to discourage trips outside. This is not to say that Saint Benedict was not interested in the arrangements of buildings, for we read in his life, written by Saint Gregory the Great, that in founding the monastery of Terracina, in the province of Rome, he told the disciples he was sending out instructions where they should build the oratory, the refectory, the guest house, and all the other necessary buildings. But he said nothing about their arrangement.

The oldest building plan we know of is one prepared for the Abbey of Saint Gall in Switzerland (ca. 817–820), founded in the seventh century in the diocese of Constance under the *Rule of Saint Columban*. (A century later this monastery adopted the *Rule of Saint Benedict*.) The plan of Saint Gall is a wonderful design drawn on parchment, preserved in the library of the city of Saint Gall.[1] We do not know who designed this plan, but in centuries past it was attributed to either Abbot Einhard, who was the building director under Charlemagne, or to Gerung, the court architect. We now believe that this plan was drawn up in the scriptorium of Reichenau Abbey, located on one of the islands in Lake Constance, in the days of Abbot Hetton (802–822), perhaps by the abbot himself. In spite of the fact that we are not sure of the designer of this plan, and whether or not it was ever really built, the plan itself is an extremely precious document in which we find precise indications for the placement and purpose of each building.

A VIEW OF THE ABBEY OF SAINT RIQUIER IN THE ELEVENTH CENTURY

One of the oldest and most important abbeys of Gaul at the end of the eighth century, for which the architecture is well known, is that of Saint Riquier. Originally named Centula, it was founded in the seventh century in the diocese of Amiens, not far from Abbeville. An illumination from the *Chronicle of Hariulf,* an eleventh-century manuscript, gives a view of the abbey. Although the original was lost in a fire in 1719, many copies of it have been preserved. The original buildings at Saint Riquier were built by Abbot Angilbert, a great dignitary and friend of Charlemagne, who was his greatest benefactor. These buildings were completed in 788. We learn from Angilbert's life that he gave the buildings a triangular arrangement in honor of the Holy Trinity. The cloister was built in the same manner, with a church erected at each of its angles. The abbey numbered three hundred monks who officiated, by the hundred, at each of these churches. One hundred young children, taught in the abbey school, were divided into three groups to chant the Office with the monks.

Figure 3.2. Engraving of Saint Riquier Abbey. This bird's-eye view of the former Centula, founded in the seventh century, was drawn in 1612, reproducing an eleventh-century manuscript now lost. Note particularly the church with its double transept in the background, and the large cloister in the foreground.

A century later, this monastery was entirely destroyed by the Vikings. The plan we have, therefore, comes from the reconstruction made according to the original plan between 1071 and 1097. In this plan we find three churches. The largest, on the northern side, was dedicated to the Saviour, the Virgin, and Saint Riquier. To the south, the second church, comprising a small nave and a rotunda, was dedicated to the Virgin and the Apostles. On the eastern side, the third church was dedicated to Saint Benedict. These three churches have all disappeared. The first was replaced by another church built in the thirteenth century and enlarged in the sixteenth. This building still remains. The second church was destroyed during the French Revolution, and the third was demolished at the end of the Middle Ages.

Against the walls of the triangular cloister were galleries connecting the three churches. The monastery buildings were in the midst of the triangle. A whole village was built around the abbey, which was surrounded by a wall, and the Church of the Holy Saviour served as the local parish. The plan of Saint Riquier differs in many respects from that of Saint Gall. Little by little, however, at least in the West, the plan for monasteries took on a definitive form conforming to the plan of Saint Gall. The places regularly used by the monks were grouped around a square cloister with galleries opening onto a central courtyard—the garth—in an arrangement resembling a roman villa. The cloister was usually sited to the south of the church although on occasion the terrain or the climate necessitated building to the north. In that case, the buildings were symmetrically arranged in the same order relative to the church.

THE ORIENTATION AND PLAN OF THE CHURCH

According to a tradition which dates back to the first centuries of Christianity, the Church faces in the direction of the rising sun, not in the direction of Jerusalem, as we sometimes hear. Our best proof for this lies in the fact that the churches built in Syria and Palestine between the fourth and sixth centuries all face the east and not Jerusalem. It was an ancient pagan custom to pray facing the east and the early Christians continued this practice. Perhaps as they did so, they recalled the passage from Matthew's Gospel announcing that Christ will come from the East and judge all the living and the dead. As for the direction of monastic churches, only the terrain sometimes made it necessary for the sanctuary to face another direction, as is the case, for example, with the abbey of Senanque in Provence, built in a narrow valley running from north to south.

The church included the sanctuary, with the high altar at the center, and the nave, the eastern bays of which were occupied by the monks' choir. This was separated from the rest of the church by two partitions: a rood screen and the more solid *pulpitum*, or lidem from which the lessons were read at the office of Vigils.[2] This *pulpitum* marked off the section of the church reserved to choir monks. The back of the nave was available to the laity and, once they were introduced, the laybrothers had their choir there as well.

The monks went to the church for Vigils in the middle of the night and for Lauds early in the morning. The name, Lauds, comes from the Latin words: *Laudate Dominum*, 'Praise the Lord', the words begin most of the verses in the final psalms (148–150) which are sung at the office. The Divine Office brought the monks together six more times during the day according to the roman arrangement of hours: Prime (the first hour) around 6:00 AM, Terce (third hour) around 9:00 AM, Sext (sixth hour) at noon, None (ninth hour) around 2:00 PM; Vespers in the evening, and Compline at the end of the day before the community retired. The church included a bell tower and throughout the day bells were rung to announce various community exercises: the Office in the church, chapter, meals, end of work, and so on.

THE ROLE AND ARRANGEMENT OF THE CLOISTER

The cloister gallery alongside the church is called the reading cloister, for there the monks did *lectio divina*, their spiritual reading of the Scriptures or the Church Fathers. The monks would end this reading in silent prayer in the nearby church. Books were kept in a cupboard or *armarium* built into the cloister wall. It was an ancient monastic custom that once the period of *lectio* was over, the books were immediately to be put back in their places. It was also said that the monks should not have their faces so obscured by their cowls that they could not be seen, lest they let themselves drift off during that period.

The cantor was in charge of the books and held the title *armarius*. In modern times we would call him the librarian. Many abbeys still have the small cupboards—*armaria* (aumbries), the forerunners of our libraries—where the manuscripts were kept. At the abbey of Escale-Dieu, not far from Bagnères-de-Bigorre, the *armarium* is made up of three semi-circular niches eighty centimeters deep. The grooves which held the wooden shelves can still be seen. At Boquen in Brittany there were also three niches, but the shelves there were made of stone. At Silvanes in the Rouergue, the *armarium* measures three yards in both length and width and is seventy-five centimeters deep. The largest known *armarium* is that of Garde-Dieu, close to Montauban, which is about 5.80 meters high and 3.7 meters deep.

The cloister gallery which stretched the length of the church also gave the community a place where they could gather in the evenings for the Office of Compline. They all sat on benches along the walls on both sides and the monk sitting across from the abbot read aloud, generally from the *Conferences*, (in Latin, *Collationes*) of Cassian. The word *collationes* gradually came to designate the evening meal, very frugal most of the year, which immediately preceded the reading. This is a typical example of the evolution of a word which completely changed its meaning until its original monastic connection is lost to most of the people who use it.

It is also in this section of the cloister that most monastic orders, as well as Canons Regular, hold the ceremony of the *mandatum* every Saturday evening before Compline. The *Rule of Benedict* states that the kitchen server, as he relinquishes his post on Saturday, should wash all the monks' feet, helped by the person who will succeed him as server for the following week. The name *mandatum* comes from the ceremony which is performed in memory of Jesus who on Maundy Thursday, washed the feet of his disciples to give them another example of humility and love before his passion. During the ceremony, the words used by Jesus are chanted, *Mandatum novum do vobis*: 'I give you a new commandment: love one another as I have loved you'. The word *mandatum* therefore came to be used to designate the washing of feet. This is also the origin of another name for the cloister gallery: the *mandatum gallery*.

In his biography of Saint Louis IX, William, a monk of the benedictine priory of Saint Pathus, recounts that the saintly king spent some time at Royaumont Abbey, which he had founded. It was located close to his chateau, Asnières-sur-Oise. While at Royaumont, the king attended the *mandatum* and wanted to wash the monks' feet.

> And it came to pass that after the holy king was seated beside the abbot during the *mandatum* he told the abbot: 'It would be fitting that I wash the feet of the monks'. And the abbot replied, 'You would do well to abstain'. The holy king asked, 'Why?' The abbot answered that some of the monks would think it was good while others would be critical of this action. And so the king abstained on the abbot's advice.

SOME BENEDICTINE AND CISTERCIAN CLOISTERS

Among the oldest and most beautiful benedictine cloisters is Moissac, near Montauban, a cloister of alternating simple and double columns, with wide, finely sculptured capitals. The cloister of Saint Michel de Cuxa, now partly in New York, is made up of a series of small, short, stocky columns.

Among gothic cloisters, the most unique and beautiful is at Mont-St-Michel, built between 1225 and 1228. It consists of two rows of slender columns arranged quincuncially and having small pointed arches. This arrangement, at the same time it gives the cloister a light, joyful effect, constitutes an ingenious solution in resisting the downward thrust of the framing.

The Cistercians also constructed very beautiful cloisters. Thoronet, Senanque, and Silvacane are counted among the most celebrated romanesque cloisters, as is that of Fontenay, which is less austere and more ornate.

Notable among gothic cloisters are Noirlac in Berry, and Fontfroide, near Narbonne, which dates back to the second half of the thirteenth century and the beginning of the fourteenth century. From a much later period we have the cloister of Cadouin in Périgord with a flamboyant style and exuberant decoration, not to mention innumerable figures on pillars, capitals, and keystones.

THE CHAPTER HOUSE

Monks finished the Office of Prime in the chapter house. The martyrology announcing the next day's feast was read and, after a few prayers imploring God's blessing on the work of the day, a chapter was read from the Holy Rule. From this practice the chapter house got its name. This is another example of a word whose meaning expanded bit by bit. At first the word 'chapter' referred to the chapter in the Rule, then to the place, and finally to those who met together in it. After the reading from the Rule, the abbot gave a brief commentary. In this room young monks were clothed with the habit, and in this same room, the abbot called the members of community, the chapter, together for important decisions concerning the administration of the house and admission to the novitiate or to religious profession. Here, too, the new abbot was elected. The plan of Saint Gall makes no mention of the chapter house. We

Figure 3.3. The Chapter House at Fossanova Abbey (Italy).

assume that the community gatherings were to be held in the cloister's eastern gallery.

The chapter house was most often built as a square or a rectangle, although in England, several places, such as Westminster and Worcester, are built in a polygon or even in a circle, as was the Welsh cistercian abbey of Margam. Among the cistercian abbeys, the most beautiful chapter houses are those of Fontenay and Senanque in France, Casamari and Fossanova in Italy, Poblet and the nuns' abbey of Las Huelgas in Spain, to mention just a few.

Near the chapterhouse in many monasteries there was a small wooden table, either portable or fixed to the wall. It was used as a sounding board to announce the death throes of a monk and to call the community to his bedside to recite prayers for the dying. This is mentioned in old customaries as far back as the tenth century. Among Cistercians, this table was also used to call the monks together for assigning of manual labor. Dom Martène noted the following verses written on the table at the abbey of Clairmarais:

> *Dirae sum sortis, quia sum praenuncia mortis*
> *At me clangente, turbantur corda repente.*
> *Quando quis moritur, ad me currendo venitur;*
> *Et certis horis praetendo signa laboris.*

> I am a bad omen, for I am death's harbinger.
> And when I knock, hearts suddenly lurch.
> When someone dies, they come running to me.
> And at the assigned hours, I give the work signal.

Off the cloister there is also a passageway with a staircase leading to the middle of the dormitory which occupies the upper floor of the east wing of the monastery. The Grandmontines located this stairway in the cloister proper. Opening from the cloister to the outside is the parlour, also called the *auditorium*. There the superior made work assignments and the monks changed their cowls for their work clothes.

A long room extends the east range southward beyond the line of the cloister. This is generally called the community room. It is thought that this room was originally used for indoor work during bad weather. In certain monasteries, it was reserved for the novitiate.

Figure 3.4. The calefactory of Longpont Abbey.

THE CALEFACTORY, THE REFECTORY, AND THE KITCHEN

On the southern wing of the cloister, facing the church, was the calefactory, or warming room. Originally it, and the kitchen, were the only heated rooms in the monastery. In the winter, the monks warmed themselves a bit after the long service of Vigils, chanted in the glacially cold church, or after outdoor work. There too, the monks were shaven—left with only a small 'crown' of hair—and there they polished their shoes.

On the door of the no longer extant warming room at Clairvaux, an inscription mentioned Saint Bernard's disciple, Pope Eugene III, who, as a simple monk, had performed the humble task of calefactorian, or caretaker of the calefactory. He had kept the fire going.

> *En ce chauffoir le bon religieux*
> *Se doit chauffer sans bruit et en silence,*

Soi Démontrant de maintain gracieux,
Et mêmement tenant paix et silence.
Car comme on dit, ici en patience
Fut chaufournier Eugene le saint homme.
Mais sa vertu et sa grande sapience
Tant l'exalta qu'il fuit pape de Rome.

In this calefactory the good monk
Quietly and silently tended the fire
While remaining gracious and peaceful.
Here, in patience, sat holy Eugene,
His virtue and great wisdom so
Exalted him that he became Bishop of Rome.

One of the most beautiful cistercian calefactories still in existence is found at the abbey of Longpont, near Paris. Dating back to the thirteenth century, it was disfigured after the Revolution, and then rebuilt according to its original plan with a central fireplace whose hood rests upon four beautiful columns. There is also a wonderful warming room at Senanque, where the fireplace is up against the wall.

Close to the calefactory is the refectory. Among both Benedictines and Grandmontines, the refectory was parallel to the cloister while the Cistercians built it perpendicular to the cloister, facing south, with a few exceptions where the terrain necessitated some other arrangement. Built into the wall and projecting into the refectory was a pulpit from which a monk read aloud during meals. He would read the section from the Bible that corresponded to the liturgical season being celebrated at the Divine Office. In this way, the monks had the entire Bible read to them over the course of a year. This explains, in part, the ancient monks' great familiarity with the Bible, a familiarity attested to in their writings. A small bell-turret over the refectory announced the meal times. Aside from the church, the refectory is often the most beautiful room of a monastery, and was sometimes decorated with murals.

Figure 3.5. The kitchen of Fontevault Abbey.

One of the most impressive refectories to have been preserved is that of the Benedictines of Saint Martin-des-Champs in Paris. The monastery now shelters the library of the National Conservatory of Arts and Crafts. This library is forty-five meters long and ten meters wide, and is divided into aisles of nine bays by eight tall columns supporting the vaulting. This edifice is attributed to Peter of Montreuil, the architect of La Sainte-Chapelle.

Among the notable cistercian refectories is Aiguebelle,

overlaid with a barrel vault, and the beautiful thirteenth-century refectory at Royaumont. A row of five columns, four meters high, divide this refectory into two sections of six bays each. The similarity of this refectory to that of Saint Martin-des-Champs leads us to believe that it, too, was the work of Peter of Montreuil. The large refectory at the college of the Bernardines can still be seen in Paris. Dating back to the fourteenth century, it is divided into three sections of seventeen bays by two rows of columns measuring seventy meters in length. It is now occupied by the Rue Poissy fire station. Also worth mentioning are the refectories of Maulbronn in Germany, Fossanova in Italy, Huerta, Rueda, and Poblet in Spain—the last unique in having its fountain in the center of the room—and the immense refectories of Fountains and Rievaulx in England.

In the Middle Ages it was a general custom to wash one's hands before going to table. In his beautiful book, *Le château fort et Caire au Moyen Age*, Jacques Levron informs us that in Châteaux there was a fountain for hand washing at the entry to the banquet room. It was the same in monasteries. Before entering the refectory, the monks washed their hands in a fountain built into the wall of the cloister or sheltered in a small building in the garth. One of the most remarkable of these small, courtyard buildings is still intact at the abbey of le Thoronet. The fountain, sheltered in a small, very simple hexagonal building, consists of a hollow column through which water rose to pass through four taps into a large basin. From there, the water passed through sixteen holes into a broad tub where the monks washed their hands. Other beautiful fountains of this kind can be seen at the abbey of Valmagne near Montpellier, at Maulbronn in Germany, and at Heiligenkreuz and Lilienfield in Austria. At Fountains Abbey, there still exists a large fountain built into the cloister wall at the refectory door.

At Fountains Abbey the kitchen was next to the refectory, and a pass through built into the wall was used to transfer food from the kitchen to the refectory. The kitchen was always vaulted with the hearth generally in the center. The kitchen at Royaumont still exists. It is a spacious hall covered by nine ribbed vaults carried by four central columns.

There is also a beautiful kitchen at Poblet in Spain and a famous kitchen at Alcobaça in Portugal. Built in grandiose style in the eighteenth century, this room (28.83 meters by 5.66 meters), became the source of ridiculous stories including those of William of Beckford, who visited Alcobaça in 1794 and in his popular book, *Excursion to Alcobaça and Batalha*, described this kitchen as 'the most remarkable Temple of Gluttony in all Europe'. It must not be forgotten that this abbey numbered two hundred monks, not to mention numerous workmen and guests. Actually, the monks received their meager cistercian pittance. The injustice done them by malicious stories has been rectified with Father Maur Cocheril's documented study of the situation.

THE MONKS' DORMITORY

The monks' dormitory was located over the chapter house. The dormitory was vaulted or simply paneled, and lighted by two narrow windows. In most abbeys, a stairway, the night stairs, led from the dormitory directly into the transept of the church for the night Office.

Originally the dormitory was one room with no separation between beds. This explains why we find numerous regulations in the old monastic customaries regarding the proprieties to be observed in the dormitory. We read in the customary of Hirsau Abbey that, once in bed, the monks should avoid making signs and looking at their neighbors. We find a rubric for taking shoes off and getting into bed. It was also a rule that even on the hottest nights, a monk was never permitted to uncover himself except for his arms, chest, and feet. Prescriptions of the same kind are found in the cluniac customary. In the customs of Cîteaux we read that while changing clothes, a monk should never be seen naked, that he should never stand on his bed, and that clothes should never be shaken out in the dormitory.

But soon, small partitions between the beds were allowed. At first, these partitions were only about two yards high and a simple curtain was pulled across before the monks went to bed. Little by little, the partitions got higher, and then doors appeared. The simple alcove became a real cell. The reformed Cistercians or Trappists until very recently kept the common dormitory with small partitions and a simple curtain.

At Saint Matthias of Trier, a magnificent three-aisled dormitory with groin vaults still exists. The cistercian abbeys of le Thoronet, Senanque and Silvacane have beautiful dormitories whose slightly pointed barrel vaulting is divided into bays by transverse arches. Other beautiful dormitories can be seen at Eberbach in the Rhineland, at Heiligenkreuz close

Figure 3.6. The monks' domitory at Eberbach Abbey. This magnificent two-aisled hall was built around 1270. It is seventy-three yards long.

to Vienna, and at Zwettl, near Krems, Austria. In Spain, the catalonian dormitory of Poblet measures sixty-six meters in length and more than twelve meters in width, and has a timbered roof carried on diaphragm arches. The abbey of the Holy Cross in Catalonia has the same arrangement but in smaller dimensions.

THE LAYBROTHERS' RANGE

The western wing of the monastic buildings contained the storeroom and the pantry. Among Cistercians, this wing belonged to the laybrothers. On the ground floor was a passageway leading directly in to the cloister and separating the refectory on the south side from the large storeroom on the north. On the upper story was the brothers' common dormitory, arranged like that of the monks.

The laybrothers formed a separate group within the medieval community. They were not monks, for the monks were priests. The laybrothers had their own separate quarters and entered only the cloister on Sundays and major feastdays to hear the sermons given by the abbot in chapter. In the church their choir was located behind the rood screen, separate from the monks' choir. In many abbeys there was a corridor, either vaulted or open-air, between the laybrothers' area and the western gallery of the cloister which allowed the laybrothers direct access to the church without having to pass through the cloister. In larger abbeys there was sometimes a laybrothers' chapter room in which they received instructions from their Father-master. The chapter of faults, a time for public accusations of infractions of the rule, was also held there.

The laybrothers' refectory sometimes had only one aisle, as at le Thoronet, with three rib-vaulted bays. At Fontfroide and Valmagne, the refectories had, respectively, five and four bays uniformly rib vaulted. Other refectories are divided into two aisles by a row of columns, as in the case of

Aiguebelle and Cleremont, refectories covered with groin vaults.

The thirteenth-century refectory at Vauclair—only the walls of which remain—was one of the largest and most beautiful of its kind. The vaulting was received on five solid columns which divided the room into two aisles of six bays each. The columns are still in place. At Longpont and Royaumont, the refectories were also rib vaulted. The late twelfth-century dormitory at Clairvaux, partially preserved, is divided into three aisles by two rows of octagonal pillars supporting groin vaults on large square beams. At Vauclair, the dormitory—now entirely demolished—was a vast hall having two aisles of fourteen bays each, with rib vaults springing from corbels along the walls and received on thirteen columns along the walls.

THE INFIRMARY

Of the buildings grouped around the cloister, we must also look at the infirmary and the novitiate, although tradition never assigned these buildings a fixed position. At times there were two infirmaries (also called the Death-hall), one for the monks and another for the laybrothers. The most beautiful of the infirmaries to have been preserved is found at the cistercian abbey of Ourscamp, not far from Noyon. It measures forty-five meters in length and nine meters in width and is divided into three aisles of nine bays each, with two rows of eight columns which carry the vaulting. But these vaults, shaken many times by bombings during the First World War, have threatened to collapse and emergency measures have had to be taken to prevent this catastrophe. The walls of some large infirmaries still exist at the two great Yorkshire abbeys of Fountains and Rievaulx.

In a room adjoining the infirmary, or close by the cloister, was the lavatory, a shallowly hollowed-out trough with a pillow cut into the stone. In it the bodies of dead monks

Figure 3.7. The infirmary at Ourscamp Abbey. This admirable thirteenth-century hall—commonly called 'the death hall'—is one of the rare infirmaries still preserved. It now serves as a church. Because of its light construction, the hall had to be reinforced with numerous tie-beams which can be seen in this photograph.

were washed before burial. At the bottom, by the feet, was a hole where the water could be drained out. At Cluny, a stone slab for washing the bodies of dead monks was located in a chapel overlooking the cloister. The cluniac chronicle tells us that when the body of Peter the Venerable (d. 1156) was placed on this mortuary slab, it shown as a glorified body. 'This body was purer than crystal and whiter than snow', we read. 'It was resplendent with celestial beauty.' Clairvaux claimed that the mortuary slab miraculously kept the imprint of Saint Bernard's body after it had been washed. This imprint formed a kind of shadow or image that was still being shown to visitors in the seventeenth and eighteenth centuries. Dom Martène was able to examine the stone during a visit to Clairvaux and did not believe in the miracle. 'I do not know that this is as miraculous as we are led to believe for this shadow is not visible from every side. One has to stand in a certain spot to see it. It might be a natural reflection from the light.'

At Cîteaux, the following verses were found on the mortuary slab in the hall of the dead:

Hic deponuntur monachi quando moriuntur Hinc assumuntur
animae sursumque [de] feruntur

Here the monks are brought when they die.
from there their souls are taken up to heaven.

The word *deferuntur* at the end of the second line, has an extra syllable which spoils the verse. Whether the monks at Cîteaux were responsible for this mistake or whether Dom Martène read it incorrectly we do not know.

THE SCRIBE'S CARRELS

Finally, in many abbeys there was a cloister gallery onto which opened the carrels of the scribes, those who copied manuscripts. In an age when a library could be built up only by copying manuscripts borrowed from other places, each monastery had many scribes. They worked in small carrels specially arranged for this painstaking work. There they copied liturgical books, the lives of the saints, commentaries of the Fathers of the Church, and the classics of antiquity. At Hirsau there were twelve of these carrels or writing desks (*scriptoria*). At Clairvaux there were fifteen in a small cloister at the east end of the church.

Here, in broad outline, we have the standard ground plan found in all the monasteries and convents where religious have lived in common, whether they were Benedictines, Cistercians, or Grandmontines. Given differences in their lifestyle occasioned by their ministries, the same general pattern is found among the Premonstratensians, Franciscans, and Dominicans.

Still to be examined are the various farm buildings, granges, storerooms, and workshops. These will be the subject of a further chapter.

NOTES

1. Walter H. Horn, *The Plan of St. Gall: A Study of the Architecture and Economy of and Life in a Paradigmatic Carolingian Monastery* (Berkeley: University of California Press, 1979), and idem, *The Plan of St. Gall in Brief* (Berkeley, 1982).

2. In French this lectern is called the *jube*, from the phrase by which the reader asked the abbot's permission to begin: *Jube, Domne, benedicere*: Pray, Lord, a blessing.

Figure 4.0. Cloister.

4

BENEDICTINE
MONASTIC BUILDINGS

BENEDICTINES HAVE BUILT innumerable monasteries throughout Europe and around the world. They range from very large abbeys with hundreds of monks to the most humble rural priories where a small community tilled the surrounding land.

THE FIRST MONASTERIES

We know little about the first monastery built by Saint Benedict near Subiaco, nor do we know much about subsequent foundations in the surrounding hills and valleys. All we know is that these monasteries housed small communities of a dozen monks each under a dean, and that Saint Benedict presided over them all. Almost all these monasteries have entirely disappeared. A few ruins have been found of two of them, and one monastery still exists, still maintained by Benedictines. Originally dedicated to Saints Cosmos and Damien, it was soon placed under the patronage of Saint Scholastica, the sister of Saint Benedict.

When this saint and his monks established themselves at Monte Cassino, between Rome and Naples, they lived in simple huts. Soon they built two churches, one of them dedicated to Saint John the Baptist, the patron of monks. Only recently its walls have been unearthed. The other church was dedicated to Saint Martin and was built near the ancient acropolis. Destroyed many times in the course of history and completely razed in the Second World War, the abbey of Monte Cassino has once again been restored, an example of the beautiful saying, *Succisa virescit* (Cut down, it flourishes again).

The sons of Saint Benedict soon travelled far. Towards the end of the sixth century, Pope Gregory the Great sent some monks to England with the mission of preaching the Gospel. Soon, new abbeys were founded there, Canterbury, York, Westminster, Winchester, Malmsbury. Many of these became episcopal abbeys with the abbot as local bishop and the monks forming his chapter.

Soon France, too, became a benedictine land. New foundations included Saint Martin of Tours, Glanfeuil near Angers, Saint Denis-en-France, and Fleury-sur-Loire, to which the relics of Saint Benedict were brought from Monte Cassino in 672. This omits abbeys already in existence: Corbie in Picardy, Luxeuil in Franche-Comté, and Lérins in Provence, all of which eventually adopted the Benedictine rule. Of the early Carolingian churches we are familiar only with that in the plan of Saint Gall's, with its western and eastern apses.

Saint Philibert in Grandlieu, near Nantes, which dates back to the beginning of the ninth century, is one of the most beautiful and important monuments from this period. It forms a latin cross with chapels opening out from both arms of the transept. The double curved arches of the grand arcades rest on cruciform pillars which had alternating courses of brick and stone. Buttresses rise to the height of the walls, on which the exposed timbers of the roofing frame rest. At

Jumièges, near Rouen, the church also forms a latin cross and the nave was similarly covered with an exposed timber frame roof.

A narthex was often set against the façade of these churches, with an upper story opening out on the nave, so that it could be used as a tribune. Some examples are Saint Philibert at Tournus, Corbie, Werden-on-the-Ruhr, and Farfa near Spoleto. Often two large towers framed the façade and a third, a bell tower, was situated at the transept crossing as at Jumièges, Tournus, Saint Étienne of Caen, Paray-le-Monial, and Conques. The church of Maria-Laach in Trier had six bell towers. Cluny's second church had a bell tower which marked the crossing and two additional towers which flanked the façade of the narthex. At Saint Denis, two towers crowned with spires flanked the façade. At Saint Benoît-sur-Loire, a large porch tower had been planned but remained incomplete. At La Trinité at Vendôme, there is a tower eighty meters high. At Saint Martin-du-Canigou, the square bell tower is surmounted by a platform enclosed by crenelation.

The capitals were often decorated with simple ornaments such as interlace, rosettes, plaits, and occasionally primitive leafy designs. All these churches were lighted by windows set into the upper sections of the walls of the nave, the apse, and the aisles. The stained-glass windows were usually decorated with figures.

ROMANESQUE: THE ART OF MONKS

The beginning of the eleventh century marked an extraordinary building boom, due in large part to the construction of monasteries. In this sense it can be said that the romanesque style was the art of the monks, for it is primarily to them that we must attribute this magnificent architectural renewal. Referring to this important artistic development, the cluniac monk Raoul Glaber wrote the following famous sentence in his *History*: 'We might say that the entire world, in common accord, threw off their old tatters and reclothed themselves in a white mantle of churches'. A large number of abbeys were restored in this period: Saint Ouen in Rouen, Mont-St-Michel, Saint Taurin of Evreux, Jumièges, Fontanelle near Rouen, later placed under the patronage of Saint Wandrille, its first abbot. During the same period, William the Conqueror, the founder of Saint Étienne of Caen (Abbaye-aux-Hommes), and Trinity Abbey (Abbaye-aux-Dames), erected the first great abbeys of England.

In Anjou, Ronceray Abbey and Saint Martin of Angers were restored by the famous Foulques Nerra, who also built the abbey of Beaulieu. His son, Geoffrey Martel, founded the abbeys of Nogent-le-Rotrou, La Trinité of Vendôme and Notre-Dame at Saintes. The counts of Blois and Champagne restored Marmoutiers and Saint Florent in Saumur. The dukes of Burgundy were the great protectors of the abbey of Molesme, from which a group of monks later emerged to found Cîteaux.

Other churches in this romanesque style were Saint Guilhem-du-Désert, Elne, and St-Michel de Cuxa in France, Soleure and Romainmôtier in Switzerland, Saint Cecilia of Montserrat and Ripoll in Spain, San Salvatore at Brescia and Saint Ambrogio of Milan in Italy.

CLUNY: CHRISTENDOM'S LARGEST CHURCH

In 910, the duke of Aquitaine founded in Burgundy the abbey of Cluny, whose influence was soon to extend over all of Europe, and which was to play an immense role in the evolution of romanesque art. New cluniac foundations sprang up everywhere, prompting a reform in already existing abbeys, many of which joined the Order of Cluny while others, not wishing to go that far, at least adopted a number of its customs. In Spain there was Saint Juan de la Peña, Oña in the high Ebro valley of Aragon, Najora in Navarre, Saint Isidore in Palencia, and Cardeña near Burgos, where

Cistercians are now located. There were also foundations in Portugal.

At Cluny three consecutive churches were built. Almost nothing is known about the first, begun by Abbot Berno and finished by Saint Odo. The second was begun by the Blessed Aimard, continued by Saint Maiolus and embellished by Saint Odilo with sumptuous interior decorations. After more than thirty years of excavation, Kenneth John Conant, a professor at Harvard University and head of the project of the Mediaeval Academy of America at Cluny, could reconstruct the ground plan. It was a large church with a nave of seven bays flanked by side aisles; a vast transept and an elongated choir terminating in an apse flanked by two smaller apses which were rounded on the interior while being squared on the exterior fales. Two long square-ended chapels opened off the transept and two small apsidal chapels ranged alongside. A large narthex, flanked by two towers, fronted the façade. Two large chapels between flat walls opened out on the transept. There were also two small

Figure 4.1. View of the benedictine abbey of Cluny in an engraving by Lallemand. Bibliothèque Nationale, Paris, France.

semi-circular apses built in echelon style terminating in a straight wall. A large porch led to the façade, which was flanked by two towers.

The cornerstone for the third church was laid on 30 September 1088. Built by Abbot Saint Hugh on a grandiose plan, it consisted of a nave which had eleven bays flanked by double aisles, two sets of transepts, a massive choir with an ambulatory opening into five radiating chapels. A narthex of five bays led into the church and was flanked by two forty-seven-meter-high towers. At the crossing of the first transept rose a square lantern tower called *des lampes* and on each arm of the transept there rose octagonal towers called *des Bisans* and *de l'Eau bénite*. Finally, a belfry known as the *Tour de l'Horloge*, crowned the second transept, a total of six towers in all.

In 1095, work had so advanced that Pope Urban II was able to consecrate the main altar on 25 October. By 1125, this immense building, more than 187 meters long, had been completed.

The pointed arches of the grand arcades were surmounted by a blind triforium with a clerestory above. The barrel vault rose to thirty meters in height. Semi-circular arcades were disposed around the choir; the apse was covered by a semi-dome decorated with a painting depicting Christ in majesty.

During the Revolution, the furnishings were sold. The bells from *des Bisans* were sent to the foundry, and the tombs in the church were demolished. In 1793 the abbey was pillaged and the buildings, exposed to open air and winds, remained abandoned. In 1801 a road was cut through the nave on the pretext that it would help business in the center of town. Then in 1811, to add to the disorder, the choir steeple and the lantern were blown up. The vault collapsed, as did the belfry *des Bisans*. All that remains of this splendid church—the largest in Christendom until the construction of Saint Peter's in Rome—is the southern end of the first transept and the *Tour de l'Eau bénite*, as well as the twelve

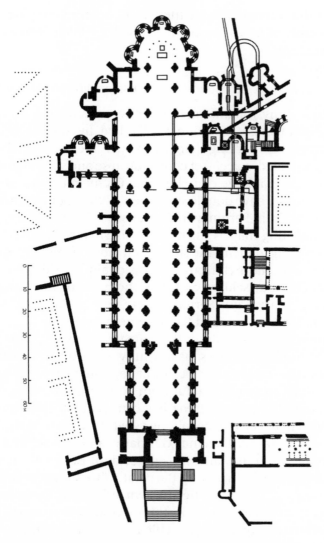

Figure 4.2. Plan of the abbey church of what archaeologists call 'Cluny III', begun in 1088.

beautiful capitals, among them those representing the various tones of gregorian chant. These have been deposited in a museum.

Like Cluny, romanesque churches generally took the form of a latin cross with a nave flanked by side aisles and transepts of varying lengths which are almost always square-ended, a deep-set choir, and apse and several smaller apses. Several large churches, like Cluny and Saint-Sernin in Toulouse, have double side aisles. With the disappearance of Cluny, Saint Sernin, with its transepts, its ambulatory and five radiating chapels and its admirable five-story tower over the crossing, remains the largest and most complete example of romanesque architecture. Occasionally the side aisles are extended, but seldom as far as the arms of the transept. Examples are Saint Sernin, Sainte Foy in Conques, Saint Martial in Limoges, and Saint Remi in Reims.

Sometimes, as at Cluny, there are two transepts, separated by a choir of two bays, as at Cluny, or as at Maria-Laach, where the transepts are located at opposite ends of the nave.

Apsidal chapels open out from both arms of the transept and there is an intervening bay connecting them with the choir whenever it is deeply recessed. Examples of this are found in France, England, Germany, and Switzerland; for example, at Bernay and St-Georges-de-Boscherville in Normandy, at Celle-Bruere in Barry, at Königslutter in Braunschweig, at Romainmôtier in Switzerland, at Ronceray in Angers, at Schaffhausen in the diocese of Constance, and in Wurttemberg at Hirsau which spread this plan into the germanic countries.

In a number of the churches, the small apses are arranged in a stepped formation against the main apse and back along the side walls. There are two of these small apses at Chezal-Benoît in Berry, at Saint Amant-de-Boixe not far from Angoulême, at Saint Germain-des-Prés in Paris, at la

Sauvé near d'Alais, at Thalbürgel in Saxe-Weimar, at Saint Mary's in York. It is this arrangement which Lefèvre-Pontalis called the 'benedictine plan' after finding more than eighty examples of this kind in a group of benedictine churches built in the eleventh and twelfth centuries. Moreover, before the middle of the twelfth century, only benedictine churches adopted this type of chevet.

PILGRIMAGE CHURCHES

In churches where the body of some saint or an important relic was venerated, crypts with ambulatories were built to encourage the crowds of pilgrims to move in one direction and to avoid jostling and sometimes fatal accidents. At Saint Martin of Tours, a great pilgrimage center, the crypt had an ambulatory with five radiating chapels. This, along with the ambulatory at Clermont cathedral, is one of the oldest known examples of this type. Later, the same system is repeated at Saint Martial in Limoges, at Sainte Foy in Conques, at la Couture in Mans, and at Saint Philibert in Tournus.

This same arrangement was adopted for the naves (of these centers). The saint's tomb was usually located at the rear. Therefore, side aisles were established around the choir. In other words, there was a semicircular ambulatory with protruding radiating chapels. There were two chapels at Saint Benoît-sur-Loire, three at Tournus built on an exceptional rectangular plan, five at Charité-sur-Loire, la Couture at Mans, La Trinité in Vendôme, Saint-Sernin at Toulouse, and Saint Martial in Limoges, and seven at Saint Leonard in Limousin. Aside from these, other chapels opened directly from the arms of the transepts.

The church of Jumièges was a prototype of the norman architecture which greatly influenced England and can be seen at Saint Augustine's of Canterbury, Bury-St-Edmunds, and the monastic cathedrals at Winchester, Worcester, Gloucester, and Norwich.

At Vézelay, at the summit of a hill on the beautiful site where Saint Bernard preached the Crusade in 1146, we find the church of the Madeleine which has been a pilgrimage center since the eleventh century. Finished in 1110, it has a long nave of ten unequal bays, with groin vaults separated by solid transverse arches. Later, a narthex of three bays was added. After a fire towards the end of the twelfth century, a large gothic choir was added. Well-lit by broadly embrasured windows, it was an expansion of the romanesque nave which, as Louis Réau says, gives 'the impression of a flower about to bloom.'

Devastated by the Wars of Religion, this church was abandoned, and gradually fell into ruins. But it was saved *in extremis* by Viollet-le-Duc who was commissioned in 1840 to restore it. The work took nearly twenty years. The spandrel and lintel of the central portal on the façade were rebuilt. As incredible as it sounds, the sincere architect, who could not tolerate the least artificiality in the materials he used, rebuilt the double bichromate arches of the nave, dispensing with the typical alternating white and grey stones, preferring painted stones! As Louis Réau comments: 'an inexcusable fraud on the part of a rationalist'. But the fact remains that Vézelay was saved.

CLUNY AND THE PILGRIMAGE TO SAINT JAMES OF COMPOSTELA

Cluniac monasteries were found at all the principal stages of the four great pilgrimage routes to Saint James of Compostela: Saint Gilles and Saint Guilhem-du-Désert; Saint Foy, Conques, and Moissac; la Madeleine at Vézelay; Saint John at Angely and Saint Eutrope in Santes.

Beyond the Pyrenees, there was a series of cluniac monasteries set at intervals along the road to Saint James: Saint John the Baptist in la Peña, Saint Colomba in Burgos, Saint Zoïle in Carrion, Saint Saviour at Lerida—which later affiliated with Cîteaux and eventually resumed its benedictine identity. Thus, the Cluniac monks held the principal stations.

Figure 4.3. The transept tower of the abbey church at Cluny.

In his beautiful book on medieval pilgrims, Raymond Oursel has shown that Cluny's benefactors intended to make Cluny an important relay-station on the route to Compostela, even if the recent claim that Cluny did not really organize the pilgrimage to Saint James Compostela has merit. It is certain that the Order intended to promote the pilgrimage as they provided hospitality and other services to all the pilgrims when they reached these relay-stations. The pilgrimage routes also became a channel for transmitting new methods of construction and styles of architecture.

AN EXPANSION IN THE USE OF THE VAULT

In most churches of the ninth and tenth centuries, only the sanctuary was vaulted. The nave was simply timbered with the rafters and the beams exposed to view. This method, as the chronicles inform us, led to a number of church fires. To avoid future catastrophes of this nature, eleventh century masons began to vault the entire church. The extended use of the vault is a distinctive feature of Romanesque architecture, as is the groined vaulting, and exterior buttresses corresponding to the pillars in the nave.

During this period, various methods of vaulting included barrel vaults, groin vaults, and cupolas whose thrust tended to push the walls outwards, a tendency counteracted by exterior buttresses. To avoid this outward thrust, it was thought best to cover the large churches with a series of juxtaposed cylindrical transverse vaults buttressing one another and resting on diaphragm arches. The only example we have of this type is Saint Philibert in Tournus, where this procedure was used to cover the nave. We find this system also in the side aisles where cylindrical transverse arches shoulder the vault of the nave.

The groin vault was advantageous in reducing the thrust, thus allowing for thinner walls pierced by windows in the clerestory. Cupolas became used much less frequently. The arcades usually rested on piers and their arches were generally rounded. But soon the pointed arch began to take over, resulting in lesser thrust and thus greater strength. Yet the rounded pattern continued to be used for a long time in the construction of doors, windows, tribunes, and blind arcades.

BUILDER-ABBOTS AND BUILDER-MONKS

Monks during this period generally built their monasteries themselves, drawing up the plans and using outside help only for unskilled labor. One great figure among the builder-monks was William of Volpiano. Born in 960 at Novare to a large family related to Otto-William, Count of Burgundy, William's godmother was the Empress Adelaide, wife of Otto the Great. He entered the benedictine order in Locedio in Piedmont and was soon called to Cluny by Saint Macolis, who commissioned him to lead a small group of monks in reforming the abbey of Saint Bénigne in Dijon. William became its abbot in 990. Many of his compatriots came to join him and to live under his direction, quite a few of them capable artists. This was a great asset in the reconstruction of his abbey which he began in 1000. This church, consecrated in 1017, soon served as a model for other churches of the Order, beginning with those dependent on Saint Bénigne. And so, while introducing his reform everywhere, William of Volpiano was also being asked to build and rebuild a large number of monasteries, particularly those of Bernay, Saint Ouen in Rouen, Mont-St-Michel and Fécamp—of which he was the first abbot. Also he rebuilt Fruttuaria which he founded in the Piedmont. A great person, a counselor to kings and princes, a diplomat at times, an architect and musician, William of Volpiano had a considerable influence on the architecture of the Cluniac order.

Saint Odilo, the fifth abbot of Cluny and a contemporary of William of Volpiano, was also a great founder and builder of monasteries. At Cluny he built the church, the cloister and other buildings on the traditional plan. The marble pillars for the cloister were brought in from a remote region in

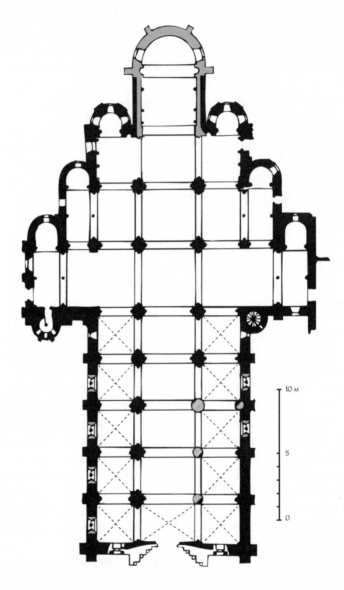

Figure 4.4. Plan of the abbey church at Saint Sever. The apses, stepped on either side of the chevet, are characteristic of benedictine architecture. It reached truly excessive proportions at Saint-Sever.

Provence. He rebuilt the monastery of Romainmôtier which had been given to Cluny by Adelaide of Burgundy in 928, and this priory became the first of some two thousand Cluny would later count among her dependencies. He rebuilt the monasteries of Payerne, Saint Victor in Geneva, Charlieu, Ambierle, Sauxillanges, Souvigny and many others.

About the year 1000 at Saint Florent in Saumur, the monks themselves built the church and other buildings of their monastery. Around 1005, Frederic, the Count of Verdun—a brother to Duke Thierry the First of Lorraine—became a monk at Saint Vanne Abbey and worked on the construction of the monastery. At the same time, Abbot Thierry of Saint Remi in Reims rebuilt his church, while in Normandy, Herluin, the founder and first abbot of Bec, took a personal part in the construction work of the monastery.

In 1079 Abbot Durand of la Chaise-Dieu in Auvergne sent three of his monks, the Prior Artaud, Theodard and Robert, to help with the construction of the Saint Gemma Priory which Geoffrey, Duke of Aquitaine, had just founded in Saintonge. The following year this same Duke of Aquitaine founded the monastery of Montierneuf near Poitiers; the monk Pons was put in charge of the building.

It was at this time that Abbot William of Saint Benoît-sur-Loire rebuilt his church. The monk Galbert oversaw the work. This magnificent building has a famous porch-tower still admired today. After 1944, the benedictine monks of La Pierre-qui-Vire returned there and are rebuilding the monastery. From 1081 to 1093, a monk Alcher rebuilt the church of the abbey of Saint Peter, near Saint Omer, which was later placed under the care of Saint Bertin, the most illustrious of its abbots. At Correns in Provence, a priory dependent of Montmajour Abbey, there was an epitaph to monk Humbert, noting his work on the monastery building at the end of the eleventh century.

Sometimes an architect-monk was asked to do non-monastic side work. At the beginning of the twelfth century the monk John of La Trinité at Vendôme was asked to rebuild the nave at the cathedral of Mans. In 1105 the reconstruction of Saint Jouin-de-Marnes Abbey in Lower Poitou was entrusted to the monk Raoul. From 1151 to 1165 the reconstruction of the church of Saint Pére at Chartres was done by the monks themselves under the direction of one of them, Hilduard. In rebuilding the abbey of Andres, near Boulogne-sur-Mer, around 1164, Abbot Peter took part in the work with his monks. We are told that he was equipped with a measuring instrument called a *virgula geometrica* and worked at cutting the stones.

We could give other examples of monks building their own monasteries. Little by little, however, this practice was lost, and gradually the abbeys had recourse to secular master-builders. Later we will see that when Suger rebuilt his church at Saint Denis, he brought in from all over the best architects, stone-masons, sculptors, and stained-glass artists he could find.

RICH DECORATION AND THE 'BIBLE OF THE ILLITERATE'

In most Romanesque churches and particularly in many cluniac monasteries, decoration abounded. As at Moissac, the tympanum and spandrel of the west portal were ornate with sculptures, as was the interior of the church where the capitals were replete with figures of all kinds. Not only Old and New Testament scenes or moral topics were represented, but so were all kinds of other subjects with preference given to various sequences such as the seasons of the year, the signs of the Zodiac, the sciences and liberal arts, and the eight musical tones. These were meant to be educational, of course. There is frequent mention of a synod held at Arras in 1025 where it was stated that the illiterate and the simple could in this way study and contemplate the images they were not able to read about in books. Saint John Damascene also commented on this in his treatises on images, which are found in a canon of the eighth ecumenical council, the Fourth Council of Constantinople in 869. There we find the phrase, *esto visibile parlare* as Dante notes in the tenth stanza of his *Purgatorio*. Or there is the beautiful verse by François Villon in the Hymn to the Virgin which he composed at his mother's request, to help her pray to Our Lady:

> A poor old woman am I.
> I know nothing, I cannot read.
> At the minster where I worship
> There is a painting of paradise
> with harps and lutes, and
> of hell where the damned are burnt.
> The one frightens me;
> the other brings me joy and relief.

This painting representing heaven and hell was located in the church of the Celestines in Paris, now the fire station at Boulevard Henri IV.

These were the sort of pictorial images that constituted the 'Bible of the Illiterate'. Saint Bernard did not approve of this book for his monks as we shall see, and Hugh of Fouilloy of the canons regular had strong opinions on it.

The artists of the Middle Ages went a step further. They found their subjects from just about everywhere: in epic poems, in *Æsop's Fables* such as 'The Crow and the Fox', 'The Wolf and the Lamb', 'The Rat and the Frog', 'The Wolf and the Stork' — and in *Phedrus' Fables* such as 'The Donkey and the Lyre' or in fabliaux.

This encyclopedic art was used to instruct the simple. But how do we explain all the monsters portrayed in churches: centaurs, mermaids, chimera, sphinx, griffins, winged quad-rupeds, unicorns, fish-women, bird-women, a wanton, a swarm of strange and fantastic animals; half-men and half-beast, cynocephaluses (men with dogs' faces), men with horses' hooves, one-legged men, Ethiopians, leopards, animals devouring one another, not to mention grimacing and grotesque faces, off-color and dirty jokes?

The text of the Synod of Arras—mentioned above—is often cited as proof that this profusion of images and sculptures had ecclesiastical approval. But strangely enough, this citation is always quoted out of context. Note the complete citation:

'That which the simple and illiterate can not read in books, they can contemplate through the use of images.' But the sentence does not end there. It goes on to tell us the nature of those images, that is, 'Christ in the humiliation through which he suffered and died for us. In venerating this image of Christ on the cross, Christ suffering and dying on the cross, it is Christ alone whom they adore and not the work of human hands.' This speaks to the iconoclasts. The text continues to mention the images of the Virgin, the angels, the apostles and martyrs, the virgins and confessors. There is no mention of the Zodiac, the fables of Æsop and Phaedrus, even less the monstrous and ghastly figures. What kind of instruction on the great truths of their religion could the faithful find in them? They did not understand these other symbols at all. It could only have left them confused and even scandalized.

Many authors have tried to discover various symbolisms in all this. Abbé Auber, one of the main proponents of this school of thought in the last century, offered all kinds of symbolic interpretations. Using a bit of imagination, one could find anything he wants. They managed to explain the symbolism of the clusters of small columns at the Collegiate Church of Saint Quentin. It remains to be seen if the artists really had in mind the intentions we liberally credit to them. It does not seem to be the case. Camille Enlart notes: 'In most of the romanesque capitals—those which our contemporaries have found so symbolic—the work is simply an artistic whim, the creation of a decoration, using imagination and ingenuity to please the eye'. Emile Mâle, the great authority in this area, shared the same opinion, saying: 'Our sculptors were not trying to educate; most of the time they only wished to decorate.'

CLUNY: 'AN ECUMENICAL MOVEMENT'

Was there a cluniac school? For Viollet-le-Duc there was no question about it. But the great archaeologist, Anthyme Saint-Paul set out in 1877 to prove that there was no cluniac school. He wrote: 'On the one hand, it is impossible even in Burgundy to distinguish the cluniac churches from others. On the other hand, when the order of Cluny extended beyond Burgundy, it did not bring with it this country's architecture.' He gave numerous examples to support his theory, since taken up by many archaeologists, including such men as Lasteyrie and Lefèvre-Pontalis. This thesis became so well accepted that it became commonplace to view cluniac construction as an outgrowth of the pure burgundian style without anything specifically cluniac about it.

But for some time now, in reconsidering the problem, there has been a return to the notion of a cluniac school. Charles Oursel does not hesitate to posit it. And the knowledgeable Harvard professor of architecture, Kenneth John Conant, who has been directing the excavations at Cluny for more than thirty years, remarked after his study of the first romanesque churches, Saint Bénigne at Dijon and Saint Philibert at Tournus, that Cluny betrays some foreign influences. At the great abbey of Cluny the best architects, masons, sculptors and painters composed a magnificent synthesis of the art of their time, which constitutes a special art form, 'a magnificent hybrid of exotic odors'. Raymond Oursel describes Cluny as an 'ecumenical monument'. This art form gave birth to such masterworks as Paray-le-Monial, la Charité-sur-Loire, and, outside the order, Saint Lazare at Autun, Notre Dame in Beaune, Saint Andoche at Saulieu, Saint Hilary at Semur-en-Brionnais. We have a right, then, to conclude that a cluniac school does exist.

Figure 4.5. The abbey church at Paray-le-Monial.

THE RISE OF ARCHITECTURE IN THE MIDDLE AGES
AND THE ROLE OF THE MONKS

Gothic churches were characterized by the systematic use of cross-ribbed vaulting, by the pointed rather than the rounded arch, and by flying buttresses to counter the thrust of the nave vaults.

The first, rather poorly built pointed arches appeared around 1125, on the periphery of the choir at the benedictine church in Morienval, not far from Senlis. Then they were used around 1130 in the choir of Saint Martin-des-Champs in Paris. At St-Germer-de-Fly, not far from Beauvais, a vast church rebuilt around the same time consists of a nave of eight bays with side aisles, a transept, an ambulatory with five radiating chapels, all rib vaulted. But it is Saint Denis which displays the first example of ribbed vaulting done in an accomplished way. Calling in architects and master craftsmen, Abbot Suger had them rebuild the façade and the base of the nave from 1137–1140 and then—from 1140 to 1144—build a new choir with ambulatory and seven radiating chapels that are still to be admired.

In England, the first ribbed vaulting appeared in the transept of Winchester Cathedral and at Malmesbury Abbey. At Saint Remi of Reims, Abbot Peter of Celle (1162–1181), the future bishop of Chartres, restored and enlarged the nave, covering it with a ribbed vault, replacing the romanesque apse with a vast choir and an ambulatory with five radiating chapels. During the same period, Saint Germain-des-Près in Paris acquired a choir and an ambulatory with five radiating chapels which were consecrated by Pope Alexander III during his trip to Paris in the spring of 1163. This same type of rib vaulted choir, resembling Saint Germain-des-Près, was added around 1181 to the romanesque nave of the Madeleine at Vézelay. Later examples were the churches of Saint Nicasius in Reims, now entirely demolished, and Saint Étienne in Caen, where a magnificent gothic choir was added to an old nave at the beginning of the thirteenth century.

Even later was the reconstruction of Saint Ouen in Rouen, the most perfect of the norman churches. Begun in 1339, it was not completed until the end of that century. The portal was not finished until the nineteenth century under Louis-Philippe, a bit like the construction of Cologne Cathedral. Not to be overlooked is Mont-Saint-Michel Abbey, a striking and splendid collection of monuments high on a rocky cliff, a celebrated pilgrimage center where the romanesque church was given a flamboyant choir and ambulatory with five radiating chapels in the fifteenth and sixteenth centuries. It is also famous for the thirteenth-century buildings built into the north side of the rock and called 'The Marvel' (*la Merveille*). From bottom to top, the three tiers shelter the chaplain's residence and the cellarer's, the guest house and the chapter house, the refectory and the charming cloister.

The end of the eleventh century witnessed the founding of the Order of Cîteaux, whose rapid expansion dotted all of Europe with monasteries. The Cistercians first spread buildings inspired by romanesque burgundian architecture, but they soon adopted the ribbed vault in all their foundations. Enjoying prodigious growth, they were soon called the 'missionaries of gothic art'. By this we see that, up until the thirteenth century, monastic churches far outstripped cathedrals in advancing the art of building.

5

THE ASCETIC REACTION: A CONCEPTION OF MONASTIC ARCHITECTURE

FROM THE END OF the eleventh century and especially in the beginning of the twelfth, a reactionary movement began which gave birth to a new concept of monastic architecture. Although they did not initiate the movement and were not its sole proponents, nevertheless, the Cistercians played a leading role in its evolution. This was due both to Saint Bernard, who took advantage of the authority he acquired through his growing prestige and founded all over Europe monasteries which used these new forms of architecture.

THE BASIC PRINCIPLE OF CISTERCIAN REFORM: THE CHURCH AS A 'WORKSHOP OF PRAYER'

The Cistercian reform undertaken in the last years of the eleventh century aimed at restoring the *Rule of Saint Benedict* to its original purity and integrity. For the Cistercians, the Rule of the holy Patriarch was, next to the Bible, the book in which they sought principles to direct their entire lives. The whole of this Rule conveys a spirit of poverty and simplicity.

111

Consequently, they wanted to reject totally all superfluity, to renounce all creature comforts, and to live poorly with the poor Christ.

The Rule says not one word about architecture. Yet the chapter dealing with the oratory begins with these words: 'Let the oratory be what it is called, a place of prayer; and let nothing else be done there or kept there'. It was perhaps on the basis of this text that Saint Stephen Harding, the third abbot of Cîteaux, asked the Duke of Burgundy to discontinue holding his court in the monastery church as he had been accustomed to do on great feasts. On this same text, Saint Stephen decided to banish from the oratory anything that was not directly related to prayer and divine worship.

Prayer and contemplation are a delicate and difficult work. And so, in order to avoid all that could be distracting, the Cistercians wanted to banish from their churches all superfluous ornamentation—all gold, silver, and precious stones, anything that stimulated the senses.

Saint Benedict also says in his Rule that the monastery is a workshop where a monk practices the spiritual art. In the monastery, if there is a place where this art is exercised in its highest and purest form, it is the oratory. We are not surprised, then, to find that Cistercians wanted to make their churches 'workshops of prayer' where absolutely nothing would detract from this fine art.

Saint Benedict's word 'workshop' (*officina*) is well chosen. Imagine a workshop encumbered with a thousand anomalous objects, none referring to the art that was being practiced there, and all doing nothing but distract the artisan from his work.

The more of an art something is, the more painstaking and precise must be the workmanship, the more need there is to rid the place of every distraction. This explains why modern businessmen work in offices with bare walls stripped of all decoration that could take up their attention and distract them from their abstract work with figures. The same could be said of an operating room, where nothing should distract the surgeon from the practice of his art and risk putting the life of his patient in jeopardy. By the same token, cistercian churches as workshops of prayer should also be stripped of all that could stimulate the senses and distract the monk from prayer. In all these examples, the stripping serves the same purpose; the only difference is that in the one instance it is for a temporal reason and in the other for a spiritual.

These principles prompted the Cistercians to adopt a life that was poor and austere and in which the most difficult and unappealing manual work was given a place of honor. This development was such a contrast from the lives of the benedictine monks of the time that it could not help but create great scandal to all who professed a life according to the Rule of Saint Benedict. These new religious were not spared mockery and sarcasm. It was maintained on all sides that this reform clung to the letter at the expense of the spirit, and could only be of short duration. 'For the letter kills and the spirit gives life,' it was said, using the expression Paul had directed to the Corinthians. The Cistercians riposted. Unfortunately, indiscreet remarks were made by monks with a false zeal, criticizing the customs at Cluny, adding venom to the debate and soon touching fire to dry tinder.

A COUNTER-ATTACK FROM THE ABBOT OF CLUNY

The abbot of Cluny, Peter the Venerable, a good friend of Saint Bernard, was affected by this activity and soon this great master of the immense abbey of Cluny—which controlled almost a thousand abbeys and priories all over the world—took up the defense of the customs and usages of his abbey. He wrote a long letter—forty-seven columns of Migne's *Latin Patrology*—to Saint Bernard, the Cistercians' most popular representative. Abbot Peter began the letter with a vigorous counterattack:

Figure 5.1. Cistercian monks building their abbey. This lively picturesque scene appears in a wood-painting adorning a retable at Maulbronn Abbey.

Oh Pharisee, you are prosperous. You
are worldly. Your sons see themselves
as being beyond comparison, and esteem
themselves above others. Tell me,

strict observers of the rule, how
can you claim to be so faithful to it
when you have so little concern for the
chapter where a monk is asked to consider
himself as the least of men, not only
in his words, but at the bottom of
his heart?

Then comes a discussion of all the injuries dealt to his Order in the area of food, clothing, manual work, and many other details. The abbot of Cluny demonstrated the legitimacy of the cluniac customs, justifying them to the least detail without ever departing from his serene manner, appealing to reason and good sense. He mentions that the letter kills and the spirit brings life. He explains that in comparison with the immutable precepts of charity, humility, and chastity, there are laws which can vary according to circumstances of place, time, and person. In brief, he reproached the Cistercians for being too attached to details which were of secondary importance, forgetting charity which was the main principle.

But it must be noted that while he was careful to explain the reasons for certain mitigations of the Rule, he did not try to justify any of the cluniac aesthetics or its sumptuous decoration.

BERNARD'S RESPONSE: THE APOLOGY TO WILLIAM

At the suggestion and insistence of his friend William, abbot of Saint Thierry in Reims—a Benedictine—Bernard decided to respond. After hesitating for a while, he eventually took up his pen. It has been said that honey flowed from his lips, but he also knew how to dip his pen in vinegar. In the *Apology* addressed to William of Saint Thierry, Bernard began by justifying his intolerance and then he took issue with those members of his Order who might have ignited the quarrel through their misplaced words and criticisms. Suddenly, however, the *Apology* changes into the most biting and virulent pamphlet imaginable against the monks of Cluny. The abbot of Clairvaux gave free course to his truculent and unflappable verve as he wrote the most striking pages known on the disorders which degraded many of the Benedictine abbeys. He mentioned the intemperance of cluniac monks in food and drink, the extravagance of their clothing and bedding as well as their buildings. In those monasteries, he wrote:

> Abstemiousness is accounted miserliness, sobriety strictness, silence gloom. On the other hand, laxity is labeled discretion, extravagance generosity, talkativeness sociability, and laughter joy. Fine clothes and costly caparisons are regarded as mere respectability, and being fussy about bedding is hygiene. When we lavish these things on one another, we call it love.[1]

This still does not concern architecture, but one cannot resist mentioning these lines as well as those which follow. The saint continues:

> 'How removed you are from the time of Anthony and of those early monks who sought food for their souls with such ambition that they forgot about food for their bodies. Those monks knew real ardor, the summit of discretion, true charity.'

Then he moves to a description of the food served to the monks at table.

> . . . course after course is brought in.[2] Only meat is lacking, and to compensate for this two huge servings of fish are given. The cooks prepare everything with such skill and cunning that the four or five courses already consumed are no hindrance to what is to follow, and the appetite is not checked by satiety.

And then we come to concrete details:

> . . . who could describe all the ways in which eggs are tampered with and tortured, or the care that goes into turning them one way and then turning them back? They might be cooked soft, hard, or scrambled. They might be fried or roasted, and occasionally they are stuffed. Sometimes they

are served with other foods, and sometimes on their own. What reason can there be for all this variation except the gratification of a jaded appetite? A good deal of care is given to the appearance of a dish, so that the sense of sight is as much delighted by it as the palate. In this way, even when the stomach rumbles its repletion, the eyes can still feast on novelties. The eyes delight in colors, the palate in tastes, but the poor stomach can't see colors, and isn't tickled by tastes. It has to carry everything, and ends up being more oppressed than refreshed.

How can I recommend water drinking, when we won't countenance adding water to the wine? All of us, because we are monks, seem to have stomach troubles, and so we have to follow the Apostle's advice and take some wine. I don't know why it is that we overlook the fact that it is a *'little wine'* that he recommends.[3] Even so, I only wish we could be content with plain wine, even though it be undiluted. It is embarrassing to speak of these things,[4] but it should be more embarrassing still to do them. If you are ashamed to hear them mentioned, you needn't be too ashamed to amend. The fact is that three or four times during a meal, you might see a cup brought in, half-full, so that the different wines[5] can be sampled, more by aroma than by taste. It is not swallowed, but only caressed, since a seasoned palate can quickly distinguish one wine from another, and select the stronger. It is even alleged to be the custom in some monasteries to give the community honeyed or spiced wine on the major feasts.[6] Is this also on account of stomach troubles? As far as I can see all this is so designed to make drink as plentiful and pleasurable as possible. When the monk gets up from table and the swollen veins in his temple begin to throb, all he is fit for is to go back to bed. After all, if you force a man to come to the Office of Vigils before his digestion is complete,[7] all you will extract from him is a groan instead of a tone.

After discussing this lack of restraint in eating, the abbot of Clairvaux then makes a great deal over the clothing and the extravagance of abbots who travel with a lordly entourage. There is no doubt that these lines were directly aimed at Abbot Pons of Cluny and Abbot Suger of Saint Denis.

WHAT IS GOLD DOING IN THE SANCTUARY?

The reader must forgive me this digression, but the passages quoted here, rich in satire, reveal a whole environment, and it is in this context that we must study the architecture of the time. This background will help us better to understand Bernard's reactions: 'I shall say nothing about the soaring heights and extravagant lengths and unnecessary widths of their churches'—the abbey of Cluny was thirty meters to the vaulting, one hundred eighty-seven meters long, the nave flanked with double aisles, and the church measured a total length of twenty-eight meters!— 'their expensive decorations and their novel images, which catch the attention of those who go in to pray and dry up their devotion.' Then, citing a verse from the *Satires* of Persius: *Dicite, Pontifices, in sancto quid facit aurum?*, he applied it to the monks: 'Tell me, O poor men,' this is my question, 'tell me, O poor men—if you are really poor men— why is there gold in the holy place?' Saint Bernard had no difficulty distinguishing what could be useful to the piety of the simple faithful from what he considered superfluous for monks:

> It is not the same for monks and bishops. Bishops have a duty toward both wise and foolish. They have to make use of material ornamentation to rouse devotion in a carnal people, incapable of spiritual things. But we no longer belong to such people. For the sake of Christ we have abandoned all the world holds valuable and attractive. All that is beautiful in sight and sound and scent we have left behind, all that is pleasant to taste and touch. To win Christ we have reckoned bodily enjoyments as dung. Therefore, I ask you, can it be our own devotion we are trying to excite with such display, or is the purpose of it to win the admiration of fools and the offerings of simple folk?

A bit further on he writes:

> Churches are decked out, not merely with a jewelled crown, but with a huge jewelled wheel.

Figure 5.2. The crown of lights at Saint Remigius, Reims. Measuring six yards in diameter, the corona is girdled with towers representing the metropolitan see of Reims and its archbishopric. It holds ninety-six candles, each commemorating a year in the life of the great archbishop, Saint Remigius.

Without doubt this refers to the large and magnificent crown chandelier, ten meters in diameter, which decorated the nave in the abbatial church of Saint Remi at Reims. It dated back to the ninth century, the time of Archbishop Hincmar. There were twelve towers representing the metropolis of Reims and its eleven suffrage episcopates, Cambrai, Soissons, Laon, Beauvais, Châlons-sur-Marne, Noyon, Amiens, Tournai, Thérouanne, Senlis, and Arras. The crown held ninety-six candles representing the years of Saint Remigius' life. The Gospel of Saint John was engraved in uncial letters on a golden band. Having been once destroyed, this crown was replaced by another during Henry II's reign. This second one was broken in 1795 by the *sans-culottes*. A new replica in turn disappeared during the First World War and was replaced by a third which faithfully reproduced it. As for the 'candelabrum as big as a tree' this refers to the immense seven-stem candelabrum, more than five meters high, located at the entry of the sanctuary at Saint Remi. There was another of the same kind at Cluny, a gift from Queen Mathilda, wife of King Henry the First of England. What is the point, Saint Bernard asked:

> Oh, vanity of vanities, whose vanity is rivalled only by its insanity![8] The walls of the church are aglow, but the poor of the Church go hungry.

And referring to the illustrated pavement tiles such as Saint Remi had, Bernard commented:

> What sort of respect is shown for the saints by placing their images on the floor to be trampled underfoot? People spit on the angels, and the saints' faces are pummelled by the feet of passers-by. Even though its sacred character counts for little, at least the painting itself should be spared. Why adorn what is so soon to be sullied? Why paint what is to be trodden on? What good are beautiful pictures when they are all discolored with dirt? Finally, what meaning do such things have for monks, who are supposed to be poor men and spiritual?

Spitting, we might remark, was a common practice in the Middle Ages, even in churches.

DEFORMED BEAUTY AND BEAUTIFUL DEFORMITY

It was not only the churches that were decorated.

> What excuse can there be for these ridiculous monstrosities in the cloisters where the monks do their reading, extraordinary things at once beautiful and ugly? Here we find filthy monkeys and fierce lions, fearful centaurs, harpies, and striped tigers, soldiers at war, and hunters blowing their horns. Here is one head with many bodies, there is one body with many heads. Over there is a beast with a serpent for its

Figure 5.3. Carved capitals of the kind emphatically opposed by Saint Bernard. Above: Battle of Demons (from North-West), Nave, 6th North Pillar, west Capital at Ste. Madeleine, Vezelay, France. Below: Capital from cloister of Saint Pierre, Moissac (before 1125). Musée des Monuments Français, Paris.

tail, a fish with an animal's head, and a creature that is horse in front and goat behind, and a second beast with horns and the rear of a horse. All round there is such an amazing variety of shapes that one could easily prefer to take one's reading from the walls instead of from a book. One could spend the whole day gazing fascinated at these things, one by one, instead of meditating on the law of God. Good Lord, even if the foolishness of it all occasion no shame, at least one might balk at the expense.

We must remember that Bernard was not speaking as an art critic and aesthete but as a monk and ascetic. If he criticized certain works of art that found their way into the house of God, it was for the sake of purity in a monastic life which requires poverty, a radical rejection of the superfluous, and unceasing prayer. Henry Focillon once wrote that Bernard 'enclosed within an austere wall the ardent austerity of his faith.' He never went as far as Angelique Arnauld, who wrote: 'I love all that is ugly. Art is only a lie and a vanity. Everything that feeds the senses takes away from God.'

The abbot of Clairvaux was not unique in his opinions. Blessed Aelred of Rievaulx, a cistercian abbot in the diocese of York, alluded in a sermon to the distractions to prayer that came from too many exterior decorations. He said, 'Surrounded by all these chants, ornaments, lights, and so many other kinds of beauty, a monk can't help but think about all the things striking his eyes, ears, and other senses'.

The cistercian abbots who gathered for General Chapter even drew up legislation in this regard around 1150: 'We forbid any sculptures or paintings in our churches or in other parts of the monastery, because as often as we look at them, we neglect the graces that come from a good meditation and the discipline of religious gravity'. In other words, these images merely distracted Cistercians from their prayer and meditation, to say nothing of the large expenditures they entailed, which could better be used to help the poor.

No particular decision on architecture itself was ever taken in the Order of Cîteaux, except that stone belfries were forbidden, something which they felt was superfluous and contrary to poverty. There were to be only two bells, and they were to be light enough that only one person was needed to handle them. They were placed either in very simple belfry arcades on the gable-end of one of the transepts, or in a small wooden bell-tower over the transept crossing. The Cistercians saw stone towers as symbols of feudal power, whose advantages they radically rejected in all their abbeys. All this was done to safeguard simplicity and monastic poverty.

In our day, this simplicity and poverty is attractive. The ecumenical movement pushes more and more in this direction. Statements coming from very different sources express the same sentiments: John Guitton, in his *Journal de Captivité* quotes one of his protestant friends as saying:

> I like the spiritualities of less. An abundance of statues in churches embarrasses and irritates me, obstructs my prayer. That's why I like cistercian chapels. There is only stone, wood, a vague odor of dust, soot, and incense. I like the desert. We Protestants can only pray in an environment stripped of things.

Then, Isidro de las Cogigas tells us in his book, *Los Mudejares*:

> The white limestone of a muslim mosque, glistening in the refracted light from the patio or the lamps, is as noble and as inviting to prayer as the stone of a cistercian church. To compare with the wonderful play of light and shadow in a muslim mosque, there is nothing better than the peace and austerity of a cistercian chapel.

ABELARD FOUNDS THE ABBEY OF THE PARACLETE AND GIVES IT TO HELOISE

The same poverty and simplicity can be seen at the Abbey of the Paraclete, founded by Peter Abelard. So different from Saint Bernard in many respects, Abelard completely agreed with him in his interpretation of the chapter of the

Rule on monastic poverty and simplicity. He wanted to see this simplicity expressed in the liturgical ceremonies and vestments as well as in the architecture. His ideas were formulated in a long letter—actually a rule for nuns—written to Heloise a short time after she became abbess of the Paraclete.

The circumstances surrounding this foundation bear repeating. After his emasculation, Abelard sought refuge at Saint Denis Abbey, where he donned the habit of a benedictine monk, more out of embarrassment than out of devotion, as he himself admits. After his condemnation at the Council of Soissons in 1121 and his internment at Saint Médard Abbey, this sad figure returned to his abbey, Saint Denis. One day, soon after his return, he was reading Bede the Venerable's commentaries on the Acts of the Apostles and discovered that Denis the Areopagite—converted by Paul before the Areopagus—had been bishop of Corinth, not Athens, and had nothing whatever to do with the Bishop Denis who later came to Gaul and occupied the episcopal seat in Paris. Consequently, the patron of Saint Denis could not have been converted by Saint Paul's convert. He could not resist sharing these findings with his confrères. There was a general outcry in the community. He had dared question the authority of Hilcuin, abbot of Saint Denis three centuries earlier, who had supposedly proven that the patron of Saint Denis was the very person mentioned in the Acts of the Apostles. Abelard's situation became even more precarious, for Saint Denis was one of the patrons of the kingdom of France. The affair was brought to the abbot, who threatened to bring Abelard before the king.

In despair, feeling that the whole world was against him, Abelard sought refuge on the property of Count Theobald in Champagne, originally to a priory at Provins and then in a wilderness not far from Nogent-sur-Seine. With the bishop's permission, he built himself a small hermitage and dedicated it to the Holy Trinity.

As soon as his whereabouts were discovered, a flock of students came to study under him. They built cabins around his place and soon began to farm and live off the land. After a time they built a larger oratory of stone and wood. In the joy and consolation of seeing a return of the good times of the past, Abelard consecrated the oratory to the Paraclete, the Consoling Spirit.

But Saint Bernard and his friend, Saint Norbert, founder of the Premonstratensians, were irked by Abelard's renewed success, for they considered his teaching suspect. Also, the turbulence and lack of discipline among his students were causing great scandal all over the country. All this put Abelard into an even darker despair. He fled deep into Brittany. There he was offered the direction of Saint Gildas Abbey at Rhuys. But all he found there were wild, unruly monks who persecuted him and even tried to kill him.

At this point Suger had just been elected abbot of Saint Denis and wanted to bring some order to the monastery possessions. He reclaimed his rights over the monastery of Argenteuil where Heloise had taken the veil after her secret marriage with Abelard and was now abbess. Suger won his case and the nuns at Argenteuil had to find refuge in other monasteries. Abelard offered the Paraclete to Heloise and her nuns, and he went to set them up. Soon afterwards he wrote the long letter that became their rule of life. In it he mentions that all excess and superfluity must be radically rejected, in food as well as in liturgical vessels and decoration and in their goods and buildings.

Like Bernard and the Cistercians, Abelard prohibited all silk vestments and altar cloths except for the stole and maniple. He forbade expensive vessels, anything in gold or silver, paintings or sculptures. On the altar there was to be a plain wooden cross on which the image of the crucifix could be painted, if desired. No other image would be permitted. Only two bells. All these regulations were to be found almost word for word in the cistercian usages.

Figure 5.4. Pillars in Le Thoronet church. This well-known church in the south of France is a typical example of the cistercian reaction to benedictine exuberance. The disposition of the massive structures, the sheer weight and volume of the stonework, and the superb workmanship attest to the severity, but equally to the harmonious and human qualities of this architecture.

WHERE NOTHING SUPERFLUOUS IS TOLERATED

The same applied to possessions and buildings: nothing superfluous was to be tolerated. 'If anything we build is larger and more beautiful than necessary, if it is decorated with paintings and sculptures, then it is not a house for the poor that we build, but a palace for kings.' Abelard ends by quoting Jerome: 'The Son of Man had no place to lay his head and you lay out vast porticos and immense roofs.' He goes to the point of saying that anything superfluous is robbery and that when engaging in this extravagance, we are responsible for the death of the poor we could have saved through more frugality.

In the eighteenth century there was a sculpture of the Blessed Trinity in the oratory of the Paraclete. The Three Persons were symbolized by three men of the same height. The central figure wore a gold crown with this verse in hand: *Filius meus es tu* ('You are my Son'). The figure on the right wore a crown of thorns and in his hand he held a cross with the verse: *Pater meus es tu* ('You are my Father'). The one on the left wore a crown of flowers with the words: *Utriusque Spiraculum ego sum* ('I am the Spirit of both'). Is it conceivable that Abelard, contrary to his own Rule, would have had this monument made in remembrance of his monastery's first dedication? Might he have wanted to affirm an orthodox view of the mystery he had audaciously pretended to understand and explain in his *Opus clarum de Unitate et Trinitate divina* (*Clear Treatise on the Unity of the Divine Trinity*) which had been condemned at the Council of Soissons where he had to throw the document into the fire? The founder of the Museum of French Monuments, Alexander Lenoir, was of the compelling opinion that this sculpture had not been executed before the end of the fourteenth century. In any case, in the eighteenth century, the memory of Abelard and Heloise was still very vibrant at the Paraclete and the sisters were proud to possess some ashes of their founder and their first abbess. Quintin Crawford, who visited the Paraclete in 1787, tells us:

> Upon entering the guest parlor of the abbey, I was struck by the many portraits of Abelard and Heloise. The abbess had them on her table and in every room in her apartment, even at the head of her bed. I entered many of the Sisters' cells where these same portraits were among their crucifixes and relics. I would venture to say that the Paraclete is the only convent where the joys and pains of two lovers are a continual subject for discussion and reflection.

Figure 5.5. Nave of the abbey church at Fontenay.

The abbey was demolished after the Revolution. The sixteenth century enclosure wall is still there, as are the thirteenth-century grange and wells and the abbatial apartment built around 1686.

THE AUSTERITY OF THE 'BONHOMMES'

Simpler, more barren and austere than even the cistercian buildings were the poor and humble surroundings of the Grandmontines, who were also called 'the gentlemen'.

The order of Grandmont came to birth at the end of the eleventh century. In 1076, Stephen, son of the Viscount of Thiers in Limousin, withdrew to the midst of the forest of Muret to live as a hermit. After about a year, a few companions came to join him. When his disciples had reached a certain number, he wrote one of the most severe rules known, in which poverty was pushed to its extreme in food, clothing, and every other area. It was forbidden to have anything beyond the bare necessities, or to have any fixed revenues, cattle, Mass stipends, or even to claim legal rights. Shortly after they made their foundation, the Canon Regulars of Ambazac reclaimed a few acres of land being used by Stephen's disciples, who left the property immediately without the least resistance. With the Bishop's permission they went to Grandmont in the midst of a dense forest. This is how the Order acquired its name.

The Grandmontines grew rapidly under the protection of the Plantagenets and by the middle of the twelfth century, from England to Provence and from Champagne to Navarre, there were already one hundred and fifty houses, each composed of twelve monks, a superior, and a few laybrothers.

In order to devote themselves exclusively to contemplation, the Grandmontines decided to delegate the entire temporal administration to laybrothers. Outside the General Chapter which met annually on 24 June, the Feast of Saint John the Baptist, authority rested with the prior of Grandmont, and in each house all the religious—lay or cleric—were considered equal. However, the real authority in each house (cell) was actually in the hands of the treasurer, or *dispensator*, who was a laybrother. This absence of hierarchical structures was a serious danger and the Grandmontines soon became aware of it, at their own expense.

Figure 5.6. The abbey church at Fontfroide. Most of the buildings at this cistercian foundation have survived, presenting a remarkably intact monastery. The twelfth-century church exhibits a harmony and sobriety very much in keeping with the cistercian tradition.

The laybrothers, who had grown to a large number, soon wanted to rule in every area. This caused unending quarrels and eventually, the laybrothers were in open revolt against the monks. Even the Prior General was put into prison and then forced to resign. Various popes had to intervene and severely punish the rebels, but nothing worked. Eventually recruits dwindled and monks began to leave the Order. The Hundred Years War also took its toll and dealt such a blow that the order never recovered. After an effort at reform in the mid-seventeenth century, this order, which numbered 144 cells in France, three in England and two in Spain, was suppressed in 1722 by the Commission of Regulars.

Their cells had usually been located in solitary, wooded areas which formed a natural enclosure. There were exceptions like that of Bois-de-Vincennes, now Minimes Lake at Nogent, and Notre-Dame du Parc in Rouen. In these cases, the monastery was entirely surrounded by walls.

POVERTY PUSHED TO THE EXTREME: GRANDMONTINE CHURCHES

The poverty of their buildings was extreme. In one of the early statutes of the Order we read that all excess is to be banned. The churches and other buildings must be simple and humble. All paintings and useless sculptures were strictly prohibited and the statute also declared: 'just as on judgement day we will have to render account for all unnecessary talk, so too will we render account for all needless works'. This ideal of poverty exemplified in the buildings was observed more scrupulously and tenaciously among the Grandmontines than anywhere else. Their churches were small and low, between twenty and forty meters long, five to six meters wide, and six to seven meters high under the vault. They generally faced the east, and had but a single nave covered by a pointed barrel vault, usually with no groins. Only one church—Petit-Bandouille in Poitou—has cross-ribbed vaulting springing from columns which rest

Figure 5.7. The abbey church at Saint-Jean-des-Bonhommes, near Avallon. This is one of the few extant examples of the architecture of the Grandmontines, who reached new heights of rigor and simplicity.

on foundations. The naves had no windows and usually ended with a semi-circular apse vaulted in *cul-de-four* like Étricor Church not far from Chabanais in Angoumois. There are also a few churches with a flat east end with radiating chapels, such as that of *Grand-Bandouille* near Bressuire in Poitou and Trézen in Limousin. Others have a polygonal apse, covered with a fillet vault like that of Breuil-Bellay near Montreuil-Bellay, and la Primaudière, both in Anjou. The choir was often a bit larger than the nave and it is assumed that this departure, peculiar to the Grandmontines, corresponded to some technique they used in constructing their choir vault.

Since they originally had few priests, there are few altars in their churches. Moreover, there was no separation between the monks and laybrothers.

The main portal was on the north side at the end of the nave, to allow the few lay people who came entrance into the church without coming into the monastery.

The churches had no framework and the roofing rested directly on the ribs of the vault. Two churches at Poitou have a belfry over the choir: at la Primaudière where it seems to originate and at Bois-d'Alonne where the belfry was rebuilt.

The monastery itself, usually on the south side, was small. It was built pretty much on the traditional plan, with a number of buildings arranged around a cloister. The only cloister that has been preserved is that of Saint Michel at Lodève, not far from Montpellier. The sides are fourteen meters long. Entering from the church door that goes to the cloister, one comes into a passageway leading to the cemetery, to which the religious processed three times each day. In this hallway they changed from their choir robes to their work clothes. A little further along is the chapter, usually vaulted. It can still be seen at Bois-d'Alonne, Breuil-Bellay, Badeix in the Limousin, Puy-Chevrier in Poitou, and at Grand and Petit Bandouille.

Next to the chapter door there was usually a stairway leading to the dormitory. Some of these staircases are preserved, as at Saint Michel in Lodève and at Grand and Petit Bandouille. Further along was a large, dimly-lit room with a large doorway to the south. It is thought to have been a storeroom. The common dormitory of the monks and laybrothers occupied almost the whole length of this upper level, lighted from both sides by small windows.

Running the length of the south gallery and facing the church was the refectory. It was parallel to the cloister and the kitchen could easily serve both the refectory and guest house. The west wing was taken up by community rooms and the guest house.

The simplicity of these buildings did not prevent them from being well-constructed. The stones were well arranged and carefully cut and adjusted. Here or there, a door or

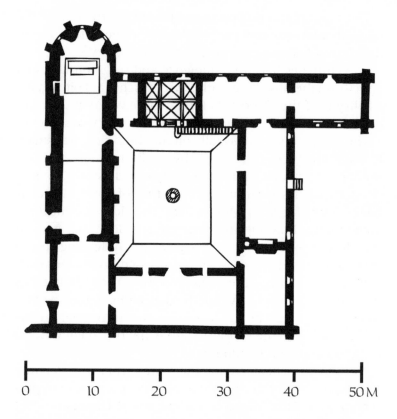

Figure 5.8. Plan of the grandmontine priory of Saint-Jean-des-Bonhommes showing the single-aisle church at the upper left.

bracket reveals a subtle decoration through which some artist could not resist displaying his inventive spirit as well as leaving his memorial. These ornaments are particularly evident on the doors leading to the outside. They include very simple base columns bearing leafy capitals sustaining some coving. Also, in the chapter rooms there are a few decorations, particularly in the bays that open onto the cloister. In the fourteenth century less attention was paid to these principles, as is evident from the walls of the churches, which began to be covered with frescoes. In spite of this, there was a great unity and uniformity in the buildings of the Order. And even in their extreme simplicity, the Grandmontines were able to achieve harmonious proportions, particularly in their churches and chapter houses.

NOTES

1. Translation by Michael Casey, ocso, *Saint Bernard's* Apologia *to Abbot William*, CF 1A (Kalamazoo: Cistercian Publications, 1970.

2. Casey, p. 55. For the literary genre of this passage, cf. Introduction, p.17. See also Leclercq, *The Love of Learning*, pp. 137f.

3. Casey, p. 56. I Tim 5:23. Cf. Sermon 30.9, *On the Song of Songs* (*S. Bern. Op.* I, p. 218; trans. Luddy, I, p. 363). According to William of Saint Thierry, Bernard himself, partly because of his digestive ailment, took wine only rarely, and then well diluted: *Vita Prima*, I, viii, 39 (PL 185:250a).

4. *Ibid.*, In the primitive edition this sentence reads: 'It is embarrassing to speak of such things that, had I not seen them with my own eyes, I would scarcely have credited . . .'.

5. *Ibid.*, p. 57. The primitive edition reads: '. . . so that the different wines can be sampled and tested, and the best among them selected. It is even alleged . . .'.

6. *Ibid.*, Bernard had already attacked the use of spices and mulse at Cluny in his letter to Robert of Chatillion; *Letter* I, II (PL 77b; trans. James, p. 8). Peter the Venerable condemned the practice in *Statute* II (PL 1028). The author of the *Riposte* staunchly defends the principle of giving something special on feast days, saying that it is only human, *humanum est* (1.590, *op.cit.*, p. 324. Saint Bernard's attitude is sketched out more fully in Sermon 3.2, *On Advent* (*S. Bern. Op.* IV, pp. 176f.; trans. Luddy, *Principal Festivals*, I, p. 24).

7. *Ibid.*, Cf. *Rule of Saint Benedict*.

8. Cf. Eccles 1:2.

Figure 6.0. Our Lady of Guadalupe Abbey, Oregon.

6

CISTERCIAN ARCHITECTURE: STARK BEAUTY

W E HAVE NOTED THAT the few norms given by the General Chapters of the Cistercians made not the least allusion to aesthetic principles. It is not there that one looks to find the inspiration for the stark architecture so common to and characteristic of the Cistercians. That inspiration is to be found instead in the spiritual principles enunciated by Saint Bernard in his *Apology* and also in the poverty which the first Cistercians regarded as the 'guardian of virtue'.

The principles set forth by the founders of Cîteaux were vigorously taken up and articulated by Saint Bernard and Blessed Aelred. Their resolve to refrain from artistic works developed into a new art style, one stripped down to essentials, an art whose beauty, stripped of all decoration (*venustas*), resides solely in simple functional forms, that is, in their harmonious composition (*compositio*) and proportions.

Certainly the first Cistercians, particularly Saint Bernard, would have been astounded to learn that they had laid the principles of a new style of art. Mme de Maillé has rightly remarked that the construction of the Cistercians became great art although they never planned it that way. 'In sacrificing all that was secondary, the Cistercians brought out the best of the monumental art of their time.' Peter Dalloz, who discovered Saint Bernard through the architecture of such churches as Fontenay, Le Thoronet and Silvacane, comments: 'One cannot imagine anything grander than cistercian construction: nothing more virtuous, more virile, more satisfying, more spiritually accomplished'. It is a truism, to echo Paschal's words on eloquence, that one architecture ridicules another.

When the Cistercians dropped romanesque methods of building to adopt the new gothic techniques, which they spread throughout Europe, they knew how, in the words of Henri Focillon, to 'preserve its power and original sobriety'.

FIRST CHURCHES OF THE ORDER

The first cistercian churches were distinguished only by their modest dimensions and extreme poverty. The first stone chapel built at Cîteaux and consecrated in 1106 consisted of a single-aisled nave twenty-four meters long ending in a polygonal apse. It was well-constructed and Dom Martène, who visited it during his literary tour, was able to say that it was 'quite small, vaulted, and very pretty'. Of the chapels built by the monks of Cîteaux's first daughter houses, we know only those of Pontigny and Clairvaux. At Pontigny the oratory was a small building of some twenty meters with a semi-circular apse. At Clairvaux the oratory had an odd square construction, seventeen meters on the sides with an aisle along the edge. Nothing here suggests there were norms dictating a model for construction, but only the injunction to poverty and simplicity.

But soon the number of recruits entering necessitated larger churches. Foundations were multiplying in extraordinary numbers. Everyone was building new abbeys. It was

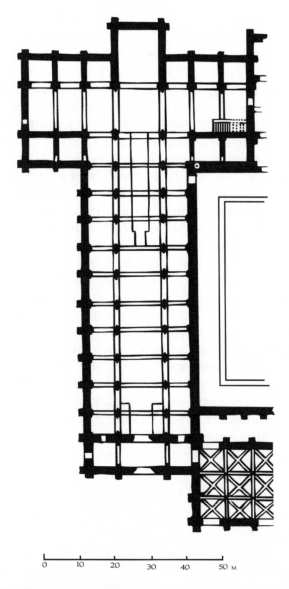

Figure 6.1. The plan for Clairvaux's second church, built from 1135–1145 under Saint Bernard. This typical twelfth-century cistercian plan is the product of strict geometry, with a narrow choir and chapels strictly aligned and open on all sides.

then that a plan emerged to serve as a model for a number of churches in the Order.

The first of these churches whose plan we know is Clairvaux, built between 1135 and 1145, conceived by Saint Bernard according to the principles enunciated in his *Apology*. When the monks of Cîteaux—the mother abbey of all the cistercian houses—built their first large church between 1140 and 1150, they used the plan of Clairvaux, which soon became the model adopted by the majority of the churches of the Order. This plan takes the form of a latin cross with a small square sanctuary, a nave with side aisles, a large transept with two or three contiguous chapels opening to the east from each of the arms. Almost invariably, a simple wooden porch was attached to the façade.

One often hears that the square east end characterizes cistercian churches. But we must remember that the Cistercians simply adopted a plan which was already widespread, and of which there are numerous examples much earlier than Cîteaux. This plan was used in the simplest burgundian churches, and adopting it facilitated their work and cut down their expenses. On the other hand, there were a large number of cistercian churches that had a semicircular or polygonal apse, according to regional customs, not to mention the large east ends based on the cathedral model, with ambulatories giving access to a series of chapels. Many examples will be given below.

THE BERNARDINE PLAN

The abbeys in the filiation of Clairvaux—which experienced a prodigiously rapid growth—were very faithful to the plan of their motherhouse. Saint Bernard's sons followed this plan everywhere: in England, the Rhineland, Italy, Ireland, France, Norway, and Sweden. This was so true that after realizing that this plan was nearly always followed in the cistercian churches built during Bernard's life, Dr Esser of Mainz began calling it the 'bernardine' rather than the 'cistercian plan'. Foigny, not far from Vervins, was Clair-vaux's third foundation, made in 1121, and very faithfully reproduces Clairvaux. Although it was entirely demolished after the Revolution, excavations in 1959 resulted in my uncovering the foundations of a large church, ninety-eight meters long, which can be dated to between 1150–1160, judging from the debris of various columns and ribs. It almost exactly reproduces the church at Clairvaux.

The oldest church of this type still intact in France is Fontenay, Clairvaux's second daughter, founded in 1119, and located not far from Montbard in Burgundy. It was consecrated in 1147 by Pope Eugene III, a former monk of Clairvaux. It is one of the best preserved and purest models of cistercian architecture. The abbey church of Noirlac, not far from Saint Amand-Montrond in Berry was also built on this plan. The church and entire monastery have recently been magnificently restored and all kinds of documents concerning the Order are being gathered there with the intention of creating at this ancient bernardine foundation an international center for the history of the Order and its artistic and economic role in the Middle Ages. Also worth mentioning is the twelfth-century church of Clermont. Recently saved from impending ruin, it exemplifies the absolute starkness of cistercian architecture. Done with care and in very good taste, the restoration has brought the church back to its primitive appearance. We find this plan with a number of variations in numerous churches all over Europe: in Italy, Ireland, Switzerland, Great Britain, Germany, Spain, Poland, Denmark, and Sweden. It also developed into many other types to the degree in which master-builders allowed themselves to be influenced by local architecture.

As the number of priests continued to grow, a way had to be found to increase the number of chapels. After lengthening the arms of the transept to accommodate three or four chapels, the monks eventually provided some chapels along the west wall of the transept. But this was a makeshift

Figure 6.2. The abbey of Fontenay in an aerial view (above) and the garth or interior courtyard (below).

arrangement. The problems went unresolved while the number of monks called to the priesthood continued to increase.

The solution adopted was to build large east ends consisting of an ambulatory with radiating chapels along the sides, modeled on the large cathedrals and pilgrimage churches. At Clairvaux, where Saint Bernard's fame brought a considerable number of recruits, the abbey—including workmen—housed as many as seven hundred people. Between 1154 and 1174 they built an east end with an ambulatory and eight radiating chapels. But because of a cistercian concern for economy and simplicity, these chapels did not project beyond the ambulatory but were contained within its segmented periphery wall with interior partitioning walls set in at angles. Later, between 1185 and 1210, this type of east end was built at Pontigny, but in a more grandiose style with thirteen chapels around the ambulatory. This model, with some variations, was used for churches in France, England, Germany, Spain, and Portugal. To this type were added ambulatories whose chapels projected beyond the main building line.

It can be said, however, that the solution which best conformed to cistercian poverty and simplicity consisted in building a square ambulatory on the model of the English abbey church of the Benedictines at Romsey, in Hampshire, which dates back to 1110. This option was first adopted by the Cistercians around 1160 in the church at Morimond, Cîteaux's fourth daughter, as we see in excavations carried out by Henri-Paul Eydoux in 1954 and 1955. This formula was successful and soon Cîteaux Abbey adopted it when they had to enlarge their church, which was consecrated in 1193. Many other churches were built on this plan in Germany, Austria, and Czechoslovakia.

At the beginning of the thirteenth century, the Cistercians began building immense basilicas modeled on the great cathedrals. Among these are Royaumont, a royal abbey built by Saint Louis IX near his chateau, Asnières-sur-Oise; Ourscamp near Noyon, and Vaucelles, not far from Cambrai, where the building is 132 meters long, the Cistercians' largest church. Other churches of this kind were built in Germany and Austria.

But these constructions were already a step removed from the simplicity of the founding fathers. Peter the Chanter mentions that the Cistercians, too, fell victim to the sickness of building (*morbus aedificandi*). Besides acquiring a reputation for monopolizing land, they also became known for their luxurious churches. General Chapters intervened many times to prevent abbeys from building monasteries resembling palaces. As one statute put it, they were 'destroying the integrity of the Order'. Many of these undertakings also put the abbeys into debt. There is an echo of all this in a sermon by Hélinand, a cistercian monk of Froidmont in Beauvais, who had converted from his former vocation as a troubadour, and took his new life very seriously. He asks:

> You Cistercians who have left all and professed
> poverty, why do you erect these elaborate edifices?
> You should have renounced all of this and given the
> money to the poor.

These same reasonings are found in Bernard's *Apology*. Hélinand continues:

> I admit that these temples are holy because the
> Divine Office is celebrated in them. Yet,
> because they are so luxurious, they excite envy
> in the faithful rather than piety.

A strange sermon given by a cistercian abbot named Justin to the General Chapter in 1300 makes it obvious that things had got worse. Alluding to the scandal the Cistercians were giving in departing from the poverty and simplicity of the founding fathers, Justin said:

> It is impossible to deny it. How can anyone help
> seeing the superfluity of our buildings? And in
> seeing it, how can we prevent them from being
> scandalized? The art seems invented by Daedalus,
> the grandeur built by Giants and the expenses
> covered by Solomon.

Yet it must be noted that even though the Cistercians succumbed to constructing large churches with matching conventual buildings, during the entire Middle Ages they still managed to keep a certain note of simplicity and restraint which remains characteristic of their constructions. Churches such as Pontigny and Poblet bear testimony to this.

THE STRUCTURE OF CHURCHES

In the structure, as in the plan of their churches, the Cistercians followed the old monastic traditions and the techniques typical of Burgundy and Champagne. Monks built their own monasteries, particularly in the early years. Therefore, Cîteaux's first foundations were built by monk master-builders from Burgundy who were naturally inspired by the architecture of their own abbey and those in the area. The same applied to Clairvaux, whose foundations were built by monks from Champagne. While there are a number of plans, the techniques employed are the same. During the period when Cistercians began to cover the whole of Europe with their monasteries, i.e., the second half of the twelfth century, romanesque architecture was gradually developing into the gothic style. In many cistercian churches of this period, we note the simultaneous use of the barrel vault, the groin vault, and, soon, the ribbed vault. Often the nave was barrel-vaulted or cross-ribbed while groin vaults covered the side aisles. We also find the rounded arch used more often for doors and windows, while the arches of the grand arcades were almost always pointed.

Figure 6.3. Nave of the cistercian church at Eberbach. This Rhineland abbey is one of Clairvaux's few direct daughter houses in Germany and can be considered one of the masterpieces of cistercian construction. The nave is relatively small (nine yards wide and sixteen yards high), but its harmonious proportions give an impression of ample volume.

Supports were often made from portions of walls, or cruciform piers, with a simple impost to which the engaged columns were soon added as the rib made its appearance. In the nave, the columns ended two or three meters above the ground, resting on corbels in the form of cones or inverted pyramids; sometimes, they were bevelled at the base. This technique was adopted to provide room for the choir stalls which were set up against the supports.

The capitals were usually very simple, sometimes smooth or with a few water leaf designs faintly outlined. Later the monks began to decorate them with crockets folding under the abacus of the column; but at least for the next two centuries, there were never any capitals designed with figures. This is where the bernardine influence is most keenly felt. Doors and windows were equally simple.

General Chapters had forbidden stone belfries, as we have seen. Most often a simple wooden belfry was placed over the transept, or else the bells were housed in a small bellcote crowning the gable of one arm of the transept. Nevertheless, there are examples of stone belfries erected at the crossing, particularly in Provence, at Senanque, Le Thoronet, and Silvacane. But they were small steeples which held only two bells. The English, following the customs of that country, built veritable towers at the crossing.

Generally, the sanctuary was of very modest proportions, for the Cistercians had done away with ceremonies requiring a large number of officiating clergy. It must also be noted that there was a definite preference for triple windows in the façade of the church as well as the east wall, and also for large rose windows.

WAS THERE A CISTERCIAN SCHOOL?

We have just sketched the distinctive traits of cistercian architecture. In all this, there is nothing that could be considered a cistercian school, properly speaking, any more than there is a benedictine school. The most that can be said is that the family characteristic discernible in all these churches is their starkness and simplicity. The similarities we do find in plan and structure come only after Cîteaux began making foundations. Once the monks of Cîteaux, Clairvaux, Morimond, and other abbeys made remote foundations all over Europe, they not only implanted their cistercian life, but also brought methods of construction that had been practiced at their abbeys. This resemblance is found in most abbeys, including those in Spain, Portugal, England, Ireland, Norway, Sweden, Italy, Germany, Greece, Poland, Cyprus, and Syria. One additional factor was Cistercian master-builders rarely submitted to the architectural influence of the countries in which they made foundations.

Is there a cistercian architecture? In spite of Marcel Aubert's opinion, everything indicates that there was not. Instead, let us say that this architecture is marked by the poverty and simplicity which Bernard defined in his *Apology* and which subsequent General Chapters frequently upheld. But this does not constitute a specifically cistercian architecture.

CISTERCIAN MASTER-BUILDERS

The historian Orderic Vitalis, a benedictine monk of Saint Evroult in Normandy, claimed that the Cistercians built their monasteries themselves. He was not alone. William of Saint Thierry, the friend and biographer of Saint Bernard, mentions in his biography that the monks at Clairvaux built their own monastery:

> Some cut down trees. Others shaped the stones;
> still others built the walls. Some constructed
> underground canals to bring water from the Aube
> river to the monasteric buildings and to
> establish waterfalls to activate the mills.
> This work advanced so quickly that the abbey
> seemed to spring into life.

Figure 6.4. The nave of the abbey church at Alcobaça, Portugal.

No master-builder is mentioned in William's account, but we know from other sources that there were several at Clairvaux. Among them was Gerard, Saint Bernard's brother, the cellarer of the monastery. In his famous funeral eulogy at Gerard's death, Bernard mentions that he is not equal to his brother in construction work and that Gerard was a master-mason as well as a master-blacksmith.

From the *Life* of Bernard we also know that another monk of Clairvaux, Achard, the novice master, had built many monasteries and that in 1134 he was sent to Himmerod in the Rhineland to build the monastery there. The following year, Geoffrey of Aignay, a monk of Clairvaux, was sent to the foundation at Fountains in the diocese of York in England to direct the construction work. This same *Life* of Bernard mentions that Geoffrey built other monasteries in France and Flanders. In 1142, when Saint Malachy, archbishop of Armagh in Ireland, asked Saint Bernard for monks to found an abbey in his diocese, the abbot of Clairvaux—in a letter we still have—replied that he was sending a number of religious and that one of them, Robert, would be good at overseeing the construction work.

It is obvious that Clairvaux had no lack of master-builders. This explains why in so many different countries from Spain to the Rhineland and from Norway to Sicily, we find the same basic unity in construction and embellishments, the same starkness and simplicity in all of Clairvaux's daughter abbeys.

In the life of the young King Louis IX we read that when he resided in his manor at Asnières-sur-Oise, he would go to Royaumont Abbey, which he had founded, to help the monks put up their buildings, joining them in silently carrying litters of stones and mortar. In Germany, the chronicles of Maulbronn Abbey in Wurttemberg tell us that laybrothers succeeded each other as master-builders during the entire construction of the church. At Walkenried Abbey in Braunschweig, the plans were drafted by two monks who then built the monastery. We know the names of many of monks and laybrothers who were master-builders or masons in the construction of Marienfeld Abbey in Westphalia, Georgenthal in Saxony, Loccum in Hanover, Lehnin in Brandenburg, Doberan in Mecklenburg-Schwerin, and Eldena in Pomerania.

There were also monk master-builders in Italy, particularly at Fossanova Abbey near Piperno, south of Rome. Camille Enlart even posited that there was an architectural school at this abbey. As was the common practice, the abbey taught the liberal arts, divided into two cycles, the *trivium* (grammar, rhetoric, and logic) and the *quadrivium* (arithmetic, geometry, astronomy, and music). This alone would certainly not constitute a school of architecture. Fossanova

Figure 6.5. The façade of Fossanova Church, Italy, about sixty miles south-east of Rome. The church, begun in 1187, was consecrated in 1208 and is an example of the gothic style introduced into the pennisula by the Cistercians.

had its master-builders and it influenced the architecture of italian cistercian abbeys as well as that of many other churches, cathedrals, parishes, and franciscan and dominican convents in the region. The cistercian abbeys influenced by Fossanova's style included Casamari in Campagna, Arbona in Abruzzi, and San Galgano in Tuscany, where the religious themselves directed the works.

Figure 6.6. Detail of the pillars at Fossanova.

The fossanovan influence can be seen even in some polish abbeys affiliated with Morimond. Wachock Abbey, founded in 1179 near the russian border, is so markedly influenced that its church is considered the work of an italian master. Its structure, still intact, bears an extraordinary resemblance to Fossanova, as does the arrangement of alternating layers of reddish and grey sandstone, a clear indication of italian influence.

In a special study of this abbey, Krystyna Białoskorska of Warsaw, unearthed important finds in the excavations of the demolished buildings and discovered, carved in the stone of one of the buttresses of the church, the signature of a certain F. Simon—undoubtedly the master-builder. Of still more interest is the fact that the same signature is found in the church of nearby Koprzywnica Abbey, also a daughter of Morimond, and we know in 1239 a monk named Simon worked in the building of San Galgano Abbey in Tuscany, for Camille Enlart discovered the name in the cartulary preserved in the archives at Siena. Could these all be the same person? This is a tempting hypothesis, particularly since Washock bears many resemblances to San Galgano, Casamari, and Fossanova abbeys. Miss Białoskorska does not hesitate to call the church at Washock 'a reduced version of Fossanova' and she is working hard to prove this point.

IN THE WAKE OF THE CISTERCIANS:

THE PREMONSTRATENSIANS

At the same time the Cistercians were beginning to dot Europe with their monasteries, the Order of Premonstratensians, founded twenty years later, was also experiencing a very rapid development. Saint Norbert, their founder, was a canon from the Cologne diocese who wanted to restore the Order of Canons to its pristine purity. His project was promoted by the bishop of Laon, Bartholomew de Jur, who offered him land at Prémontré on the Saint Gobain plateau in a deserted dale in the midst of the forest of Coucy.

Figure 6.7. The abbey church at Varnhem. Sweden. This church, situated in Vastergotland, was built in the first part of the thirteenth century; its belfry is from a later period. Here we see an interesting combination of the cistercian rules and the scandinavian experience, calling to mind their wooden houses.

The order of Cîteaux was enjoying great success because of its strong constitution as well as the manifold activities of Bernard, so the new canons felt they could do no better than to base the organization of their Order on that of the Cistercians. They decided that each year there would be a canonical visitation of all the communities of the Order and a General Chapter at Prémontré on the feast of Saint Denis, 9 October. As the Cistercians had done for the first three daughters of Cîteaux, the Norbertines gave the abbots of their first three foundations the title of founding fathers of the Order. These foundations were Saint Martin in Laon, Floreffe in Belgium, and Cuissy in Thiérache. They adopted most of Cîteaux's observances, copying many word for word. As did other Canons Regular, they adopted the Rule of Saint Augustine.

When Hugh of Fosses—who had succeeded Saint Norbert in 1126—was named archbishop of Magdeburg, he issued a series of rules concerning the poverty and simplicity to be observed in regard to the sacred vessels, church ornaments, and clothing. There were also some regulations about buildings. First of all, an abbot could not build a convent without the approval of the Father Abbot, or without having consulted the abbots of that region. And if the annual visitors found the constructions too extravagant, they were to suspend the work immediately until the matter could be referred to the General Chapter.

We know nothing of the first church at Prémontré. It was apparently demolished at the end of the seventeenth century. When Dom Martène visited Prémontré at the beginning of the eighteenth century, he noted that the abbot's garden had all the charm possible in a restricted area, but added that he was angry that 'in order to make it more beautiful, they have destroyed the chapel and Saint Norbert's first building'. The oldest known church of the Order is that of Saint Martin of Laon. It dates back to the twelfth century and has remained intact, very much resembling the cistercian churches both in its plan and in its simplicity. It has a long nave of nine bays with side aisles. The church terminates in a small, squared chevet. From each arm of the large transept open three square-ended chapels. Also worth mentioning are three other churches whose ruins still exist. Their plans are in every way identical to those of the first cistercian churches. Beauport Abbey founded in Brittany near Paimpol around 1184, had two chapels in each arm of the transept. Easby Abbey, founded around 1152 in Yorkshire, had three chapels in each arm of the transept, while Torre Abbey, founded in 1197 in Devon, had two chapels in the same location.

Quite often the master-builders yielded to local influences. One of the first examples is the no longer extant abbey church of Dommartin near Thérouanne. The choir was built between 1153 and 1163 with an ambulatory opening on to five small chapels built into the wall, literally reproducing the one at Thérouanne Cathedral, razed in 1153 by Charles V along with the whole city. The cathedral choir was built between 1131 and 1133 by Bishop Milo, former abbot of Dommartin. His successor wanted to build another abbey exactly like it.

AN ABBEY IN CYPRUS: A TESTIMONY
TO THE PREMONSTRATENSIAN EXPANSION

On the island of Cyprus, the Premonstratensians had abbeys at Nicosia and Paphos, but their most famous was the abbey at Lepais (or Bellepais) where, in 1206, they occupied the former residence of the greek bishops of Kernynia. In the course of the fourteenth century, the abbey was completely restored. Begun through the generosity of King Hugh IV (1324–1359), it was completed under the reign of Peter I, his successor (1359–1369). At the end of the fifteenth century, the abbey was placed *in commendam*. After that, the community grew lax and the buildings were no longer kept up. At the end of the sixteenth century, the abbey was devastated

Figure 6.8. Façade of the premonstratensian abbey church at Beauport.

by the Turks and abandoned. For all that, some valuable ruins remain, and from a distance one can see the imposing ramparts with their powerful buttresses looming out of the trees. The buildings north of the church are arranged in the traditional order. Built on a small scale, the church has a cistercian look to it. It includes a nave of two bays with ribbed vaulting, flanked by side aisles which are also ribbed. The non-projecting transept is barrel-vaulted. There is a small square east end with three windows. The transverse arches of the nave are supported by thick columns. On the west side, the portal is preceded by a beautiful porch of three bays. The rib-vaulted cloister, on a lower level than the church, dates back to the end of the fourteenth century. The refectory is among the finest known. Parallel to the cloister gallery, it is thirty meters long, covered with six rib-vaults whose keystones are about eleven meters high. The lector's chair has been completely preserved. All these give remote testimony to the premonstratensian expansion around the world in the Middle Ages.

7

ABBOT SUGER AND
LUXURY FOR GOD

WHEN SUGER WAS ELECTED ABBOT of Saint Denis in 1122, the royal abbey founded by Dagobert and rebuilt by Pepin the Short and Charlemagne, this necropolis sheltering the remains of french kings was in a bad financial state and the lives of the monks there were hardly exemplary. Three years later Saint Bernard wrote his *Apology* to Abbot William of Saint Thierry. Copies of it spread with amazing speed to every cloister, especially among the Benedictines who could not mistake their part in it.

THE REFORM AT SAINT DENIS RECEIVES

SAINT BERNARD'S APPROVAL

Suger himself was not spared. When Saint Bernard blasted the extravagance of abbots who could not leave their abbeys without being accompanied by a suite of sixty mounted valets, or carrying their own dishes and kitchen utensils on a trip of four leagues—to the extent that people

159

mistook them for great lords rather than fathers of monasteries—everyone recognized the abbot of Saint Denis.

But Suger was a humble and saintly man. He quickly
showed that he had profited from the lesson. While re-
establishing the financial status of his abbey through his
careful administration, he undertook a personal reform and
put an end to the abuses which had provoked Bernard's
sarcasm. Bernard soon became aware of Suger's efforts and
he wrote him a long letter in which he used many biblical
phrases to reinforce his own endorsement of Suger's reform.
Bernard rejoiced that Suger had not only renounced his
pompous way of life but had also renewed the fervor and
discipline of his community, turning aside lay people who
until then had had free access to the cloister, putting an end
to the sport of boisterous youth who had steadily disturbed
the silence of this house of God.

Bernard's letter did not go unnoticed and the voice of
the cistercian abbot was heard throughout the benedictine
world. But although Suger leapt to follow Saint Bernard's
advice regarding the extravagance of his life and that of his
monks, the sections in the *Apology* concerning Suger's luxurious church remained for him a dead letter. In this area,
his ideas were completely contrary to those of Bernard. The
abbot of Clairvaux might close his eyes to all natural beauty
to think only of spiritual realities, but Suger believed that
beauty which touched the senses helped to raise the spirit
to invisible beauty. He was to show in an impressive way
that in this area he kept a free hand. To Bernard's *Apology*
Suger responded with his own *Apology*, which was simply a
recital of the accomplishments of his administration at Saint
Denis, particularly the consecration of the church which he
had enlarged and restored with great splendor. He aimed to
show that nothing was too beautiful for the house of God.
He said:

> If under the Old Law, we used gold vessels and utensils to
> hold the blood of goats, veal and cows, we have all the more

Figure 7.1. A representation of Abbot Suger at the feet of the Virgin on a stained-glass window at Saint-Denis.

reason to use golden vessels decorated with precious stones to hold the Blood of Jesus Christ.

The time had come to demonstrate his concept of worship through the use of unprecedented extravagance. All he could find that was most precious and rarest he procured at considerable cost to bring glory to God and to draw souls to Him by using visible beauty to draw them to spiritual splendors.

THE THRONG OF PILGRIMS AT SAINT DENIS

The buildings at Suger's abbey were too narrow to accommodate the growing community, particularly the church where the constantly increasing crowds could no longer be handled during pilgrimages and on great feasts. Educated by the monks, Suger had entered Saint Denis in his youth, so he had seen the vast crowds that gathered in the church to venerate the relics of Christ's passion—the holy nail and the crown of thorns—as well as the remains of the monastery's patron martyrs, Denis, Rusticus, and Eleutherius. On certain days, the throng was so dense and the pressure so strong— from those wishing to enter as well as those wanting to leave—that among the thousands of pilgrims, no one could move a foot. Fixed like statues, they kept up a continual din. For the women—who did not have the men's stamina— this pushing became so intolerable that they would blanch and begin to cry out in pain as if they were in labor. Many of them looked so ghastly that the men would hoist them up above the heads of the crowd. Suger said that when the crowd was thick these women could have walked on the heads of the throng as if on a pavement. This may have been an exaggerated comparison but it gives a good picture of the scene. These women sometimes managed to get themselves to the nearby brothers' garden, where they breathed their last. The monks who were in charge of the relics were in the same position. Succumbing to fatigue and pressure on all sides, no longer able to hold themselves up, they escaped through the windows, taking the holy relics with them.

This was the appalling picture drawn by Suger himself. Except in the small detail mentioned above, it was no exaggeration. Even if such disorders are no longer common, thanks to well-organized police forces, there are still extraordinary circumstances which give us a glimpse of these medieval episodes. Those of us who were in Paris on November 11, 1918, at the announcement of the Armistice, for example, can remember crowds on the boulevards that afternoon so dense that we could hear the cries of choking women. Many of them fell, were trampled by the crowd and died without receiving the least bit of help.

SUGER RECONSTRUCTS THE CHURCH

To avoid such recurrent scenes, Suger began as soon as he was made abbot to rebuild the church on a larger plan. Using considerable sums of money which had been saved through his prudent administration, he undertook the huge task of renovation. By 1130 he began the restoration of the carolingian nave, strengthening the walls, along with the columns supporting the grand arcades, their capitals and bases.

In the *Acts of his Administration* Suger explained how he rebuilt his church. The door of the façade was too narrow for

Figure 7.2. An aerial view of Saint-Denis.

the pilgrims and enclosed between two towers which were neither high nor useful and on the verge of decay. It was there that the work began around 1135, with the building of a narthex to be flanked by two high towers. The masons, the sculptors, and the stone cutters began their work. This section of Suger's construction is the best preserved. It consists of two bays covered by very beautifully executed rib-vaults with vaulted side aisles. Above, there is a gallery of the type previously described. The façade suffered great damage in nineteenth century restorations. Guilhermy did not hesitate to write that 'the damage which the most savage vandals had not time to do, the architects managed to accomplish. They leveled, scraped and patched things up so well that the monument has nothing left of its primitive aspect'. The northern tower, rebuilt in 1838 by the architect Debret with materials that were too heavy, soon cracked and was razed in 1846.

We can assume that this façade was completely romanesque with its three portals, a rounded archivolt, a blind arcade above and semi-circular windows. It was surmounted by a crenellated terrace and included a south-facing tower. The three door jambs were decorated with statues which have since disappeared. This was the first experiment with the statues which were eventually to appear at the portals of many gothic churches.

On the tympanum there is a Last Judgement scene which, in spite of its mutilation and unfortunate restoration, remains Suger's authentic work. On the lintel are two verses he wrote in which he refers to the Judgement:

> *Suscipe vota tui, Judex districte, Sugeri:*
> *Inter oves proprias fac me clementer haberi.*

> Accept, O just Judge, the vows of your Suger.
> Mercifully number me among your sheep.

This façade has three portals with carved columns, and the sculptured tympanum contains a vast iconographic program. Along with its buttresses and central rose window, this arrangement initiated the royal portal theme found in all gothic cathedrals.

Once these first projects were completed, the new pieces had to be adapted and joined to the old. There was a particular need to find marble columns or their equivalent to create a continuity with those already there. But where could they be found?

THE SEARCH FOR MATERIALS

Suger worried, searched, inquired, traveled to all kinds of distant places without finding anything. Then he remembered having seen some beautiful marble columns that would be a perfect match in Diocletian's palace in Rome. He planned to have them sent by sea as far as the English Channel, and then brought up the Seine to Paris. In spite of the considerable cost, this seemed the best solution for a number of years. Suddenly God revealed to him the existence of hard limestone blocks in an abandoned quarry around Pontoise, on the edge of the abbey property. Immediately the transportation problem was solved by this unexpected windfall. Stone-cutters were put to work. With considerable difficulty the columns were pulled up from the bottom of the quarry. The drovers were helped with their work, not only by the monks, but by a method used in many monastery quarries, as we have noted: a large number of local people, nobles and peasants, harnessed themselves with ropes to the team of oxen, and served as beasts of burden.

The work advanced rapidly. Once the new pieces had been joined to the old, it was time to think about the framework. A new problem. Suger consulted carpenters at Saint Denis and in Paris. Everyone told him not to count on finding the necessary wood in that region because of the sparse forests. He was told he would have to look in Burgundy, around Auxerre. But aside from the expense this would involve, it would also slow down the work considerably.

Suger searched for a better solution. One night after he had gone to bed after Matins, the problem prevented him from sleeping. The idea came to him that he should scour the surrounding forests himself to find the wood he needed for the framework, particularly for the large pieces such as wall-plates and tie-beams. He immediately got up and, leaving all other duties aside, left that morning with some carpenters, having noted down the measurements of the pieces he needed. He went to the forest of Yveline, north of Rambouillet. Crossing the Chevreuse valley where the abbey had some land, he called for the caretakers as well as those who were familiar with the forest, and asked if he had any chance of finding the wood he needed. Hardly able to hold back their laughter, they told him not to count on it. Milo, the lord of Chevreuse, who held half the forest in fief from the abbey, had cut down the wood he needed for his fortifications and war machines in drawn-out battles against the king and Count Amaury of Montfort. But Suger paid no attention to what the caretakers told him, and with bold confidence, he began to scour the forest in all directions. During the first hour he managed to find a beautiful oak the size he needed. Then he plunged into the underbrush, the most dismal thickets, through thorn bushes, and finally discovered—to everyone's astonishment—the twelve beautiful trees he needed. Overcome with joy, he had them hewn down and sent to Saint Denis to span the new nave.

They were able to consecrate the narthex on 9 June 1140, in the presence of Archbishop Hugh of Rouen, Bishops Eudes of Beauvais and Peter of Senlis, and a large crowd of people. Afterwards Suger had a latin inscription placed over the door, a prayer to Saint Denis, in whose honor Suger had undertaken these renovations.

The great american archaeologist Sumner MacKnight Crosby of Yale University, in the course of several excavations at Saint Denis between 1938 and 1948, found part of the foundations for the carolingian church and was able to determine its exact plan. He also discovered the foundations of Suger's construction, including the junction with the original wall of the church.

Because the choir needed to be enlarged, Suger left the upper storey of the façade and the crenellated terrace alone. The vaulting of the choir had first of all to be raised to the same height as that of the apse, that is, as far as the area over the crypt. He then laid the floor of the choir over the vaulting of the crypt so that it was raised above the level of the nave. He then proceeded to build the chevet.

The cornerstone was laid by King Louis VII of France, surrounded by many bishops and abbots, on 14 July 1140. The crypt was enlarged by adding an ambulatory with radiating chapels. Above it was erected the choir and its ambulatory. This consisted of nine radiating chapels whose cinquefoil rib vaults were supported by small ornamental columns with beautiful capitals.

The work lasted nearly four years during which Suger never, winter or summer, slackened in recruiting workmen and directing the work, striving to finish the construction as soon as possible. He was anxious to offer the Lord a new house as magnificent and grandiose as the old. On January 19, while they were putting up the capitals and arcades before beginning the vaults, a terrible storm rose, accompanied by torrential rains. The wind shook the unfinished construction, threatening to destroy everything. Bishop Geoffrey of Chartres was there at the time, celebrating a solemn Mass at the main altar to mark the anniversary of the death of King Dagobert. Aware of the danger, the bishop took fright and more than once during Mass extended his hand in blessing in the direction of the construction area. In spite of the violent winds, catastrophe was avoided and the

Figure 7.3. Interior view of Saint-Denis church looking from the ambulatory onto the nave. In the foreground are Suger's choir columns.

uncompleted section suffered no harm. Suger took this as a special blessing from heaven.

The work on the choir and radiating chapels was finished in October of 1143. They then turned their attention to join the choir to the narthex by a nave with side aisles and a transept with lightly projecting arms. Construction began with the north walls of the transept and nave. At this point, however, the king left for the Crusade and Suger had to interrupt his work to become the regent of France in accordance with the king's request. Only during the thirteenth century, in 1231 under the reign of Saint Louis, was the work of building resumed under the direction of the architect Peter de Montreuil.

ORNAMENTS OF UNSURPASSED LUXURY

The abbot of Saint Denis wanted his church to radiate splendor in every detail and to be truly worthy of God. He also wanted it to be worthy of the martyrs, Denis, Rusticus, and Eleutherius, to whom it was dedicated, as well as the French kings who were buried there. Suger knew Rome. He had also heard of the marvelous Hagia Sophia at Constantinople. He drew some of his inspiration from these places and wanted to endow his own edifice with all possible magnificence and splendor. This explains why he embellished his church with numerous ornaments of unsurpassed luxury. He had an altar frontal made out of gold set with many precious stones, amethysts, sapphires, emeralds, and topazes. Bishops and other dignitaries gave up their rings as an offering to God and the saints. A large crucifix was ornamented with gold and small stones by the best artists, gathered by Suger from far and wide. This piece required so many precious stones that they soon ran out. But just at that point, three monks arrived on business. Two were Cistercians, one from Cîteaux and the other from an unnamed abbey. The third came from Fontevrault. They offered him a quantity of precious stones originally from the treasury of the king of England, Henry I. At his death these treasures had passed to his nephew and successor, Stephen of Blois, who had given them to his brother Theobald, Count of Champagne. The count, in turn, offered them as alms to various abbeys. Thrilled with this unexpected windfall,

Figure 7.4. The Eleanor of
Aquitaine vase from the
treasury at Saint-Denis.
Musée du Louvre, Paris.

Suger did not hesitate to buy these stones for the considerable asking price, four hundred pounds.

These gems and many more were used to decorate the
cross, whose base was ornamented with the faces of the four
evangelists. This magnificent work of goldsmithing, created
over two years by artists from Lorraine, was finished in
1147. Pope Eugene III, a former monk of Clairvaux, was
in France that year and came to Saint Denis on Easter
day, 20 April, accompanied by Saint Bernard, his former
abbot. The monks of Saint Denis used the occasion to have
the pope solemnly bless the cross. One can easily imagine
the inner reaction of these two Cistercians to this work of

art so contrary to their own concept of monastic poverty and simplicity.

It would take too long to go through the entire list—which Suger eagerly details—of all the splendors at Saint Denis. Something must be said, however, of the stained glass windows, not only because they left a mark on the history of stained glass work, but also because, by their beauty, warmth, and life, they constitute one of the most beautiful examples of the 'aesthetics of light'.

Inaugurating the system of cross-ribbed vaulting, Suger was able to bring light into large bays by which light streamed into the immense nave, while the thousands of colors in the historicized stained-glass windows representing scriptural scenes cast their reflections everywhere. 'The entire church sustains a wonderful, resplendent light spilling through the luminous windows', as Suger described it. This light also illumined the gems and precious stones generously distributed on the reliquaries, chandeliers, and candelabra.

All these splendors ravished Suger's heart. Totally caught up in the enchantment of this house of God, he wrote:

> The charm and beauty of this house of God,
> the splendor of the multicolor gems, lifts
> me beyond my everyday concerns, and in medi-
> tation I reflect on the diversity of the virtues,
> transposing what is material into what is
> immaterial. I feel as if I am living in
> some strange part of the universe which lies
> somewhere between the slime of earth and the
> purity of heaven. And so, by God's grace, I
> rise anagogically beyond the inferior to the
> superior.

SUGER, VICTIM OF A DOUBLE ILLUSION

Suger's entire aesthetic of light can be found in the writings of Pseudo-Denis, whom Suger had read, persuaded that they were the writings of the patron of his abbey, Denis, first bishop of Paris, a martyr beheaded by the sword. Christian iconography recalls the death of these martyrs by depicting them holding their heads in their hands. Saint Denis is one of the most famous of this group of *cephalophores* (saints holding their heads). A confusion dating back to Hilcuin, the ninth-century abbot of Saint Denis who translated the works of the Pseudo-Denis, identified this first bishop of Paris with the Denis converted by Paul's discourse at Athens, as recorded in the Acts of the Apostles.

The first confusion: Suger thought that the patron of his church was the same person converted by the Apostle to the Gentiles, despite Abelard's findings. The second confusion: Suger was equally convinced that Denis the Areopagite was the author of several writings which are actually the work of another author about whom little is known. Modern criticism has brought order to these legends and the writings in question are now commonly attributed to 'Pseudo-Denis the Areopagite'. Among his most famous works is a treatise on *The Celestial Hierarchy*, which Suger read in latin translation with a commentary written three centuries earlier by John Scot Eriugena. This treatise deals primarily with light, brightness, splendor, luster, and illumination. And as Suger commented himself, he was somehow 'enlightened' by these readings.

THE 'AESTHETIC OF THE MARVELOUS AND LUMINOUS'

These writings awakened in Suger a taste for material opulence, precious stones, brilliant stained-glass windows, and a well-lighted church—all the elements which constituted the aesthetic of the marvelous and the luminous which is found throughout Suger's work. The proof lies in the numerous verses he had inscribed in his church to explain the hidden symbolism of the ornamentation. They are mere paraphrases of texts found either in Pseudo-Denis or the commentaries by John Scot Eriugena. Two characteristic examples will convey the idea. On the basilica door a latin inscription prepares the visitor to appreciate the true sense of all the beauty being offered him:

Portarum quisquis attollere quaeris honorem
Aurum nec sumptus, operis mirare laborem
Nobile claret opus, sed opus quod nobile claret

Clarificet mentes, ut eant per lumine vera,
Ad verum lumen, ubi Christus janua vera,
Quale sit intus in his determinat aurea porta.

Mens hebes ad verum per materialia surgit,
Et demersa prius hac visa luce resurgit.

Admire not the precious or costly materials in these doors, but rather the craftsmanship of the work. It is brilliant and noble.

All noble work, through its beauty, illumines souls to the genuine splendors, lifting them to the true light, of which Christ is the true door. This gilded door merely prepares you for what shines beyond it.

Through this perceptible beauty, the burdened soul rises to true beauty, and as it lies outstretched, engulfed by the earth, it may rise to heaven by seeing the light of its splendor.

This last phrase sums up Suger's thought. It also betrays the famous neoplatonic theme that what is material can be transmuted into the immaterial by the elevation of the spirit.

The church was consecrated with great pomp and ceremony on 11 June 1144. King Louis VII attended with Queen Eleanor and (of Aquitaine) and other dignitaries of the kingdom. Also present were the archbishops of Reims, Rouen, Sens, and Canterbury, and the bishops of Chartres, Soissons, Noyon, Orléans, Beauvais, Auxerre, Arras, Châlons-sur-Marne, Coutances, Évreux, Thérouanne, Meaux, and Senlis.

The inscription over the door at the east end concludes with this verse:

Annus millenus et centenus quadragenus
Quartus erat Verbi, quando sacrata fuit.

In the Year of the Word, 1144,
This church was consecrated.

To this Suger added the following verses on the stained glass windows on the east end, words which point once again to light and brilliance. The last lines are Suger's signature.

Pars nova posterior dum jungitur anteriori
Aula micat medio clarificata suo
Claret enim claris quod clare concopulatur
Et quod perfundit lux nova, claret opus
Nobile, constat auctum sub tempore nostro
Qui Sugerus eram, me duce dum fieret.

When the new construction is joined to the original,
Its glistening halls space will shine with light.
For light clearly linked to light,
Glows and a new light sweeps
Through it, as it does this noble work, this building
made during my lifetime. I, Suger, myself directed
the work.

BENEDICTINE EXTRAVAGANCE AND CISTERCIAN AUSTERITY

The magnificent realization of this grandiose project must be credited to Suger, one of the greatest men in the Middle Ages. As regent of the kingdom, he deserved to be called a father of his country and through his extraordinary gifts and energy he made Saint Denis one of the most prodigious sanctuaries of France, a church which marks one of the most important stages in the history of architecture. Suger had every reason to be proud of his work.

We are left with the question of how to deal with such contrary concepts of monastic architecture as that of Cluny and Suger on the one hand, and that of Cîteaux and Bernard on the other. Both views have had and still have their ardent defenders, both of whom can cite excellent arguments in defense of their theses. The debate is not about to end. Gradually the Benedictines did away with extravagance, either because their taste evolved in a more sober direction, or because hard times forced them to be more economical. On the other side, the Cistercians mitigated their absolute austerity, so the conflict has for a long time been pointless.

While extravagantly decorating the church at Saint Denis, Suger was equally busy rebuilding the abbey's conventual buildings, notably the dormitory and refectory as well as the guest house and various workshops. If Suger was convinced that nothing was too beautiful or too luxurious for decorating the house of God, he was equally firm in maintaining strict poverty for himself. In the biography written by Suger's disciple, the monk William, we read that Peter the Venerable, abbot of Cluny, while on a visit to Saint Denis marvelled at the splendor of the church. Then, when he saw the small cell Suger had built for himself, the cluniac abbot said, 'This man puts us all to shame. He builds not for himself, but for God alone.' In fact, during the rest of his abbacy, Suger had only this humble cell adjoining the church, a cell which measured barely three meters by five. This was his way of sharing Saint Bernard's concept of monastic poverty.

Figure 8.0. Comberoumal (Aveyron). Grandmontine Priory.

8

THE DWELLINGS
OF HERMITS

EREMITICISM, OR LIFE in the desert, was, as we have seen, the first kind of religious life to appear in Christianity, both in the East and in the West. But these first hermits or anchorites (the two words mean the same) lived in caves or huts made out of branches which they built themselves. From an architectural standpoint, therefore, there is not much to say about them. Later, however, hermits began to build stone hermitages and a few of them are still in existence.

SAINTS ON COLUMNS: THE STYLITES

There was a particular type of hermit much favored in the fifth century, and as extravagant as they may appear, a number of great saints were among them. These were the Stylites, hermits who spent their whole lives living atop a column (a *stylos* in Greek). In our day, there is a tendency to regard them as pious eccentrics craving attention. We would do well, however, to refrain from judging them by our twentieth-century concepts and categories and to see

Figure 8.1. Icon of the Stylites from Balamend Monastery. This lebanese cistercian monastery was founded from Morimond in 1157. The stylites represented are Simeon Stylites and Symeon the Younger. This painting dates from the very end of the seventeenth century.

them instead as men who lived in a world utterly removed from ours both in time and in space.

The late Father Hippolyte Delehaye of the Society of Bollandists has written an entire book on the stylites, many of whom were authentic saints and whose lives have been written down and preserved. He writes:

> Rather than stop at the external form of their asceticism—which sometimes shocked their own contemporaries as much as it does us—we should study the thought which inspired it, and this will force us to admit that these sty-lites, whom we know through their biographers, in spite of certain inevitable exaggerations, possessed character and virtue, that they were not feeble-minded, proud or fanatic. . . .
>
> It has been said that the stylites constituted a deviation in monasticism. Why a deviation? It would be more just to consider them a branch of the eastern monastic institution. It flourished in a situation which no longer exists and, we must honestly add, under conditions which we hope will never return.

The stylites deserve to be mentioned because their columns are of architectural interest and also because monasteries were built around them as memorials. The stylite column usually consisted of the following parts: the stairs to climb to the base of them, the base itself, the shaft, the capital. At the top there was a low railing and a tent made out of skins or a shelter made out of boards.

SAINT SYMEON STYLITE AND HIS IMITATORS

The best known of the stylites is Saint Simeon the Elder, the son of a shepherd from Cilicia. Simeon was completely illiterate and, after staying in the company of a few ascetics, decided to live in the village of Telanissos (Telneshe), not far from Antioch, perched on a column first nine feet, then eighteen and finally, about sixty feet high. By way of comparison, Trajan's column in Rome is ninety feet high and the Vendôme column in Paris about one hundred thirty-five feet high. At the top of Simeon's column—which was

Figure 8.2. The porch of Saint Simeon Stylites basilica in
northern Syria.

sectioned into three drums in honor of the Holy Trinity—
was a platform which provided a surface about four meters
square, as far as we can surmise from the debris.

People came from everywhere to see this new type of
hermit, and a number of miracles attest to Simeon's sanctity.
He died in 459, at the age of seventy, after spending thirty-
seven years atop his column. Father Delehaye writes:

> Even if there were no other proof of Simeon's fame,
> we would need only to note the incomparable number
> of monuments erected soon after his death at the very
> place he made illustrious through his penance. The
> imposing ruins continue to attract visitors to Qala'at
> Sama'an, or 'Simeon's fortress', as the Arabs call it.
> The basilica is the same one that the syrian historian
> Evagrius visited and described. The architect gave it
> a unique shape. It was an immense cross with arms that
> rested on the sides of an octagonal court, in the center
> of which stood the stylite's column. The base of the

column still stands. In its dimensions, this monument can rival our cathedrals. It stuns us by the boldness of its conception and the somber elegance of its detail. In a language more eloquent than the spoken word, this majestic edifice transmits the enthusiasm of the syrian people for the hermit of Telneshe.

Saint Simeon had a number of rivals: Saint Daniel in the fifth century died at the age of eighty-four; Saint Symeon the Young died in 592 at seventy-two; Saint Alypius in the seventh century lived on his column until he was ninety-nine years old; Saint Lazarus the Galisiote in the eleventh century died when he was more than a hundred years old. There were many others. Obviously this way of life did not shorten the life expectancy of these men.

There were still a few stylites in the thirteenth, sixteenth, and even the nineteenth centuries. Among their imitators we might even venture to name a young intellectual who in our own day withdrew to become the lighthouse keeper at Ar-men in Brittany—perhaps a new type of stylite!

The solitary hermit who depends on no authority and submits to no superior can be subject to many illusions, however, and Saint Bernard noted, not without humor, that the hermit can start to consider whatever he prefers, as holy and anything that displeases him as forbidden. Left to himself without any kind of guidance, he risks becoming a rule unto himself. To counteract this danger, it was thought necessary to organize groups of hermits under a rule and a superior, so beginners could receive serious formation before being allowed to live in solitude. These groups came to be modeled on the great lauras of Syria and Egypt in the early centuries of Christianity.

THE FIRST GATHERING OF HERMITS: THE CAMALDOLESE

Only at the beginning of the eleventh century did Saint Romuald make the first attempt to provide for a group eremitical life. A nobleman from Ravenna, Romuald first entered the Benedictines at Saint Apollinare in Classe, not far from his home, but he lived with them as a hermit. Others came to join him and around 1015, he founded the hermitage of the Holy Saviour at Camaldoli in Tuscany, in the high Apennine valley of Arno. These hermits lived the benedictine Rule in small cells with adjoining gardens, separated from one another without being connected by a cloister. Nearby they had a church with a small cloister, but there was no chapter house or common refectory. All these buildings together constituted the hermitage, the *Sacro Eremo*. A number of daughter houses were soon founded and the Order's constitutions were drafted in 1085 by Blessed Rudolph, fourth successor to Saint Romuald.

Close to some of these hermitages were monasteries where religious lived a cenobitic life and where novices were formed for the eremitical life which they would later live in the hermitages. Besides this, the Order had—and still has—a few among their number who live as recluses. The Camaldolese are now represented by two congregations: one in Tuscany with its center at Camaldoli, and the other at Monte Carona. There are two Camaldolese monasteries in the United States.

HERMITS LIVING UNDER ONE ROOF: THE CARTHUSIANS

It was left to Saint Bruno and his disciples at the charter house to experience a large expansion in their order. They adopted a formula similar to that of the Camaldolese which allowed the monks to live as real hermits, alone in the silence and solitude of the cell, but as members of a community which was organized hierarchically, under a rule and a superior. This approach removed the dangers which threatened hermits living on their own with no supervision. Luchaire very correctly called this *l'érémitism collectif*, collective eremitism. Even though the life of the Carthusian contains both eremitical and communal elements, primary place is given to the eremitical element and the Carthusian should be considered a true hermit. The order has a few monasteries of carthusian nuns whose life is similar to that of the men.

Saint Bruno, originally from Cologne, was a canon and scholar in Reims where he had taught for twenty years. His students included Anselm of Laon and Eudes of Lagery, who became Pope Urban II. He and a few companions decided to withdraw together into the desert. After an initial attempt in the forest of Sèche-Fontaine, a dependent priory of Molesme Abbey, they headed for the mountains of the Dauphiné where Saint Hugh, the bishop of Grenoble, directed them to the mountains of Chartreuse, an inaccessible solitude at an altitude of some 3000 feet. He himself led them there, and there Bruno settled with his six companions.

First they built an oratory and a few huts. The bishop gave them full title to the Chartreuse valley, as did many lords in the region, and he built them a wooden monastery. This first monastery, with buildings arranged according to a new plan, was designed for hermits rather than cenobites and came to serve as a model for Carthusians everywhere. Unfortunately, Pope Urban II, who had been Bruno's student at Reims, soon called his former teacher to be with him in Rome. Deprived of their leader, the first disciples left Chartreuse and the new foundation seemed in jeopardy. Landuin, Bruno's successor, however, managed to get them back together and the Chartreuse was saved. Bruno, meanwhile, wasted no time asking the pope for permission to return to the desert. Around 1090 he founded a Charterhouse in Calabria, where he died in 1101.

In the Order's first customary, drafted by Guigo I, the fifth prior of La Grande Chartreuse (1109–1136), we see already many regulations concerning poverty and simplicity. The church was to contain no gold or silver decoration except for the chalice and the straw used to drink the consecrated wine. Rugs and draperies were forbidden. Later, in 1261, paintings were also forbidden and those already in the churches were removed.

Guibert of Nogent, who praised the silence and recollection of the Carthusians as much as their extreme poverty, added that their norms did not prevent them from collecting rich libraries while copying manuscripts. He wrote: 'The less they had in material bread, the more diligently they worked to secure food that did not perish but lasted eternally.' Before the invention of the printing press, the Carthusians' main work was the copying of manuscripts. This was how Guigo managed to collect an important library. He urged his religious to take great care of the books, which he considered imperishable food for the soul.

The first monastery at Chartreuse was demolished in 1132 by an avalanche in which many of the monks died. Those who survived went with Guigo to *la Correrie*, a house at a lower level where the Father Procurator lived with the laybrothers. Then they searched for a better location in which to rebuild the monastery. They decided to choose a lower elevation, the site of the present monastery. Eight times in the course of its long history, the Chartreuse has burned down because of its wooden shingle roofing. The present buildings at La Grand Chartreuse, built from 1676 to 1688 after the last fire, are the work of Dom Le Masson. This time the roof was made of slate.

Dom Le Masson wrote up a directive forbidding anything in the construction to be superfluous or contrary to carthusian simplicity. Dom Martène, the benedictine scholar, could say after his visit to La Grand Chartreuse in 1708 that 'The house is beautiful but it has nothing which is too spectacular or which detracts from religious simplicity.'

THE ARRANGEMENT OF THE BUILDINGS IN A CHARTERHOUSE

Everything in a charterhouse is arranged so that the religious can spend the greater part of the day in solitude, recollection, and silence in their cells. The cenobite, particularly

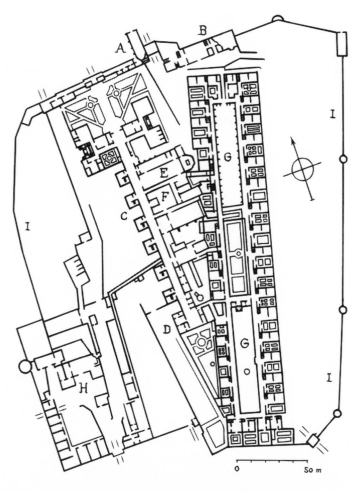

Figure 8.3. Plan of the Grande Chartreuse. The main entry is on the north where we first see a large building which lodges all the carthusian priors who gather annually for their General Chapter. (A) the exterior chapel open to women. (B) the laundry. (C) a long corridor called the officers' cloister where those who deal with outsiders have their cells. (D) cell of the Father General. (E) the church which opens onto the officers' cloister. (F) the small cloister (G) the large cloister, nearly 220 yards long. Around this are the cells, thirty-five of them, each with its small garden. (H) the outbuildings with the various workshops: the former brewery, the bake-house, the stables and the garages.

the Cistercian, lives from morning until night in the company of his brothers, whether in the common dormitory, the cloister, the library, the church for the Divine Office, the refectory, or the area for manual work. The Carthusian, in contrast, usually lives in his three-room cell, separated from everyone else. There, in his little oratory, he says his Office as soon as the bell rings, at the same time as his brothers do. There he meditates, does his spiritual reading, manual work, and garden chores, takes his meals, and sleeps at night, fully dressed, on a poor straw mat. On ordinary days, he gathers with his brothers only for the conventual high Mass, for Vespers, and for the Office of Matins, sung in the church in the middle of the night. On Sundays and feast days he also joins them for the little hours (Prime, Terce, Sext, None), for chapter and for lunch at noon. Add to this the weekly recreation when the monks come together for a long walk of several hours in the areas surrounding the monastery, during which they are allowed to converse freely with one another.

This way of life required a unique arrangement of the buildings, a radical departure from the monastic tradition. To provide each monk with his own hermitage and small garden, the monastery had to be good-sized.

A Charterhouse can be divided into three parts. The first, which takes up the most space, provides for the solitary life of the monks. It includes the large cloister (or *galilaea major*) around which the cells are arranged, each designated by a simple letter in alphabetical order, as was the custom in the ancient monasteries of the Thebaid. Each cell, a small, self-contained hermitage, has three rooms and a small enclosed garden. It is built so that it is impossible for the monk to see anyone outside or for anyone outside to see him in his hermitage. At the center of the large cloister is the cemetery where the Carthusian is buried right in the soil without coffin, as in the cistercian tradition. A plain, unmarked wooden cross marks the grave. Only the Superiors General have a stone cross.

Each cell has three rooms. The first is called *Ave Maria* because, upon entering it, the Carthusian recites that prayer before an image of the Virgin. This room is an antechamber to the next, the oratory, which has a stall and a prayer desk where the monk prays the Little Office of the Blessed Virgin and the little hours when the bell sounds, following the ceremonies observed in choir. There is an alcove with a bed consisting of a straw pallet, a sheet and some blankets, a table, books for study, and, in the window recess, a table for meals. The third room is a workshop and woodshed with a bench and a lathe. There a monk does small carpentry jobs, sawing and cutting the wood he burns in a stove during the winter months. There is also a porch which enables him to take a bit of exercise when the weather is inclement. Close to the door, built into the cloister wall is a little hatch through which a brother passes his food each day. In the twelfth century Guigo had water diverted to all the cells of the Charterhouse through the marvelous system of stone conduits. In all charterhouses, conduits of this same type distribute water to all the cells.

In this hermitage the Carthusian spends his entire life, and from it he emerges only three times a day: for the Office of Matins, for High Mass, and for Vespers. Spiritual writers have not failed to point out that in this hermitage, this cell (*cella*), the Carthusian experiences a foretaste of heaven (*caelum*). Others use a comparison dear to the monks of the early centuries and repeated by Blessed Guigo in his statutes: the Carthusian cannot remain outside his cell longer than a fish can stay out of water. Saint Bruno wrote to his friend, Raoul le Verd, dean of the chapter at Reims, that: 'In the cell we give ourselves to an active work and rest in a quiet action'.

The second part of the monastery is set aside for the common life. This includes the church, the small cloister (or *galilaea minor*), the chapter house, the refectory, and the kitchen.

Finally, the third section includes the laybrothers' quarters with various workshops and farm buildings: stables, sheds, granges, and garages. The laybrothers do various kinds of work. They function as cooks, bakers, shoemakers, blacksmiths, carpenters, gardeners, cowherds. Their quarters are usually as far away as possible from the large cloister so they will not disturb the silence of the monks in their cells. It would be futile to search for a style unique to the Carthusians. They have been content to follow local customs, but always with a real sense of simplicity.

In the charterhouse buildings there is no infirmary because a sick Carthusian stays in his cell and is treated there.

La Grande Chartreuse since it is the motherhouse, also includes an official cloister besides the regular buildings. And it has a house for the priors of the Order who come together each year for General Chapter. Four large groups of buildings are reserved for them, according to regions, France, Burgundy, Italy, and Germany.

La Grande Chartreuse is famous all over the world. Tourists come from everywhere and many hope to visit the monastery. In order to be sheltered from these continual visits and to stay in the silence for which they have come, Carthusians absolutely refuse to open their doors to visitors. In an attempt to satisfy the visitors' curiosity, however, some years ago they had the happy idea of organizing a museum at *La Correrie*, lower down the mountain. This museum is open from Easter until All Saints Day, and includes abundant documentation on the Chartreuse with plans, drawings, photographs and a beautiful scale model of the monastery. There is even a replica of a carthusian cell. In this way the visitors are satisfied and the Carthusians can fulfill their vocation to prayer and contemplation in the peace of solitude.

Figure 8.4. Aerial view of the charterhouse at Valbonne.

A RULE NEVER DEFORMED AND NEVER REFORMED

The Carthusians have been able to remain faithful to their original rule and simplicity. Pope Urban V (1362–1370), a Benedictine, wanted to give the prior of *La Grande Chartreuse* pontifical privileges (i.e., the use of the mitre, the cross, and the ring), with the title of abbot. He also tried to require the Carthusians to pray the Office in choir, to take their meals in common, and to use meat in cases of sickness. But the Carthusians were able to convince him that such mitigations would destroy the Order. This fidelity to the spirit of their founders has prompted two popes, Alexander IV (1254–1261) and Pius II (1458–1464), to assert in papal bulls that the Carthusian Order has never needed to be reformed because it has never been deformed: *Cartusia numquam reformata, quia numquam deformata.*

While the Carthusians have remained true to their poverty and simplicity, their benefactors, have not always shared these principles. Offering to take over construction of a building or to put up a cell, they often tried with the best intentions, to build large, beautiful edifices, adding ornaments and refinements to the austerity of the Order. We see evidence of this in the famous twelfth-century *Golden Epistle* written by William, once abbot of Saint Thierry and a friend of Saint Bernard, to his neighbors at the Charterhouse of Mont-Dieu. Among other things, William advised them to avoid in their buildings anything which would give an impression of quaintness and affectation.

> We remember certain artisans who put aside the
> poverty that our fathers left us as an heritage
> to build us cells that were more aromatic than
> eremitic (*cellas non tam eremeticas, quam aromaticas
> aedificimus nobis*).

Several of their benefactors built entire monasteries and made it a point of honor to erect immense edifices, sometimes luxuriously decorated, expecting, in return, to be buried there. This was the case at the famous *Certosa* (Charterhouse) of Pavia. Yet in spite of these exceptional monuments, which the Carthusians were obliged to accept in order not to offend their benefactors, it should be noted that in the great majority of their buildings, they were faithful to the norms of poverty and simplicity established by their founding fathers.

THE MOST FAMOUS EXTANT CHARTERHOUSES

Among the best-known charterhouses is one founded by Saint Louis IX in Paris. In 1258 he gave the Carthusians his château at Vauvert, outside the city walls in the area of Gentilly, now in the Avenue de l'Observatoire. Abandoned, and in semi-ruins, this château was thought to be haunted by spirits and demons. The parisians even referred to 'the devils of Vauvert', and in speaking of a distant place, they would say it was '*au diable vauvert*'. The devils did not stop the Carthusians from taking over the château and building a church under the architect Peter de Montreuil, the architect of Sainte-Chapelle. Saint Louis laid the cornerstone in 1260. After the king's death, the work was interrupted for a while and the church was not finished until 1324. Under the reign of Charles V, this monastery was outfitted with beautiful buildings and became one of the most flourishing places in the Order. The large cloister had at least forty cells. For this charterhouse at Vauvert, Lesueur painted twenty-five scenes of the life of Saint Bruno which are still admired at the Louvre. This monastery was razed during the Revolution and only the small street *des Chartreux* perpetuates its memory.

The charterhouse at Champmol at the gates of Dijon—where Charles V wanted to be buried along with his burgundian ancestors—is one of the most beautiful buildings of the period. It was founded in 1379 by the Duke of Burgundy, Phillip the Bold, who called in the most famous artists to decorate it, and chose it for his burial place. Only the church portal remains, decorated with a large number of statues. The trumeau, the central column, has a carving of the Virgin with Child by Claus Sluter. At her feet, on either sides of the door, are statues of Phillip the Bold and his wife, Marguerite of Flanders. These statues are on both sides of the door. Sluter also did a famous Well of Moses at the center of the large cloister; only a few sections of it remain. It was decorated with statues of Moses, Daniel, Jeremiah, Zachary, and Isaiah which have been preserved.

The charterhouse at Ville-neuve-les-Avignon, with its beautiful fourteenth-century church, is being restored, and the buildings of another charterhouse, at Valbonne, near Pont-St-Esprit, founded in the thirteenth century and rebuilt in the seventeenth, are completely extant and now serve as a leprosarium. The charterhouse at Val-Sainte, not far from Fribourg in Switzerland, was founded at the end of the thirteenth century and rebuilt in the eighteenth after a fire. In this charterhouse Dom Augustin de Lestrange's Trappists found refuge during the Revolution.

We must mention the charterhouse at Pavia even though it departs completely from the poverty and simplicity dear to the Carthusians. One of the most luxurious monasteries in the world, it was founded by John Galeas Visconti, Duke of Milan, in expiation for the murder of his uncle, Barnabo, and built between 1396 and 1398. No attempt will be made to describe the church of unprecedented wealth or the large cloister which is at least 125 yards long. In 1525, the famous Battle of Pavia took place on the plain below this charterhouse, and Francis I was taken prisoner. The conquered king had himself taken to the charterhouse and that night he wrote to his mother the famous line, 'Madam, all is lost, save honor.'

The charterhouse at Florence was founded in 1341 by Niccolo Acciaioli, seneschal of Queen Juana of Naples. This beautiful church is decorated with (among other things) the frescoes of Bernardino Poccetti, who represented the main episodes in the life of Saint Bruno. A subterranean chapel contains the tombs of Niccolo Acciaiolo and the members of his family. The cloisters are decorated with numerous statues and small oratories.

In Spain, the charterhouse of Miraflores, a magnificent monastery is located near Burgos. Founded in 1441, its church contains the tombs of King Juan II, his wife, Isabel, and their son, Alonso.

AN ORDER UNIQUE TO THE IBERIAN
PENINSULA: THE HIERONYMITES

In the fourteenth and fifteenth centuries many congregations were founded under the patronage of Saint Jerome. These religious, called Hieronymites or Hermits of Saint Jerome, originally lived as hermits but soon embraced the cenobitic life. The most famous group was the Hieronymites of Spain founded near Toledo by Pedro Fernandez Pecha, the king's chamberlain. Pope Gregory VI gave approval to this congregation in 1373, and presented the hermits with a cenobitic rule. Their constitutions stated that important repairs to their buildings should be submitted to a designated council. Major new constructions could be made only with the approval of the General Chapter. Moreover, the priors of new foundations were to submit the plans for their proposed monasteries to the General Chapter, or in the interim, to the Father General of the Order. Their most famous monasteries were Guadalupe and Yuste in Estremadura, the Escorial, not far from Madrid, and Belem near Lisbon in Portugal.

As it would be prohibitive to describe all these monasteries, let us take Yuste as an example. It is located forty kilometers from Placentia. Its name, taken from a stream running on the edge of the property, has no connection with Saint Justin to whom it is often attributed. In 1402 some hermits established themselves there. In 1408 a monastery was founded which passed to the Hieronymites. A spacious church with a small gothic cloister was built. Soon the neighboring forest was full of hermitages and chapels. When Charles V, suffering from gout, tired from traveling, and embittered by reversals, decided to abdicate in 1553, he thought of retiring to the monastery of Yuste. In greatest secrecy, he had a house built adjoining the monastery, large enough to lodge his suite and servants. He abdicated in 1555 and withdrew to Yuste in 1557. From his chamber he had a view of the church choir and could hear Mass and follow the Offices without leaving his room. From his work desk he had a splendid view overlooking the Vera de Placentia Basin, with the mountains of Guadalupe bordering the horizon. Stricken with a dismal monomania, like Phillip the Fair, his father, and Juana la Loca, his mother, he wanted to have his funeral celebrated with great pomp while he was still alive and could be present. He died at Yuste in 1558 but was buried at the Escorial.

Figure 9.0. Santa Croce, Florence: Church and Cloister.

9

THE ARCHITECTURE OF
THE MENDICANT ORDERS

THE FRIARS MINOR and the Friars Preacher belong
to the canonical order and, as we mentioned above,
should not properly be called monks. Their houses
are neither monasteries nor abbeys, terms which relate to
monks and abbots. The superiors of the canonical orders do
not bear the title of abbot. The term 'convent', from the Latin
conventus, connoting a gathering, a community of religious,
best describes them and is the one we will use. Both the
Friars Minor and the Friars Preacher were great builders,
especially in the thirteenth and fourteenth centuries when
these two Orders spread with astonishing rapidity.

'HOLY POVERTY': THE FRANCISCAN IDEAL

The Order of Friars Minors was founded in Assisi in 1209.
In the chapel of the Portiuncula, on February 24 of that
year, the feast of Saint Matthias, Saint Francis heard the
gospel reading in which Our Lord says, 'Go and preach,
saying: the kingdom of heaven is at hand. Take neither gold
nor money in your belts, nothing for the journey, no spare

tunic, no sandals, no walking stick.' His program was set. Following the example of the apostles, he wanted to witness to Jesus Christ.

Saint Francis established himself in the chapel of the Portiuncula, which he received as a gift from the benedictine abbot at Mont Subasio. Soon disciples came to share his life and he had to find a larger place to house his small community. They settled at Rivo Torto, not far away. The Order was born in utter destitution. Pope Innocent III approved Saint Francis' rule in 1209. The religious were to live in absolute poverty, engaging in manual work and accepting alms from the faithful, preaching repentance everywhere. Poverty was pushed to such an extreme, for the individual as well as for the community, that receiving monetary gifts was forbidden.

Saint Francis' first companions were content to live anywhere, anyhow, to eat when they could, to live from day to day, without any possessions, along with their little poor man, 'God's fool', in Chesterton's phrase. But this ideal could not be maintained in an Order which was growing with astonishing speed and which, by 1217, already had houses in Germany, Spain, France, Hungary and even Syria. Thought had to be given to forming new recruits, educating them, providing churches in which they could sing the Office and preach, collecting libraries, building infirmaries, organizing a secretariat, archives, in brief, everything that is necessary to the life and administration of a religious order. They had to build. Saint Francis could not resign himself to it all. He wanted 'A ditch, a hedge, nothing more, no wall in honor of Holy Poverty; huts of wattle and daub, small churches. Neither preaching nor any other consideration should bring the Brothers to build large, richly ornamented temples.'

Despite this, and by necessity, poverty came, little by little, to be no longer observed strictly. The saint unhappily had to amend his first rule and draft a second, which was approved by Pope Honorius III in 1223.

Saint Francis' original companions remained ferociously attached to absolute poverty, however, and to them building was a luxury. When construction began on the church at Assisi, this project seemed like an affront to the spirit of their patriarch. When some of the friars put up a poor-box to receive money for their construction work from pilgrims, one of Francis' companions found a way to blow it up, an act of sabotage. Another, after visiting the conventual rooms which he considered too luxurious, cried: 'Nothing is missing! And will we soon have women too?'

The order divided on the manner of observing poverty. To go into the details of these quarrels would take too long. We need only say that after this the Order split into several branches, and eventually the Franciscans regrouped into three distinct Orders: The Friars Minor, the Friars Minor Conventual, and much later, the Friars Minor Capuchin.

Figure 9.1. Exterior view of the basilica and cloister of Saint Francis, Assisi.

THE CHURCH OF ASSISI

The most important and best known building of the Friars Minor is the basilica at Assisi. It contains two superimposed churches with their 'east end' at the west, contrary to custom. This building was begun in 1239 and consecrated in 1253. The two churches together form a latin cross with a nave of forty rib-vaulted bays and a transept without sideaisles. The lower church has a semi-circular apse vaulted in semi-dome with a barrel-vaulted transept. A whole series of chapels was added in the sixteenth century at the entry, along the length of the northern side of the nave, and at the end of each transept. The vaulting is supported by enormous transverse ribs which are received on short, thick piers. It is very dimly lit by small, narrow windows.

In the upper church, on the contrary, the vaults soar up, supported by clusters of tall columns while light floods in through the large choir windows, through the double rose windows in the façade, and through the painted windows in the nave and the transepts. A gallery at mid-height and a trifolium along the choir give this edifice a monumental appearance. The exterior is very simple, without sculptures or the least ornamentation except for the portal, which was added during the Renaissance. A square belfry, rebuilt in the sixteenth century, stands near the southern transept. This gothic basilica betrays a strong cistercian influence. For a long time it served as a model for most of the churches built by the Friars Minor in Italy and other countries.

PREACHING HALLS

The Friars Minor built vast churches in which they sang the Office and preached, unconcerned with embellishing them with sculptures and other decorations. Often their churches were not even vaulted but instead were covered with simple wooden shingles. These churches were merely large preaching halls, like the fourteenth and fifteenth-century German *Hallenkirchen*, with a prominent pulpit attached to the wall as an integral part of the church. Their simplicity was such that Camille Enlart commented: 'The austerity of Cîteaux only frightened architecture; the poverty of the mendicants brought it to destitution'.

By 1216 the Friars Minor had a house in Paris and in 1262, the church which Saint Louis had built for them was consecrated under the patronage of Saint Madeleine. In 1225 Jeanne of Constantinople, Countess of Flanders and Hainaut, founded a convent of friars at a place in Valenciennes called *le Donjon*, insisting that the building be undertaken without regard to cost. She sent architects from Lille to examine the site, to see if it was good and decide on the arrangement of the buildings. The religious asked that the buildings not be luxurious but small and humble, conforming to poverty, austerity, and simplicity because Christ had become poor and had been able to say, 'The foxes have their dens, the birds their nests, but the Son of Man has no place to lay his head'.

Countess Jeanne laid the cornerstone and the site was marked for the church and conventual buildings: dormitory, cloister, chapter, refectory, infirmary. In two years a large church, nearly sixty yards long up to the choir, and ten yards wide with twelve columns, four altars, a very elaborate belfry containing a large bell, and magnificent stained glass windows had been erected. To this was added a smaller dormitory, a cloister and some other buildings. There the church was consecrated by the bishop of Cambrai in 1223.

At Valenciennes, there was another convent of Friars Minor, dedicated to Saint Bartholomew. For some unknown reason, the question came up of moving this community to the convent at *le Donjon*. The Guardian—the title of the superior—of Saint Bartholomew was consulted. He replied that he did not want to live in so luxurious a convent because, as he said, 'by our rule we are to be imitators of Christ and the apostles and so we condemn all pomp and extravagance in our buildings'. The religious there sided with their

Guardian and refused to move. But the General of the Order wrote to order the transfer. The friars submitted but begged that the belfry and stained glass windows be suppressed as too elegant. Otherwise, they felt that they could not, in conscience, live with the brothers at *le Donjon*. And so they stayed at Saint Bartholomew until 1251 when, by mutual agreement, the bell tower at *le Donjon* was destroyed and replaced by a new one, smaller and simpler.

SEVERE RULES SOON TRANSGRESSED

When Saint Bonaventure became the General of the Order, he felt the need to draw up some constitutions. This he did at the General Chapter which gathered at Narbonne in 1260. In these constitutions many articles concerned the simplicity and poverty to be observed in construction. Everything superfluous or quaint in paintings, sculptures and stained glass windows was strictly forbidden. Nor was it permitted to erect buildings that were too large or too high, or to vault the churches except over the main altar. Belfries were not to look like towers. Glass windows were not to be colored or ornamented with designs except for the window in the east end behind the high altar where there could be some scenes of Christ on the cross, the Virgin, Saint John, Saint Francis, or Saint Anthony. Other paintings or murals were forbidden and those already present were to be removed. All infractions were to be severely punished and the responsible superiors removed. The visitors were to maintain discipline and enforce these constitutions. But in spite of the regulations, the Friars Minor were soon influenced by contemporary styles and began to decorate their churches profusely. We have already seen an example. When Pope Nicholas IV, who was a Franciscan and had succeeded Saint Bonaventure as General of the Order in 1274, was raised to the throne of Peter, he had the basilica of Saint Francis of Assisi enlarged and decorated. He commissioned the greatest artists, like Giotto and Cimabue, to cover the walls and vaults with frescoes, and to decorate the windows with magnificent stained glass which is still admired.

As soon as this slackening took place, echoes resounded in the writings of the time, particularly in a latin poem written by an english franciscan apostate who had become a follower of Wycliffe and who made the Franciscans' luxurious buildings the object of criticism:

> *Hi domos conficiunt mirae largitatis,*
> *Pollitis lapidibus, quibusdam quadratis;*
> *Totum tectum tegitur lignis levigatis.*
> *Sed transgressum regulae probant ista satis.*

They build houses of astounding size, of beautiful, well-quarried stones. The entire ceilings are of varnished wood. But all this proves that they have transgressed their rule.

SAINT DOMINIC AND THE FRIARS PREACHERS

The origin of the Order of Friars Preachers goes back to the crusade against the Albigensians or *Cathars* (from the Greek, *catharos* = pure), that is, the pure or perfect.

At the same time Simon de Montfort was trying by force of arms to reduce the number of lords defending the heretics, Dominic was able to bring a number of noblewomen and young girls back to the Catholic faith. With them he began a convent near the church at Prouille, which had been given him by the bishop of Toulouse. Prouille was Dominic's first center of activity before it became the first convent of dominican nuns.

After a few months the Cistercians grew discouraged by the poor results of their work and asked to return to their abbeys. The entire enterprise fell to Dominic, who tried to gather missionaries to preach the gospel while leading exemplary lives of poverty and mortification. After the capture of Toulouse in 1215, Bishop Foulque established Dominic and his companions as preachers throughout his diocese to extirpate the Albigensian heresy. He gave them Saint Romain Church and they established their convent nearby.

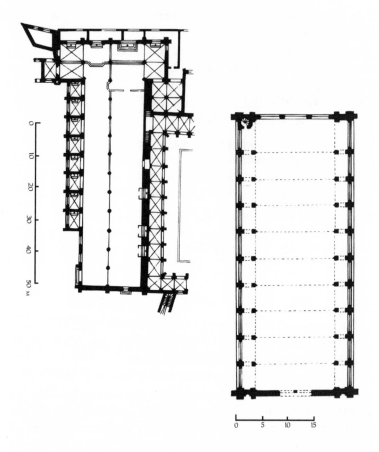

Figure 9.2. Plans of the jacobin church in Paris (left) and dominican church in Ghent (right).

This was the beginning of the Order of Friars Preachers, which was recognized and approved by Pope Honorius III in December 1216. They adopted the Rule of Saint Augustine and, for the most part, the observances of the Premonstratensians, whose origins had been closely connected to the Cistercians. Reacting against the luxury and wealth of many abbeys, Saint Dominic wanted a certain poverty to be

Figure 9.3. Interior view of the jacobin church in Toulouse. This immense space is divided into two bays by a row of columns at least twenty-two yards high.

felt in the buildings, and the convents of his Preachers to be humble and modest houses.

A CODE OF ARCHITECTURAL SIMPLICITY

Regulations were promulgated. The convent walls could not be more than four and a half yards high on the ground floor and that the total height—including the upper story—should not be more than seven and a half yards. The church was not to be more than eleven and a half yards high. It was to have not a vaulted, but a simple plaster ceiling, except over the sacristy and choir. These norms were set for the sake of poverty and also to avoid scandalizing the faithful by too much elegance. By 1220, the regulations appeared in the constitutions. A few years later it was decided to elect three of the most discreet brothers in each convent to form a council which would decide future building projects. Those who by-passed this council were to be very severely punished.

As in the case of the Cistercians, the General Chapters had to intervene countless times to safeguard the simplicity and poverty of the buildings. They forbade sculptures, paintings, stained glass windows, and all other such artifacts, delegating visitors to make the necessary adjustments where abuses had already occurred, and to punish delinquents severely. With a few exceptions, they were able to maintain these regulations, which architects, founders and benefactors often found very vexing.

The general layout of the buildings differed slightly from monasteries. The various phases of the common life were similar to that of the monks. We should note, however, that in the first years of the Order, the Preachers were given previously established churches, as at Toulouse, Paris, Rome, and Bologna. It follows that, for good or ill, the buildings erected near the churches were arranged any way possible in the midst of surrounding constructions.

Near the convent door was a small atrium and a modest courtyard surrounded by porticoes. There the friars received visitors and ministered to the poor. Dignitaries were received in the chapter. The guest house with its bedrooms and refectory for visitors was located near the main door. The cloister lay in the center of the buildings, and all around it were the other quarters, as among the monks.

The first churches built by the Preachers were used only to celebrate the Office. Preaching was always done in parishes which invited the friars. Sometimes they preached in the open air, as when converting heretics like the Albigensians. But soon, around 1240, the growing success of their preaching attracted larger and larger crowds. They began to overshadow the parish clergy, who took offense and became reluctant to call on the Preachers. Also, the people were making large donations to the Preachers at the expense of the parishes.

And so, like the Friars Minor, the Dominicans began to build large churches which could be used not only to celebrate the Office but also to hold the large crowds of people who came to hear them. They followed in the steps of the Friars Minor. Like them, they built large preaching halls in which everything was arranged to enable the people to see them and hear their preaching.

By dint of their new purpose, these churches could no longer conform to their fixed norms. For large churches, the maximum 11.5 yard height was simply inadequate and out of proportion to the rest of the building. So they began to build higher churches which soared upwards, yet still maintained a sense of poverty and simplicity.

Ordinarily the church was divided into two sections, with an enclosure surmounted by a large crucifix which prevented the people from seeing the friars enter and leave. This enclosure formed a kind of loft from which they read the lessons during the Office of Matins. A door in the center was opened at the consecration of the Mass. To the right of this door, was an altar, as in cistercian churches. The sanctuary was raised a few degrees, and the Blessed Sacrament was reserved on the main or conventual altar. In the spirit of poverty—and also to avoid provoking the clergy of neighboring parishes—the church had only one modest bell to summon the friars to the Office.

Those entering the chapter wing found a sacristy adjoining the church and cloister. Gold and silver vessels were forbidden, except for chalices, which were not to be ornamented with precious stones. Vestments, such as chasubles and copes, were also to be very simple. The cloister galleries were usually vaulted, and had colonnettes with austerely decorated capitals. The friars and their friends had access to this area. In the center of the courtyard was a fountain. The chapter house was a large vaulted hall with columns and very simple capitals. At the right end, to the left of the door, were two large bays. In this hall the friars held chapter of faults—a custom in all religious houses—where the brothers admitted their failures in living the rule. There too sermons were given to the community, the members voted on the admission of novices to religious profession, and important affairs were discussed. Distinguished visitors were introduced to the community in this same room before being taken to the guest house. A small bell over the chapter house was used to convene the friars.

Upstairs was a very modest dormitory. Sometimes, however, the builders got carried away, as was the case at the Barcelona convent, where the prior set out to build a dormitory which exceeded set norms. He was condemned by the General Chapter in 1261 and given as a penance a fast on bread and water for thirteen days and orders to use the discipline thirteen times. The building soon resumed the proper dimensions.

In the dormitory each friar had a small cell of about two yards square with no door; its partitions were not to exceed a man's height. For furnishing they had only a simple bed, a desk, and a chair. There the religious studied and slept completely dressed. Only the Master General, the lecturers, and professors were allowed an enclosed room, a privilege which was sometimes given as well to very industrious students. Little by little, the partitions between cells got higher. At Saint Nicolas in Bologna, the procurator raised the partitions an arm's length during Saint Dominic's absence. When the saint returned, he reproached him in tears, saying, 'You want to do away with poverty and build large palaces already', and stopped the work, which remained unfinished as long as he lived. But despite the interventions of General Chapters, the partitions between cells gradually rose and doors appeared. Eventually, each person had a private room. Human nature seems always to tend towards ease and finds ways of avoiding regimentation.

The library was usually near the cells and on the same level. Annexed to it was a study-room where the brothers could consult the various volumes they obtained from the librarian. There too they would find books of general interest attached by chains, as was the custom in most monasteries.

Along the length of the cloister gallery opposite the church lay the refectory, which sometimes extended the entire length of the building. It was usually vaulted and separated into two naves by a row of columns. Built into the wall was a stairway leading to a reader's pulpit. In the cloister near the refectory door was a fountain where the friars washed their hands before eating—also a custom in cistercian houses. This fountain was sometimes sheltered in a bay projecting into the garth or the cloister's inner courtyard. A small bell over the refectory called the brothers to meals and rang during the thanksgiving afterwards. The fifth Master-General, Humbert of Romains (1254–1263), noting that in certain convents the bell was not rung during the thanksgiving prayer, once facetiously commented: 'I don't blame them. If the neighbors hear the dinner bell and then hear the thanksgiving bell a long time afterwards, they'll say: "Today the good fathers had a very long meal!" '

The various workrooms for the laybrothers were removed as far as possible from the friars' living quarters so that their noise would not disturb Offices and studies.

THE JACOBINS IN PARIS

The convent of the Friars Preacher in Paris was founded in 1221 in the buildings of a hospital given them by a canon of Saint Quentin. The rue Saint-Jacques on which it was located gave its name to the religious living there, and, by extension, to all the Preachers. Saint Louis, who had been educated by the 'Jacobins', finished the church that had already been begun, and added the dormitory and refectory. His mother, Blanche of Castile, along with ladies and lords of the court, was present at the first Mass to be celebrated in the convent church. Built right up against the fortifications of Philip-Augustus, the buildings were arranged as best they could be in a very limited space. The refectory had to be built straddling the city walls.

The church had two naves of unequal width separated by a row of columns. The friars' choir occupied the narrower of the two while the other was reserved for preaching. The fixed pulpit, an integral part of the architecture, resembled a projecting balcony and had a built-in staircase. The huge refectory—which extended beyond the city walls—was separated into two sections by a row of ten columns. Eighty meters long, it could hold three hundred religious.

This convent was built in 1256 with the revenue from a fine of 12,000 pounds imposed by Saint Louis on the Sire of Coucy, Enguerrand IV, the son of Enguerrand III 'the Great' or 'The Builder' who erected the splendid Château de Coucy with its fifty-four meter high keep and walls more than seven meters thick. It took the Germans 62,000 pounds of explosive to destroy this unique monument in 1917.

Enguerrand IV, infamous for his cruelty and evil deeds, had found three young Flemish gentlemen in his forest, carrying bows and arrows. With no judicial process of any kind, he had them hanged. Saint Louis did not take this kind of sport lightly, as the Sire of Coucy soon realized. Arrested and thrown into the tower at the Louvre, he went to trial and nearly lost his head. But the king relented and Enguerrand got off with a fine of 10,000 pounds and the obligation of serving three years in the Holy Land. This fine was used for various pious works, particularly for building the Jacobin convent.

THE JACOBINS IN TOULOUSE

The Jacobin convent in Toulouse provides a classic example of the Preachers' construction. As the late Elie Lambert remarked, the church is one of the masterpieces of Old Provencal religious architecture. It is separated into two equal naves by a row of columns twenty-two meters high; from these rise the vaulting ribs. The bosses at the intersections of the vaults are eighty-five feet high, giving the building the air of extraordinary height.

This building was begun in 1230. The foundation stone was laid by Bishop Foulque of Marseille who had already done much to establish the Preachers in his diocese and episcopal city. Born in Marseille, the former troubador had converted and become a cistercian monk at La Thoronet in Provence before becoming a bishop in 1205. He was the only troubador to be placed by Dante in his *Paradiso*, among the *Spiriti amanti* in Venus' heaven. During a synod held in Toulouse to celebrate the inauguration of of the University the preceding year, 1229, another former *trouvère*, Helinand, famous for his *Poem on Death* and now a cistercian monk at Froidmont Abbey near Beauvais, came to Toulouse on 24 May, the feast of the Ascension, and gave a long talk—still preserved—to the students at the Jacobins'.

When Pope Urban V granted the Jacobins the favor of entombing the body of Saint Thomas Aquinas in their church, they decided to add an apsidal east end to their church in the

Figure 9.4. Jacobin church in Toulouse. The main column of the apse.

manner of pilgrimage churches. The ambulatory encircles the easternmost of the existing columns and seven chapels lead off it. The friars celebrated the transfer of Saint Thomas' body in 1369—he had died in 1274 at the cistercian abbey of Fossanova—in an extravagant manner and named the church after him.

One of the naves was used for the Office and the other, with a pulpit built into the western wall, for preaching. Traces of this pulpit can still be seen, including a small, exterior staircase opening onto the small cloister. This pulpit was one of the oldest of its kind. The large cloister was sited to the north of the church, and the east range housed the sacristy, chapter house, and a small mortuary chapel dedicated to Saint Antonin; all three buildings terminated in three-sided apses to the east. The east range was extended southwards to accomodate a large refectory.

The Jacobin churches in Paris and Toulouse served as models for many others. The Jacobin church at Agen, finished in 1283, is also divided into two naves by a row of three columns and has a chapter house bounded on the east by a small, semi-circular apse.

A DEPARTURE FROM THE ORIGINAL SIMPLICITY

At the convent in Cologne, the choir of the church built by Albert the Great surpassed the height decreed by the Rule. But as the saint had become the bishop of Regensburg in 1260, and escaped the Order's jurisdiction, the General Chapter of 1261 could no longer penalize him for it. They decided instead to demolish all the sections of the walls which exceeded the prescribed height. This disfigured the edifice as the height of the walls no longer corresponded to the proportions of the building. A solution was needed and it was Albert the Great who found it. After he had retired as bishop and returned to his convent in Cologne in 1271, bound once more by his vow of poverty, he requested and obtained permission from the pope to dispose of, as he wished, the sums of money he had received or would receive. He drew up his will in 1279, leaving all his money to the Cologne convent so that they could finish the construction of the church choir. The work was not completed until 1288, eight years after his death.

By the end of the thirteenth century, the Preachers had repealed many of their restrictions. Yet the Masters General never failed to remind them that they should avoid anything arrogant or superfluous, and forbade conspicuous curiosities as well as paintings, sculptures, pavements, stained-glass windows and other things similarly incompatible with the spirit of the Order. But little by little, under the pretext of embellishing the liturgy and rousing peoples' piety, they began to represent Christ, the Virgin, and the saints in paintings, sculptures, and stained-glass windows. The Masters General became less exacting. At the convent in Bologna, John of Vercelli (1264–1283) had a magnificent marble tomb made for Saint Dominic's remains.

Critics accused the Preachers of growing rich on the alms they received, but on the whole, the convents and churches of the Preachers remained poor and simple for many years. It was not until the end of the fourteenth century that they erected a stunning monument in one of the most elaborate, flamboyant styles: the convent of Batalha (the Battle) near Leiria, Portugal.

This convent, dedicated to Our Lady of Victory, was founded and built by King John I of Portugal as a votive offering after his victory over John I of Castile in the battle of Aljubarrata in 1385. Beyond the fact that the buildings were built in the most flamboyant gothic style, elaborate to an unbelievable degree, the ground plan of this church is unique. It is built in the shape of a key. The stem is the nave; the ring is the unfinished chapels, which border the church to the east; the key-bit is the founder's chapel, constructed to the south of the nave and flush with the façade. Some have claimed Islamic influence from the symbolic key engraved on the Door of Justice at the Alhambra. But the very fact that the unfinished chapels and founder's chapel were added much later shows that there was no over-all plan conceived from the beginning. Only after these later additions did the

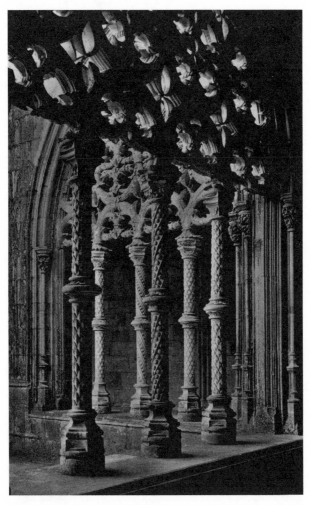

Figure 9.5. The Batalha Cloister (Portugal).

group began to resemble a key, which has no particular symbolism in this case.

The construction of the church was begun in 1388 according to the plans of Afonso Domingues of Lisbon. Interestingly, this plan was inspired by cistercian tastes. Later, King Manuel embellished the convent of Batalha yet more generously. He vaulted the chapels which would hold the royal sculptures and gave them a gigantic portal in the most ornamental, elaborate style possible. Batalha remains a great monument of national independence. There, in the chapter house, we find the tomb of the Unknown Soldier, guarded by an armed sentry.

10

MONASTIC FORTRESSES

BECAUSE OF THEIR religious vows and common life, their many similarities to monastic communities, and their unique architecture, the military orders deserve to be mentioned in this book.

THE HOSPITALLERS OF SAINT JOHN OF JERUSALEM
AND THE SYRIAN CASTLES

Not long after the capture of Jerusalem by Godfrey of Bouillon in 1099, Gerard de Tom, a Frenchman from Provence, founded an order to offer hospitality to the many pilgrims who flocked to the Holy City. Soon, as early as 1121, the Order also had to take up arms to defend the pilgrims against attacks by infidels. And so the Order of Hospitallers became a military order.

Among the fortresses built by the crusaders for the defense of their states, the new Hospitaller-knights were to guard the Krak des Chevaliers (from the Syriac word, *karak* = fortress). This castle was situated in Syria between the Mediterranean and the Orontes, in the extreme eastern part of the country of Tripoli. It commanded a strategic defensive position against invaders, and it was not without reason that the king of Hungary, Andrew II, called it 'the key to the christian lands', and the arabian chroniclers compared it to a bone in the throat of Muslims.

This immense castle is among the most complete and best preserved anywhere. It rises 2250 feet high, covers an area of some six acres, and sits on a sixty foot slope. It was redone, enlarged, and perfected many times by the Hospitallers, who occupied it until 1271.

The fortress has two precincts fortified with massive towers and a turret one hundred fifty feet high—almost as high as Coucy's, at one hundred sixty-two yards—with walls nine and a half yards thick (Coucy's were only seven and a half). The main entry was on the east. There a long vaulted ramp, bent in three sections and protected at long intervals by doors, portcullises and machicolations, with broad, low steps, allowed the Knights to ride their horses as far as the inner court. To the north was another entrance, framed by two round towers and surmounted by stone parapets. From the top of the second enclosure, wooden machicolations and brattices were constructed for defense. Stones thrown by the defenders rolled down the slope and straight onto the assailants. This method of defense was first used by the Crusaders in the Holy Land, and soon imitated in France, as at the Chateau-Gaillard, built in 1197 by Richard the Lion-Hearted for the defense of Normandy against Philip Augustus.

At the Krak visitors can still see the apartment belonging to the Master of Hospitallers, built in one of the large towers. In the esplanade is a large rectangular hall, divided in the style of Champagne, into three bays. The fortified church, which opens onto the court, was built in the burgundian style. It has a nave of three bays covered by a barrel vault, with a three-sided apse imbedded in a massive stone retaining wall.

Figure 10.1. Aerial view of the Krak (fortress) des Chevaliers in Syria.

The Krak survived many assaults, notably from Saladin in 1188 after the capture of Jerusalem, and in 1207 from Abu Bakr. It succumbed after heroic resistance only in 1271, after the disaster that terminated french domination in the Holy Land. After the attacking forces had successfully invaded the rest of the castle, the Knights took refuge in the turret and would not capitulate until the sultan, Malek ed Daher, showed them a counterfeited document from the Count of Tripoli, ordering their surrender.

Of less importance is the castle of Margot, also maintained
by the Hospitallers. They hurriedly rebuilt this fortress
which controlled the ascending slope of the Antioch-Tripoli
border. This castle also became the residence of the local
bishop who felt safer there. The fortress church became his
chapel. This pretty little church, built with great care, has
two square groin-vaulted bays with a transverse rib reposing
on two columns engaged in pilasters. A rounded apse is set
into a rectangular chevet flanked by two small sacristies.
At the east and west ends of the building are beautifully
decorated doorways with trefoil arches.

It was at Margot that Richard the Lion-Hearted imprisoned the Duke of Cyprus, Isaac Comnena, in 1192, after
he had seized the island. It is said that the proud prince
managed to have himself fastened in gold and silver chains.

After the fall of Jerusalem, the Hospitallers regrouped first
at Saint Johon of Acre, then on Cyprus, and finally on the island of Rhodes. They stayed there for the next ten centuries,
despite repeated attacks from infidels. They successfully re-
pelled them until they were forced to capitulate to Suliman
II, in 1522, after a long seige. They sought refuge in Candia,
and then Sicily. In 1530, Charles V granted them the island
of Malta, which he had inherited. From that time forward
they have been known as the Knights of Malta. They forms
an elective sovereign state. In 1789 Napolean invaded Egypt,
seized Malta, and put an end to the Order as a sovereign
state. The Knights of Malta did not, however, stop calling
themselves a soveriegn order. As recently as 1956, their new
constitution received recognition, and the Grand Master of
the Sovereign Military Order of Hospitallers of Saint John
of Jerusalem, of Rhodes, and of Malta (their official title)
holds rights to special prerogatives and sovereign honors.

THE BIRTH AND TRAGIC END OF THE TEMPLARS

The Order of Templars was also a military order. It began
in 1118 at Jerusalem when several knights gathered around
Hugh de Payns, a cousin of saint Bernard, and Godfrey of

Saint-Omer, to form a society to defend the shrines in the Holy Land, to protect Christians there, and to guarantee the safety of pilgrims along the road to the Holy Land. Always prepared to take up arms to defend their faith and Christians, they led a life of withdrawal, silence, prayer and penitence between battles.

King Baudoin II of Jerusalem granted them lodging in a dependency of his palace, near the Temple of Solomon. From this they took the name, Knights of the Soldiery of the Temple, or more simply, the Templars. Many of them attended the council at Troyes in 1128, to request that they be given a rule of life. The Rule proposed to them contained seventy-two articles and had an entirely benedictine inspiration. Saint Bernard was its principle author. He wasted no time in writing a spiritual commentary on the rule, calling it *In praise of the new knighthood*, and drawing a sharp distinction between the blustering self indulgence of worldly knights and the monastic simplicity of God's knights.

Recruits of distinction, like Count Hugh of Champagne, soon joined the first group of knights. At the same time, important donations arriving from everywhere, and exceptional privileges accorded by the pope soon made the Order one of the richest and most powerful in Christendom. They possessed castles in Palestine and Syria, as well as in most of Europe: France, England, Spain, and Portugal.

Even in the twelfth century, the castles, forts, and commanding-posts of the Templars had reached a prodigious number. There were about nine thousand of them. In addition, there were immense domains from which they collected taxes. Being excellent administrators, they managed to acquire considerable wealth, estimated at 100,000,000 *livres tournois*. This enabled them to lend large sums of money and they thus became the royal bankers to princes and kings. They lost no time in becoming a true power-block in the state and they eventually occupied an important political and diplomatic position.

All this excited hatred and jealousy. King Philip le Bel took umbrage of their power and coveted their immense wealth. Added to this was the Templars' imprudence in refusing to pay their share of a gift of 100,000 pounds which the city of Paris was giving to the king in 1296. A few years later, in 1305, the king sought refuge at the Temple when he was menaced in his palace at Louvre by the riot which broke out after he altered the value of the coinage. His stay at the Temple enabled him to really see the wealth of the Order. One beautiful morning in 1307, he ordered the mass arrest of all the Templars in the kingdom and referred them to the Inquisition. After a seven-year trial, a good number of Knights died at the stake. This powerful order was annihilated through the greed of a king and the weakness of a pope. Suppressed in 1313 by the Council of Vienna, their goods were given to the Hospitallers of Saint John of Jerusalem. However, the King of France had already taken the Temple treasures besides claiming a 300,000 pound fee for the proceedings.

THE DOME OF THE ROCK IN JERUSALEM

In 1118, Godfrey of Bouillon had given the Templars a house near the Dome of the Rock (now the Mosque of Omar) and they made it the mother church of the Order. Built in the byzantine style by Muslims in 690, it was partially rebuilt in 1022. It had originally been built in honor of the rock where tradition has it that Abraham offered his son Isaac, and where there had been the altar of holocausts in the Temple of Solomon.

Captured by the Crusaders in 1099, it was given by Godfrey of Bouillon to the Canons Regular of Saint Augustine, who restored the altar and built a monastery and cloister.

This church, which the Templars regarded as the Temple of Solomon and which must not be confused with the Church of the Holy Sepulchre, was the prototype for the other churches in a round or polygonal plan they built elsewhere.

After their Order had been approved, they began to build a monastery in the Temple enclosure. Of these buildings, there remains only the large twelfth-century hall, about seventy-five yards long with two aisles each of ten bays with groin vaults resting on cruciform pillars.

The Dome of the Rock, now again in Muslim hands, still contains fifteen magnificent wrought iron grills arranged between the columns, completely made up of a network of sprigs of various thicknesses, convoluted, surmounted with *fleurs-de-lis*, in whose centers people would place candles. These beautifully wrought grills are a masterpiece of twelfth-century ironwork. There is also a beautiful wrought-iron candelabrum, a catalonian work of the same period.

By 1182, the Templars had a house at Saint Johon of Acre which commanded the river front near the port where the vessels of their fleet were moored. One of the main fortresses was located at Tortose. In 1183, they created a fortified port next to the expiscopal city and built an entire city surrounded with ramparts. This fortress resisted Saladin in 1188 when he managed to capture the episcopal city.

Between the donjon and the great hall of the fortress of Tortose was a large chapel. It was a simple rectangular, single-aisled chamber of four rib-vaulted bays. The transverse arches rested on pilasters with roll-moulded imposts which received the ribs. The great doorway of the façade had pointed arches and protruding door jambs. Four corbels set into the wall above them indicate that there must originally have been a covered porch. The main hall dates back to the thirteenth century. It is one hundred thirty six feet long, forty-five feet wide, and has two aisles of six rib-vaulted bays which have now collapsed. The Tortose fortress was completely abandoned in 1300 after the fall of Chastel Blanc in 1271. The Templars then occupied the Island of Ruad, entrusted to their care, and soon built a castle which they had to surrender in 1302.

At Safita, mid-way between Tortose and the Krak des Chevaliers, at an altitude of 300 yards on a steep hill which overlooks two valleys, the Templars built the fortress of Chastel Blanc (The White Castle) in 1203. Surrounded by two enclosure walls, it included an important keep which sheltered a church in the lower hall. This church had three bays, was barrel vaulted with transverse arches, and terminated in a semi-circular apse flanked by two rectangular sacristies set into a retaining wall. The apse was illuminated by a loophole window, and four windows of the same kind pierced the last two bays. The western portal was very simple. There was a built-in stairway facing the southwest, leading to the main hall. In the center of the first bay was the entry to a cistern sunk deep into the rock. The upper hall, which constituted the armory, had ten aisles of four groin-vaulted bays. Each of these bays was pierced by a loophole window. Above it was a battlement.

In 1217, between Haifa and Jaffa at the foot of Mount Carmel, on a small island which was once a Phoenician city, the Templars built one of their main fortresses, naming it Chastel Pelerin (Pilgrim) Castle. According to Jean de Joinville, it was in this castle in 1250 or 1251 that Queen Marguerite—wife of Saint Louis—gave birth to their seventh child and fifth boy, who was named Peter and whose godfather was the Master of the Fortress.

The church was vast, a ten-sided rotunda with three polygonal apses. It is one of the most beautiful examples of this type, a favorite of the Templars which they reproduced countless times in Europe, as will be seen. An Arab village was later established in the castle enclosure and the chapel converted into a mosque. In 1837 an earthquake demolished the vaults and only a few of the foundations remain.

We must also mention the castle of Beaufort, not far from Tyer. It was built in 1260 by the Templars and there are still some remains of a thirteenth-century hall which has two rib-vaulted bays and seems to have been the chapel.

THE TEMPLE OF PARIS

Of the Templars' buildings in the West, the best known is the Temple of Paris, founded in 1146, now entirely demolished. It formed a kind of fortified city spreading

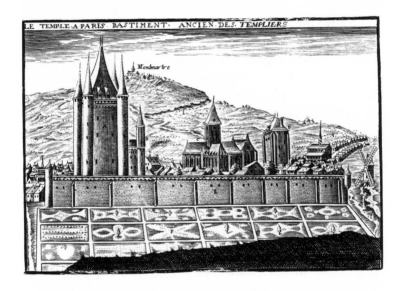

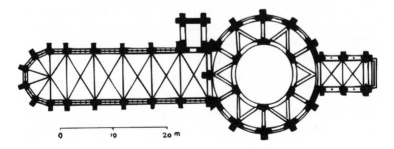

Figures 10.2a and b. Late sixteenth-century engraving of the Temple of the Knights Templar in Paris and floor plan of its church.

over 320 acres. Surrounded by battlements, protected with towers, it became the center of the Order after the loss of Jerusalem.

In the center of the conventual buildings stood the twelfth-century church in the form of a rotunda, bordered to the southeast by a square tower surmounted by a pyramidal spire. In the thirteenth century, a vast rectangular choir was built which terminated in a five-sided apse. A central dome, surmounted by a lantern, was raised on six piers encircled by a broad ambulatory. Later a rib-vaulted double-bayed porch was added in front of the rotunda.

There was a cloister and a large reception hall. There were also two towers: The square Tower of Caesar was three storeys high, and the masonry was reinforced by sturdy angle buttresses set at each of the four corners. The donjon, known as the *Grosse Tour*, had walls two and a half yards thick and reached a height of one 150 feet. Félibien has written: 'It is one of the solidest buildings in our kingdom.' It was built to a square plan and was four storeys high. At each corner were turrets slightly higher than the main tower.

It was in this Temple that the king of England, Henry III, was lodged during a week's visit in Paris in 1254 to pay homage to Saint Louis, his suzerain. It was also in this Temple—in the *Grosse Tour*—that Louis XVI and his family were imprisoned on 10 August 1792, and from which, after being submitted to every possible insult and outrage, he was led to the scaffold the following January 21st.

The church was razed in 1796. As for the *Grosse Tour*, Napoleon began to demolish it in 1808 and accomodatingly accelerated this project in 1810 for Marie-Louise of Habsbourg whom he had just married. He wanted to spare her the sight of this prison where her aunt, Marie Antoinette, had been confined. There is no longer the slightest trace left of any of the buildings. Temple Square occupies the approximate site of the Grosse Tower.

In France, chapels were built on a rectangular plan, as at Chastel Blanc: the Castles of Rudelle in Le Quercy, Vaour in Albigenses, and Voulaines in Burgundy. There is also the beautiful little chapel of the Temple of Laon, preserved intact. It was built in the form of a rotunda and was located not far from the cathedral on a piece of land ceded in 1128 by Bishop Bartholomew de Jur—a great founder of monasteries—who donned the cistercian habit in 1150 at Foigny Abbey, near Vervins, which he had founded. In Metz the Templar's chapel, also built in rotunda form, is still extant.

THE TEMPLARS' BUILDINGS THROUGHOUT EUROPE

The first Temple in England was built around 1135 in London, at the end of what is today Chancery Lane. It was demolished, but the foundations which have been uncovered suggest that it was built on a circular plan.

Later another Temple was erected in London and its name was given to a whole section of the city on the bank of the Thames. The church, consecrated in 1185, still exists. It closely resembles the Temple of Paris with a rotunda preceded by a square porch, and a vast choir of five bays flanked with straight-ended side walls. Added later, the choir was consecrated in 1240 in the presence of King Henry III. The rotunda is covered with a cupola supported by six pointed arches which repose on six clusters of slender columns surmounted by an arcade with round interlacing arches. Other Templar churches in England built on the circular plan were at Dover, Bristol, and Garway.

In Spain, the Templars built a church at Segovia resembling the Holy Sepulchre in Jerusalem. The interior is circular while the exterior wall outlining the ambulatory was a twelve-sided polygon. The sanctuary, to the east, took the form of a single-square bay terminating in a semi-circular apse flanked by two small apsidal chapels. This church, consecrated in 1208, was named the Holy Sepulchre for its resemblance to the one in Jerusalem. Its name was changed to Vera Cruz, however when Pope Honorius II gave the Templars an important relic of the true cross in a magnificent reliquary embellished with precious stones. The church was restored in 1830.

The Order of Templars was introduced into Portugal in 1126, and their first establishment was located a few miles north of Coimbre.

Later, after the recapture of the Lisbon and Santarem regions by Alphonse I in 1147, the Templars built a fortress on a hill overlooking the city of Tomar. This became the motherhouse of the Order in Portugal and the building still remains. This fortress was part of a whole system of fortifications established to resist the Muslims who still occupied the southern part of the country. It included an imposing turret which in the twelfth and thirteenth century, sheltered an octagonal chapel covered by an eight-ribbed cupola. All around it runs a sixteen-sided ambulatory covered with a barrel vault. In the thirteenth century, the fortress at Tomar became a veritable fortified city encircled with ramparts and towers. It was considered one of the most powerful Templar forts in the West.

When the Order of Templars was suppressed, this fortress passed to the Knights of Christ, and new constructions were added to the old by Henry the Navigator who was the Grand Master of the Order.

THE KNIGHTS OF CALATRAVA WITH A CISTERCIAN ABBOT AS THE GRAND CAPTAIN

The original aim of the Order of Hospitallers had been to do a work of charity while the Knight Templars had originally sought to form a kind of police force in the Holy Land and along the roads used by the pilgrims. From the very beginning, however, the Spanish Knights of Calatrava were founded to fight against the Muslims and to reconquer the occupied country by force of arms.

Surprisingly, the founder of this military order was a cistercian monk—a man who belonged to a contemplative order dedicated to prayer, totally separated from the world, not involved in any outside ministry. This stunning and paradoxical story bears retelling. Kalaat Rawaah (Calatrava) fortress occupied a strategic position on the edge of Guadiana, along the old Roman road on the border of Castile and Andalusia. By 1147 it had fallen into the hands of the infidels and King Alphonsus VII, with the help of the other christian spanish kings, had managed to secure it again and had entrusted it to the Templars. Ten years later, in 1157, a large muslim expedition from Cordova set out to capture all the christian forts which defended the route to Toledo. Kalaat Rawaah was the most important of these. The Templars felt they were not numerous enough to sustain the assault victoriously and asked King Sancha III for reinforcements. But because he faced other trouble in the North, the king was not able to supply them. Time was short. Sancha hurriedly proclaimed everywhere that he would give the entire Calatrava region with its castles and villages to the knight who would offer to defend the fortress. But in spite of his pressing appeals, no one responded.

At that point, Raymond Serrat, the cistercian abbot of Fitero was in Toledo on business for the monastery, accompanied by one of his monks. He was a native of Saint Gaudens, in France, and had entered the Cistercians of l' Éscale-Dieu in Bigorre. From there he had been sent to Spain as prior of the new foundation of Fitero in Castile, and was soon elected its abbot. His companion, Diego Velasquez, was a former soldier. When he heard the king's appeal for the defense of Calatrava, he cried out: 'To war against the Moors!' The abbot saw this heart-felt cry as a sign of God's will and hurried to ask the king for the honor of defending the endangered fortress. As can be imagined, the king accepted with joy and he named Raymond the

Captain General of the endeavor. With arms and backing from the king and the bishop of Toledo, Raymond searched for reinforcements, first among his monks at Fitero and then among the neighboring lords.

He put the fortress back on its feet, instructed and drilled the troops, recalled the peasants who had taken flight with their cattle, and put them back to work on the land, with the understanding that they would help defend the fort, if need be. And so, more than 20,000 people left for Calatrava. Diego Velasquez sent his troops on frequent excursions into the environs to train and inure them. All this activity and these many demonstrations began to worry the Muslims who finally decided not to attack the place. Although there were a few battles, the big offensive never took place.

But the abbot of Fitero had acted without the consent of his superiors. It took nothing less than the intervention of the king of Castile, the duke of Burgundy, and even the king of France to check the anger of a General Chapter ready to fall on Abbot Raymond.

The abbot, however, had organized the lives of the monks and transformed them into soldiers. As with the Templars, he worked to assure a balance between the religious life and the military life of the Knights of Calatrava, who were soon incorporated into the Order of Cîteaux and attached to Morimond Abbey, the motherhouse of l'Escale-Dieu and Fitero.

THE MAIN CASTILLOS OF CALATRAVA

Numerous recruits soon swelled the ranks of the Knights of Calatrava who occupied a series of castles (or *castillos*) guarding the frontiers of christian Spain. The Muslims also held their own forts. Between these two lines of forts was the *tierra de nadie* (as we would say today, 'no man's land'). From one side or the other, troops would make excursions to pillage and take prisoners. The Muslims called these journeys *al-garat*. The Spanish called these *cavalgadas* or cavalcades.

The Muslims were waging a holy war for which they prepared by a life of prayer and penance. Their fortresses—each containing a mosque, or *ribat*—resembled the convent-fortresses of the christian military orders. It is feasible that the Christians may have been influenced by the Muslims in the organization of their lives and the construction of their forts.

The most important fortress, after Calatrava, was Alcaniz, a gift from the king of Aragon. At the center of this rectangular enclosure is a castle with its turret as well as the convent with cloister, chapter room, and a church built with cistercian simplicity.

The fortress of Zorita, which overlooks the Tagus in the region of Alcarria, is also one of the Order's most important sites. It is in ruins but one can still make out the towers, the guard room, the turret, the site of the cloister, and a few remains of the nave of the church. The chapter is on a circular plan, covered by a cupola lighted by a single loophole window. It was from Zorita that the Calatravans left in 1212 to join the royal armies gathered in Toledo, ready to undertake the last major campaign which ended in the stunning victory of the Christians at Las Navas de Tolosa. After this victory, which drove the Muslims south of the Guadalquivir, the Calatravans were able to return home. But the old fortress had been greatly damaged. Rather than restoring it, they chose to build a new one to the south, in the foothills of the Sierra Morena. They called this new fort Calatrava La Nueva to distinguish it from the old one, Calatrava la Vieja. The Order's headquarters were established at Calatrava la Nueva in 1217. The castle, with its imposing keep, can still be seen. The convent is in ruins but it is still possible to distinguish the chapter house and especially the church, the most beautiful in the Order.

Other *castillos* were those at Guadalerza between Toledo and Calatrava la Vieja; Alarcos and its beautiful church on

Figure 10.3. The fortresss at Calatrava la Nueva. Sitting high on a rock in the bleak landscape of Castile, this construction, both fortress and convent, embodies the spirit of the Knights of the Order of Calatrava, who were both soldiers and religious.

the banks of the Guadiana; Hisn and Ukab, near Las Navas de Tolosa.

THE TEUTONIC KNIGHTS

The Order of Teutonic Knights was founded in 1190, after the siege at Saint John of Acre. A number of german lords at the time built a hospital to nurse the sick and wounded and specified that only Germans (Feuton) staff it. Pope Celestine III designated them as a hospital and military order to care for the sick and poor and to defend the Holy Land. It included knights, who were to be of noble birth, and also priests and brother-servants who would all take religious vows. The seat of the Order was established at Saint John of Acre.

Around 1230 the Teutonic Knights were called to Prussia to fight pagans in those areas. They first settled at Kulm where they built some forts. In 1238 the Order of Sword-Bearers (the Militia of Christ) were incorporated into the

Order of Teutonic Knights. This extended their power along practically the entire Baltic seaboard where they established many episcopal sees. After the capture of Saint John of Acre by the Muslims in 1291, they left the Holy Land.

In the beginning of the fifteenth century, the Order began to decline. After their defeat at Tannenberg, the Teutonic Knights retreated to Konigsberg which became the seat of the Order. In the sixteenth century the Order went over to the Protestant Reformation. It was finally suppressed by Napoleon in 1809.

CISTERCIAN FORTIFICATIONS

The Cistercians themselves built fortifications. These were not houses for military orders associated with Cistercians but simply abbeys of Cistercian monks. Nor was it a matter of adding fortifications after the monastery had been already built, although there were examples of this, particularly during the Hundred Years' War and the Wars of Religion. Mont-Saint-Michel was fortified to repel the assaults of the English. At the Cistercian abbeys of Maulbronn and Behenhausen, the remains of their old fortifications have been preserved. La Ferté Abbey in France was fortified and encircled with a moat in the fifteenth century, as was Longpont Abbey not far from Villers-Cotterêts where there is still a beautiful fortified door. Many other monasteries built ramparts and towers to protect themselves from bands of pillagers.

Yet what we will discuss here is not one of these cases. The Cistercians also had monasteries that were originally conceived and built as true fortresses with water-trenches, drawbridges and fortified gates. Many Cistercian monasteries were founded in northern Germany, among them Doberan near Rostock in 1171; Dargun in Pomerania in 1172; Olivia near Danzig in 1186; Reinfeld near Lübeck in 1190; Eldena in Pomerania in 1199. At the end of the twelfth century and the beginning of the thirteenth century, Pope Innocent III (1198–1216) and his successor Honorius III

(1216–1227) wanted to provide a fresh impetus for the missionary movement which had just been touched off in that previously neglected area. As this also involved clearing and cultivating land, the two pontiffs first addressed themselves to the Cistercians, also entrusting them with the mission of preaching the Gospel and baptizing.

And so, more cistercian abbeys were founded in the area. At the request of Albert, the first bishop of Livonia, Dünamünde Abbey was established in 1208 near Riga, at the

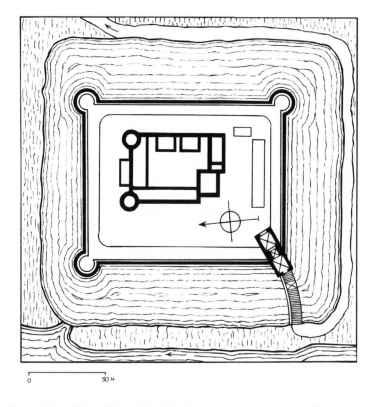

0   50 M

Figure 10.4. Plan of the cistercian fortress at Dünamünde (Lithuania). This veritable fortress, built at the end of the thirteenth century, is surrounded with towers and a broad moat.

mouth of the Duna, not far from the fortress of the Teutonic Knights. Thierry, the first abbot, became bishop of Leal (now Tartu) in Estonia in 1213. Bernard de Lippe, from a noble family in Westphalia became a cistercian monk at Marienfeld, succeeded Thierry as abbot of Dünamünde, and was named the bishop of Semgallen (Zeimjalis) four years later. Already in 1215, Christian, a monk from the Polish abbey of Lekno, had been named the first bishop of Prussia.

The next foundations were at Neuenkamp in 1223; Bukow in 1260; Peplin in 1267; Hiddensee on the island of Rügen in 1296; Stolpe in 1305. These abbeys extended all along the Baltic seafront from Lübeck to the farthest end of Estonia. They were all more or less forts. The ruins of Dünamünde and Falkenau (in particular) exemplify fortresses that were perfectly organized and powerfully protected with enclosure walls entirely surrounded by moats, with a single drawbridge entry. These fortresses served no other purpose than to protect the monks from the savage non-christian peoples living along the shores of the Baltic. The Cistercians purposely established themselves in the midst of the pagans, and offered shelter, when needed, to the christian colonists who had followed them.

At Dünamünde, the first rectangular enclosure wall was built with towers at three of the corners. In the fourth, southwestern corner, there was a fortified door which protected the drawbridge. In the center, a second enclosure with thicker walls encircles the monastery. On the north, it is defended by two large round towers. The chapel is sited to the south. Built on a rectangular plan, it is forty-three feet by twenty-one. There is no cloister and it is difficult to differentiate the various buildings. There was another small chapel on the ground level of the turret. The first enclosure was further protected by a moat about forty yards wide all around, which was created by diverting the Duna. Despite all this, the pagans, in a furious assault, managed in 1228 to penetrate into the monastery which they pillaged and burned after massacring the religious. In 1263 there was another attack, a new disaster from which the monastery never recovered. In 1317 the community was transferred to the village of Padis in Estonia, a few kilometers southwest of Reval (now Tallin), where the Dünamünde monks owned some land.

Of the monastery-fortresses built by the Cistercians, these are the most characteristic and little know examples.

11

MONASTIC AUTARCHY

THE CONTEMPORARY WORD 'autarchy' best expresses the need for self-sufficiency. If the word is new, the meaning is not. Many centuries ago Saint Benedict wrote in his Rule that, if at all possible, the monastery should be built in such a way that all such necessary things as water, mill, garden, kneading-trough, might be found within the enclosure, and that the various works were to be done there, so there would be no need for the monks to go outside. Whatever the reason for the saint's insistence on this matter, it has been faithfully observed. And in the deserted area where most monasteries were founded, they had to be able to become self-sufficient.

CRAFTWORK AND CULTIVATION OF THE LAND

So it was that monks always chose places near a water supply and tilled and transformed the land, cleared forests, and dried up marshes. They also learned various trades: farming, gardening, milling, baking, vine-dressing, brewing, cooking, weaving, fulling, tailoring, currying, tanning, skinning, sewing, stone-cutting, masonry, butchering, carpentry, building, roofing, lock-smithing, brick-making, glass-making. All these skills were needed in building their monasteries. Monks were also wheelwrights and blacksmiths so they could make the tools needed for farming and for the various workshops. Not to mention their work as shepherds, cow herds, carters, ox-drovers, and ploughmen.

In the Middle Ages, because land was the only measure of wealth and agriculture the sole means of income, monasteries owned large properties. Among the large benedictine abbeys were:

In France: Saint Germain-des-Pres in Paris, Saint Wandrille and Jumièges in Normandy, Saint Benoit-sur-Loire not far from Gien, Saint Denis and Cluny; in Germany: Fulda and Lorsch in the diocese of Mainz, Corvey in Saxony, Reichenau on an island in Lake Constance; in Belgium: Savelot and Saint Trond in the diocese of Liège; in Italy: Monte Cassino, Farfa near Spoleto, Bobbio near Pavia, Subiaco near Rome; in England: Romsey in Hampshire, Evesham in Worcestershire, Glastonbury in Somerset. The monks themselves worked the land in the rural priories where small communities lived under a prior, dependent on a large abbey. But the greatest part of these huge properties were leased to tenant-farmers.

The Cistercians refused to accept churches, tithes, and other forms of revenue, preferring to earn their bread by the work of their hands. Desiring to conform to the Rule of Benedict which calls for generous hospitality, however, they also found it necessary to acquire large domains in order to meet expenses. The lay brothers helped them farm the land. This constant effort to acquire more property as soon as the community grew larger often brought them reproaches from those who felt that monks simply wanted to hoard land. This complaint was levied against them in many writings of their contemporaries: chroniclers, moralists and even the spiritual authors of their own Order. Stephen, the abbot of Saint Genevieve in Paris, who died as bishop of Tournai in 1203 and who held the Cistercians in great esteem, mentions a cellarer who was over-eager to enlarge the monastery domain: 'I believe that Cistercians are numbered among those who storm the kingdom of heaven [an allusion to the Gospel of Saint Matthew] but I have never seen it written anywhere that it is also allowable to storm the earth with violence.' However Stephen carefully adds that he blamed not the community but the Cellarer. Commenting on this reputation for hoarding, Viollet-le-Duc wrote: 'Those who reproach the Benedictines for their immense wealth, their spirit of power and propaganda might ask themselves if all these terrestrial and intellectual goods might have been better used for humanity in other hands.'

MONKS AS HYDRAULIC ENGINEERS

In each abbey, near the claustral buildings, was a whole series of workshops where various trades were carried on. Monks used nearby rivers and built dams, creating waterfalls to provide the motor force which activated their machinery. Water power is not a modern invention.

An anonymous thirteenth-century author has left us an extremely vivid picture of the workshops at Clairvaux and of the services rendered by the Aube River, which was diverted and made to run through the monastery from one end to the other.

> A branch of the river passes through the many abbey workshops and is everywhere blessed for the services it renders. . . . First the river darts forward with great impetuosity, into the mill where it is very busy and animated, as much to grind the wheat as to agitate the sieve which separates the bran from the meal. Then it moves to the next chamber. It fills the pail and prepares the fire which brews the monks' drink. Now if, perchance, the vine has responded to the vinedresser's work with sterility, and if the grape juice is lacking, it must make up for the lack with an ear of grain. [All this to say that if there was no wine, they made beer!]

Figure 11.1. Cougnaguet (Lot), France. The mill, with four wheels, was built *c.* 1300 and belonged to the cistercian abbey of Obazine.

But the river is not yet through. In turn, the fullers near the mill call it over. And so this water lifts or lowers its heavy pestles, its mallets (or rather its wooden feet—for this better expresses the work of the fullers) and therefore saves the brothers many heavy labors . . . Rather than exhausting the horses and tiring men out, the gracious river works to give us our food and clothing. It combines its efforts with ours, and after having put up with the scorching heat of the day, it asks only one reward for its labors: the permission to run freely on after accomplishing all we asked of it. After it accelerates and turns so many fast wheels, it comes out foaming. It almost seems to have been ground and become softer itself. Coming from there, it goes to the tannery where it prepares the materials needed for the brothers' shoes, demonstrating as much action as care. It gives itself to a crowd of arms, always diligently searching out those who may need it for some service: to filter, grind, water, wash or mill, never refusing its help. Finally, so that it receives no undue thanks, and leaves no work uncompleted, it takes away all the filth and leaves everything clean.

All this required considerable canalization to bring water into the various workshops and other buildings of the monastery. We noted previously that in the twelfth century at the Grand Chartreuse and at many other houses of that Order, water was channeled into every cell by a network of canals, to allow the monks complete solitude. Obazine Abbey undertook an enormous water supply project in the twelfth century. The well water supplying the monastery, which included feeding the fish-pond and activating the mills and machines in the various workshops, was no longer sufficient for the needs of the community. So the monks did not hesitate to cap the stream at Coiroux, more than two kilometers away. They built a canal which involved channelling through solid rock for over a kilometer of its length as well as building aqueducts to carry the water over ravines. This was a huge undertaking and the remains are still impressive.

THE FORGE AT FONTENAY AND
THE BREWERY AT VILLERS-EN-BRABANT

Most have disappeared of the various workshops and farm buildings. Yet a few examples have been preserved almost intact.

There is, first of all, the forge at Fontenay, a daughter abbey of Clairvaux near Montbard in Burgundy. It is a magnificent twelfth-century building, fifty-three yards long, thirteen yards high, built on the edge of a canal which produced the power to drive the bellows, the lathe and the mill wheels. This forge had four rooms, the first being the forge properly speaking, and the last room sheltering the mill. The building is lighted by high semi-circular windows and the thick walls are reinforced by powerful projecting buttresses.

Not far from Brussels, at the cistercian abbey of Villers-en-Brabant—whose ruins are among the most beautiful monastic buildings in Belgium—parts of the brewery still remain. It was built between 1270–1276, on the banks of the Thyle which provided the necessary water. This building is forty-two yards long, twelve yards wide, divided into two groin-vaulted naves, supported at the center by a row of five columns with very simple capitals. Just inside is the placement of the forge itself, with six small columns supporting the pointed arches of the chimney hood. Two stairways, one on the interior and the other on the exterior, lead to the upper floor which was used for grain storage. Only the roof is missing in this beautiful building. Along with the forge at Fontenay, it is one of the few monastery workshops dating back to the Middle Ages that have been preserved.

FARM BUILDINGS

Monastery farm buildings are not as rare. In cistercian abbeys, property was divided into a certain number of granges, each of these forming a center for an autonomous unit of farm buildings. First of all, there was the abbey

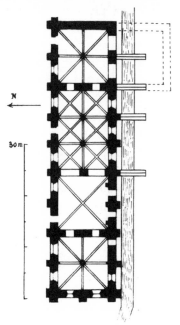

Figures 11.2a and b. The forge at Fontenay Abbey and floor plan.

grange, which included all the land on which the monastery was situated. There are a certain number of these beautiful farm buildings from the Middle Ages still extant.

At the abbey of Preuilly, Cîteaux's fifth daughter house, founded in 1118 near Donnemarie-en-Montois, there is still an important barn, called the *Grange de Beauvais* (the Beauvaux barn), dating back to the twelfth century. It is divided into three rooms, the first of which has six groin-vaulted bays resting on short, stocky columns. The vault from the other two rooms has collapsed.

Pontigny's fourth daughter, Jouy Abbey, founded in Brie the same year as Fontaine-Jean, provides another example of a thirteenth-century grange. This construction was carefully executed, thirty-four yards long, twelve yards wide with thick walls shouldered by large buttresses. It is divided into three groin-vaulted rooms.

Another lovely, somewhat later, barn is at the famous Maubuisson Abbey, founded in 1241 by Queen Blanche of Castile. It has a large central space with two side aisles, one of which was destroyed in the nineteenth century. This central space is divided by a double row of nine columns which support pointed arcades under a small wall made of beautiful, original oak woodwork.

The barn at Froidmont Abbey in Beauvais likely dates back to the thirteenth century and is still intact. Its three aisles are divided by rows of wooden posts which support the roof. At the end of one of the aisles there are two doors. Two small windows in the upper part of the gable provide some light.

Among the oldest granges is a quaint boathouse at Hautecombe Abbey in the Savoy. This abbey, founded by the Benedictines of Molesmes, passed to the Order of Cîteaux in 1135, in the Clairvaux filiation. The Benedictines of Solesmes now have it. It is situated on the west bank of Lake Bourget. In the thirteenth century, when the monks established themselves on the narrow strip of land between the lake and the foot of Mont-du-Chat, their property extended onto the banks of the lake. The simplest and most rapid method was to bring in the wheat and other harvests hauling them by boat. The industrious monks thought of building a boathouse on the water-front, so the boats could pass under cover with their heavy loads. This rectangular boathouse, thirty-six meters long and thirteen meters wide, dates from the latter part of the twelfth century. Carefully restored and given a new roof, it is in perfect condition.

Besides the barns which stored the harvests from monastery properties, we must not forget the cellars, which took up half the ground floor of the laybrothers' buildings.

THE WEST RANGES

The twelfth-century laybrothers' range at Clairvaux is fairly well preserved, and is one of the oldest and most beautiful we have. It is seventy-five yards long. The ground floor is double-aisled and rib-vaulted while the laybrothers' dormitory above is groined. The walls of the building are reinforced by powerful vertical buttresses linked at the top by semi-circular arches. This arrangement is also found in the cellars at Vauclair, Pontigny (not far from Auxerre), and at Longpont (between Soissons and Villers-Cotterets). This last was transformed into a novitiate, then to an abbatial palace, and now serves as a dwelling. It has the same kinds of buttresses as the infirmary, or 'hall of the dead' at Ourscamp, near Noyen.

In the nineteenth century, Clairvaux was made into a maximum security prison but guided visits to the lay brothers building—which has recently been restored—are allowed on weekends even though it is technically within the prison.

Another, even older wine cellar of Clairvaux, is preserved at Dijon. It is divided into two naves by a series of octagonal pillars on the ground floor and round pillars on the first floor. Its twelfth century timberwork is intact.

One of the most beautiful and best preserved west ranges is at Vauclair Abbey, Clairvaux's fifteenth daughter, founded in 1134 in the diocese of Laon (now Soissons). Built in the thirteenth century, it is seventy yards long and fifteen yards wide. Both the ground and the first floor—which was the lay brothers' dormitory—were cross-rib vaulted. As at Clairvaux, the outward thrust of the vaulting was resisted by a series of powerful vertical buttresses linked at their tops by rounded arches. The magnificent chestnut roofing timbers are original and until quite recently could be admired. Unfortunately, situated as it was north of the *Chemin des Dames*, at the foot of the Craonne Plateau, it lay in the line of fire between 1914 and 1918. Little by little, it collapsed under the constant artillery barrages and is now only a sorry ruin.

Also of note in France are the laybrothers' ranges at Royaumont, Noirlac (founded in 1136), and Clermont (founded in 1136 not far from Laval). In Belgium the west range at Villers-en-Brabant looks very like the one at Vauclair. In England, the most beautiful west range can be seen at Fountains, a daughter of Clairvaux founded in 1135, in Yorkshire. Dating from the end of the twelfth century, this range is nearly eighty yards long. The largest west range of all is at Eberbach Abbey, a daughter of Clairvaux in the Rhineland. Built around 1200, it is at least ninety-three yards long, and sixteen yards wide.

SCATTERED GRANGES

All the buildings we have mentioned so far were built at the abbeys themselves. But there were also granges distributed throughout the abbey landholdings according to the number of autonomous farm-centers, each having some five to eight hundred acres of workable fields and forests. These granges were to be not more than a day's walk from the abbey—about nine to twelve miles, so that the lay brothers living there could return to the monastery on the eve of Sundays and great feasts to attend the Offices with the community and hear the instructions of the abbot and their own father-master. The morning after the feast, they were back on the road to their granges in silence. The distance between each grange was to be at least two burgundian leagues—a bit over seven miles—to avoid disputes with other farmers in the area.

These granges were farmed by the lay brothers under the supervision of the grange-master, himself a lay brother, and under the direction of the cellarer, who was responsible for all the abbey finances and lived at the monastery. Besides the sheds, stables and other out-buildings, the grange included an oratory, a refectory, a kitchen, a dormitory and a warming room. There was also a guesthouse because hospitality was offered at granges as well as abbeys.

The most important granges sometimes looked like the abbey. A thirteenth-century author, describing Clairvaux, mentions that Outre-Aube Grange—a few buildings of which still remain—could have been mistaken for the abbey had it not been for the ox-yokes, ploughs and other field equipment lying around everywhere. The granges differed from the monasteries, however, in that only lay brothers lived there. The monks went there only to help with very heavy work, such as haymaking, harvesting, sheep-shearing, and, if they made wine, grape-harvesting. They could eat their meals with the lay brothers but were never to spend the night there, for they had no dwelling other than the cloister.

In the Cistercian Order, the granges never became autonomous houses as sometimes happened in benedictine rural priories, where the monks lived and formed distinct communities with a superior directing the work on the land.

The Cistercian granges had an oratory in which the lay brothers recited their Office together, but there was no altar, at least during the Order's first centuries. There was no bell, either, except for a hand-bell which announced meals.

The cellarer who was in charge of all the abbey finances, also directed all the granges, which he administered with great care and competence. In twelfth and thirteenth-century Europe, the Cistercians were pioneers in new technologies, and their monasteries acquired great prestige as model agricultural centers. From all around, the lords who had vast wastelands or infested marshes counted on the monks to transform them into fertile fields and pastures through their hard work.

Gerald the Welshman—or Giraldus Cambrensis—wrote in his *Journey Through Wales* in 1188: 'Give these monks a barren land and a wild forest, leave them there for a few years, and you'll find not only a splendid church, but human dwellings around the church as well,'—evidence shows that they lost no time in cultivating the land.

THE LEGENDARY PREFERENCE FOR UNHEALTHY LOCATIONS

No credence should be given to the story that the Cistercians, in founding their monasteries, purposely sought low, humid valleys where the air was foul. This legend began with Blessed Fastrede, the third abbot of Clairvaux, who died in 1163. Writing to a cistercian abbot who was making himself conspicuous by his fine food and clothing, Fastrede reminded him that this was not proper to a monk. Then, he quotes what Saint Bernard is supposed to have said on the subject: 'Early monks chose to live in low, humid valleys, so that, never sure of their health and often sick, they would always have the image and fear of death before their eyes'.

All this comes from hearsay. Besides that, Abbot Fastrede was particularly noted for his austerities. Moreover, in all of Saint Bernard's works, the letters as well as the sermons and treatises, there is not even the faintest trace of such a doctrine. As for choosing an unhealthy environment for a new monastery, there is no mention of this either in the sayingas of the ancient fathers or in the Cistercian statutes. There, there is only one stipulation: that the site chosen be secluded or 'far from human habitation'. Remember that the Cistercian Order arose during a period of great agricultural expansion, and good pieces of land had been taken up long before then, so the monks had to content themselves with what was offered, very often waste lands and marshes which the monks worked hard at draining and clearing. If in spite of their work, the air still remained unwholesome, they begged for a more favorable site and transferred their monastery. The early history of the Order mentions a number of relocations on account of the 'trouble with the air'.

Two examples alone will show that the deliberate choice of unhealthy locations never existed in the Order. An abbey was founded in the twelfth century in Franconia in the middle of a marsh. The summer months brought disease-ridden mists which changed into hail and wrought desolation to the entire area. It had been named *Hagelsbrun*—source of hail. The monks did so well with their drainage that, using a word play the Cistercians loved, they soon renamed the area *Heilsbrun*—source of salvation. The monks at Franquivaux provide another example. This abbey, founded in the thirteenth century, suffered so much from the foul air each summer that the General Chapter authorized them to relocate for that reason alone.

WATER MANAGEMENT

Very often monks had to deal with flooding and the erosion it caused to the land. A good example of the immense amount of work needed is given by the grange at Bréda. The lay brothers at Tamié Abbey in the Savoy built an embankment at this grange, located near Avalon in the Dauphiné, at the juncture of the road to Grenoble and the highway running from Lyon to Italy in the area of the Mont-Cenis Pass. While they were protecting their own land, they were rendering a great service to the countryside.

In other areas they struggled against the sea. In the eleventh century, the monks of Saint Bertin in Flanders

established polders, or land embankments, to gain pasture-
land. The monks of the Cistercian Abbey of the Dunes in
Flanders were able—after a great deal of work on dikes,
locks, and canals—to conquer the sea and the dunes and
to create thousands of acres of land which they farmed or
pastured, establishing granges. This allowed them to raise
immense flocks of sheep whose wool they sold to the drapers
of Flanders. Shipping of this wool became so important
that the abbey soon had its own fleet. These dikes and
locks had to be constantly maintained. The abbot of the
Dunes bore the title 'Count of Dikes,' or better, Chief of
Waterworks. That is, he was in charge of establishing and
maintaining dikes, locks, and drainage canals. In twelfth
and thirteenth-century Poitou, the monks, whose property
extended to the ocean front, were granted concessions for
doing drainage work.

Most of the buildings on these granges have disappeared.
A few remaining examples, however, witness to the great
care, perfection and art with which they were built.

A FEW BEAUTIFUL GRANGES THAT HAVE BEEN PRESERVED

Among the barns that have been preserved in France is
that at Vollerend, not far from Charles de Gaulle airport.
A dependency of Chaalis Abbey, the grange was founded
in 1137 by King Louis VI. The barn lies in the township
of Villeron, not far from the road running between Paris
and Senlis. It was built in the second half of the thirteenth
century and is sixty-six yards long by eighteen yards wide. It
is divided in three bays by two rows of pillars bearing pointed
arches which support the timbers of a steeply pitched roof.
The clerestory is pierced by two rows of high, narrow windows. In the façade are two doors and an adjoining round
tower housing a spiral staircase.

Gratien Leblanc, professor at Toulouse, showed me an
interesting barn at Fontcalvi, a dependency of Fontfroide,

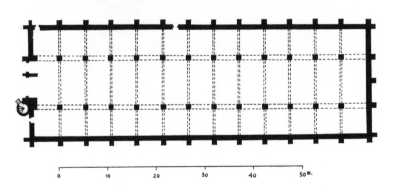

Figures 11.3a and b. The grange at Vollerand and floor plan.

on a plain about nine miles north of Narbonne. The lay brothers moved there around 1200. Besides grazing cattle, growing wheat, olive trees, and vines, they exploited the salt marshes. After the Revolution, this grange was sold and then abandoned, but there are still some important ruins which were classified in 1946. Built at the beginning of

Figure 11.4. Interior view of the grange at
Vollerand.

the fourteenth century under abbot Jacques Fournier of
Fontfroide—the future Pope Benedict XII—it resembles a
small fortress with its thick walls flanked by eight square
towers, one at each of the four corners, and one in the
center of each of the four walls. All this was designed to
resist potential plunderers.

In Belgium a beautiful cistercian priory barn still exists in
western Flanders at Lisseweghe, a dependency of Ter Doest

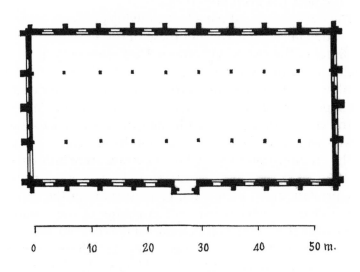

Figures 11.5a and b. The grange at Ter Doest and floor plan.

Abbey, a daughter house of Dunes. Built of brick about 1250, it is sixty yards long and twenty-four yards wide. The gable ends of the steeply pitched roof are sixty feet high while the side walls attain a height of only twenty-seven feet. The interior is divided into three bays by two rows of oak pillars mounted on bases of alternating brick and Tournai stone. The thirteenth-century roof timbering is original.

The Cistercians allowed only what was absolutely necessary in their architecture, resolutely refusing any superfluous decoration. Yet here is a typical exception that proves the rule: a farm building built in the thirteenth century includes a gable decorated with ten blind windows arranged in a very beautiful and artistic way, and have absolutely no practical use. While Cistercians wanted simplicity, they were quite capable of putting small discreet, artistic touches even on ordinary farm buildings. The barn at Lisseweghe has much in common with one at Longchamp Abbey founded for the Poor Clares in 1232 by Saint Louis' sister, Isabel, in what is now the *Bois de Boulogne*. This barn has disappeared but the plan has been preserved.

The Carthusians, who made their living primarily by raising cattle, also had barns, but these never attained the importance of the cistercian granges. They were only sheds to shelter their herds and forage, with a dwelling for the lay brothers. Each grange was entrusted to a lay brother under the supervision either of the monk in charge of the cattle or of the chief shepherd. As with the Cistercians, Carthusian monks were not allowed to reside on the granges.

The Premonstratensians who, as we saw, were influenced by the Cistercians, also had granges. Each was entrusted to a provost, aided by the grange-master under the supervision of the canon or overseer in charge of the outdoor work. But the Premonstratensians differed from the Cistercians in that on their granges they had chapels where Mass was celebrated. Often these chapels developed into local parishes.

VITICULTURE: THE CLOS-VOUGEOT AS AN EXAMPLE

Some monks also kept vineyards. They needed both Mass wine and drinking wine. Although Saint Benedict said in his Rule that wine was not a drink for monks, he never the less allows its use because, as he says, 'in our day, monks cannot be persuaded not to drink it'. And he contents himself with setting a measure.

The monks of Cîteaux had vineyards very early. The most famous was the Clos-Vougeot, a little over two miles from Nuit-Saint-Georges. The monks constantly enlarged these vineyards and in the middle of the twelfth century built a cellar with wine-presses. At the end of the fifteenth century the property, some two hundred fifty acres, was enclosed with walls. The old twelfth-century cellar as well as the magnificent sixteenth-century buildings with a fermentation vat and four large presses can still be seen. The Clos-Vougeot is now the seat of the eminently peaceable Order of the Knights of Tastevin.

During the seventeenth century, in a period called the 'war of observances', the abbot of Cîteaux did not look favorably on monastic reform movements and some wicked tongues spread the rumor that wines from Clos-Vougeot helped him to get abbots to support him. In the *General History of the Reform of the Cistercian Order* by Dom Gervaise, the second successor to the abbé de Rancé as abbot of the reformed abbey of La Trappe, we read that the abbots in favor of reform considered it pointless to attend the General Chapter scheduled to begin on 10 May 1667. The reason?

> We would be overwhelmed by the majority. The abbot of Cîteaux will preside over the Chapter. He will have everything under his control. As he endears himself to all the German, Swiss, and Polish abbots as well as the other foreigners, and as he pours them his excellent wines from his Clos de Vougeot—which have worked such wonders on similar occasions—he will get them to say whatever he wants to hear.

At Clairvaux the monks also had vineyards. The main cellar near the abbey was called *Colombe-le-Sec* (Dry Dovecot)—a strange name for a winecellar! The monks' old buildings can still be seen.

The Vineyards of the cistercian abbey of Eberbach in the Rhineland were considered among the best in the area. In the fifteenth century the monks built a giant 1000 hectoliter (26,400 gallon) cask. The bavarian philologist, Vincent Obsopaeus, who died in 1539, compared this cask to the wonders of the ancient world.

Quid vetat Erpachium vas annumerare vetustis
Miraclis, quo nec vastius orbis habet.
Dixeris hoc recte pelagus vinique paludem
Nectare, quae Bacchi nocte dieque fluit.

What keeps the Eberbach cask, the largest on earth, from being one of the wonders of the world? You are right to call it is an ocean of wine, and a pool of Bacchus where nectar flows day and night.

As their properties increased, the monks gradually produced more wine than they needed and began to sell the excess. To do this they began to attend the reat fairs of Champagne at Lagny, Bar-sur-Aube, Provins, and Troyes, where there was important international trade.

Similarly, after having created small industries to provide for the needs of their monasteries and neighboring villages, they gradually expanded and began to work for outsiders. Well-organized, having large capital, which was rare in those days, and long experience, they were forerunners of the organization and development of modern industry, just as previously they had been the great colonizers in much of Europe. After organizing themselves to live in inaccessible solitude, they became self-sufficient by force of circumstances, and then used their expertise to benefit nieghboring people and so made a great contribution to society.

12

THE SEVENTEENTH AND EIGHTEENTH CENTURY ARCHITECTURAL RENAISSANCE

INNUMERABLE TIMES THROUGH HISTORY, monks have known tragic moments. Their monasteries have been pillaged, plundered, demolished and burned in wars and revolutions. They have had to flee from their monasteries and often to leave their homeland. At times, caught unaware, they have been massacred, hanged, or burnt at the stake. Monastic history is full of these dramas and atrocities. In periods of turbulence, monks are often the first victims of popular persecutions. But every time, no matter what the country, monks have returned to their monasteries as soon as possible. Often without waiting for peace and order to be restored, they hurried to repair and rebuild a monastery whose ruins were still smoking.

In France, the Hundred Years' War was followed by a period of brigandage, the Wars of Religion, and finally the Revolution. All these brought immeasurable hardship to the monasteries and terrible massacre of the religious. In every case, at the first lull, the monks regrouped and rebuilt their monasteries. The same thing happened in England and

255

Germany after the Reformation had caused massacres and destruction.

More recently, the Spanish Revolution of 1835, the Laws of Persecution in Italy immediately after reunification, and those in France in 1880 and in 1901, expelled the religious. Always, the monks returned, at first clandestinely, then in broad daylight as they began to build new monasteries to replace the old ones which had been confiscated. It is the same in Russia, Poland and Czechoslovakia now that persecutions have begun to subside.

AN IMPORTANT REVIVAL IN MONASTIC CONSTRUCTION

As monks hurried to rebuild their monasteries after the wars and revolutions, a strong impetus also began toward monastic reconstruction in the seventeenth and eighteenth century and could be compared to that of the eleventh century. Whether monasteries had not been entirely rebuilt after the wars, or whether the buildings had not been well maintained, in the nineteenth century all the religious orders sensed a need to renew and replace their old buildings—many of which dated back to the Middle Ages—with newer ones, ones that would be larger and more practical, better lighted and ventilated. This they did in a style both noble and subdued, with the sobriety that typifies neo-classicism.

In France moreover, Louis XIV ordered all the monasteries to reconstruct their buildings. This obliged the monks to invest their capital and provided jobs for workmen. And so, a great revival in reconstruction came to birth. Most of the monasteries owned large properties and especially vast forests. The monks asked for authorization to timber these off. Those of limited resources called on their more affluent friends or took out loans.

Usually the old church was kept and it was the conventual buildings that were rebuilt, enlarged and embellished. Everywhere monasteries were built in grand proportions with spacious rooms, high ceilings, generous lighting, wide hallways, splendid staircases decorated with magnificent wrought-iron banisters, and huge dormitories with private cells. There were also beautiful reception rooms and veritable *salons*. To store the ever increasing number of books and manuscripts, large, magnificent libraries were built. Not to mention the veritable *chateaux* replete with beautiful gardens adorned with statues, ponds, and fountains, which the commendatory abbots and even the regular abbots often had built for themselves.

THE PLEIADES OF BENEDICTINE ARCHITECTS

Among the Benedictines, the arrangement of buildings remained the same, conforming to the traditional plan. Only the dimensions changed. In those places where it was rebuilt, the church usually had a very broad nave with narrow side aisles or, alternatively, a series of chapels opening directly off the nave. The transept projected only slightly while the choir itself was very large. The façade was generally divided into three tiers by rows of small columns with capitals reproducing the Doric, Ionic, and Corinthian orders. The crossing was covered with a dome surmounted by a lantern. The building was barrel vaulted with large transverse beams resting on the pillars of the arcades.

At Cluny, the monks began to rebuild the conventual buildings after 1740. Dom Athose, the prior, tore down the old cloister built by Saint Odilo, and built a larger whose arcades resemble those of the *Palais Royal*, the Royal Palace, in Paris. At great expense—and with the help of the commendatory abbot, Cardinal Frederic of Rochefoucault—a new monastery was erected on the medieval foundations. The majestic new building, with its two wings, faced the garden. Yet, the prior, while pushing on with the work, had an intuition of the approaching doom as he said: 'I'll build, but before a hundred years have passed, our house will be destroyed.' He had the time to finish the work, however, and the General Chapter of 1762 spared him no applause for his zeal and intelligence.

The Abbot General of the Congregation of Saint Maur, Dom Gregory Tarrisse, had a number of monasteries built or repaired. The type of buildings usually adopted had a long façade overlooking gardens. At each end was a square pavilion and the central section was projected beyond the main building and given a beautifully decorated pediment. The ground floor had large, semi-circular windows. The whole building was covered with a mansard roof. This same model was used for other abbeys: Fleury, Saint Denis, Bec, Saint Ouen in Rouen and Saint Etienne in Caen.

During this period, the Benedictines had counted a good number of architects in their ranks: The best known was Dom Denis Plouvier who worked on the Abbey of Préaux, not far from Évreux, and also on Saint Victor Abbey in Bayeux. He was helped by Dom Firmin de la Croix and Dom Alexis Briard. There was also Dom Anselme Boisseau who built the cloister and the infirmaries at Bec around 1644. Dom Augustine Moisset, prior at Mont-Saint-Michel, designed the plans for his abbey. Dom Pierre Lede worked on Fécamp, Bernay, and at Saint Wandrille.

Indisputably the most famous architect of them all was Dom William de la Tremblaye, a monk at Bec, who rebuilt Saint Étienne and La Trinité at Caen, and, at the Abbey of Saint Denis, using plans drawn by Robert de Cotte, the buildings now used to house the Legion of Honor. De la Tremblaye and Jean Batte also rebuilt the abbey of Saint Germain-des-Prés in Paris and drew up the plans for Saint Benoît-sur-Loire.

The Low Countries also experienced a revival in their monastic architecture during the same period. The court architect, Laurent-Benoît Dewez, rebuilt a good number of benedictine abbeys such as: Saint Martin of Tournai, Gembloux and Andenne in the province of Namur, and Afflighem and Vierbeck in Brabant. These were built in the same noble, somber style and on the same plan as the french abbeys. In Germany and Austria, too, the age was marked with numerous monastic constructions, nearly all of them in the over-elaborate baroque style which will be discussed later.

WHEN CISTERCIANS SUCCUMB TO IMMODERATION. . . .

In this sweeping current of renovation, the Cistercians were not left behind. In the second half of the seventeenth century, Abbot Dominic Georges of Val-Richer in Normandy undertook the restoration of the buildings at his monastery. The work was done under the direction of the monks. They all, even the abbot, took a hand in it. The church was decorated with statues and friezes of saints and nine bells were hung in the belfry! Nearly all these buildings were destroyed in 1802. All that remains is the west wing which a M. Guizot bought in 1836, restored, and made into a residence.

At the end of the seventeenth century, Armand de Chalucet, bishop of Toulon and a commendatory abbot (1672–1712) of Vaux-de-Cernay near Chevreuse, had a splendid abbatial palace built for himself. None of it is left. Of the medieval abbey all that remains are the ruins of the church and the east range of the monastery. The rest was demolished in 1816 by its new owner, General Christophe, who had the buildings blown up, and invited all his friends to enjoy the spectacle of the walls collapsing with a crash.

At Ourscamp Abbey, situated on a bend of the Oise River near Noyon, a large guesthouse was built at the end of the seventeenth century. It was located to the left of the façade of the thirteenth-century church. To the right, a similar building was erected in 1748, for the commendatory abbot. A new façade for the church—one reflecting the taste of the day—was modelled over the old. It had four columns and an equal number of pilasters with a combination of Doric and Ionic capitals. The structure was crowned with a pediment having a carved stone bear set into it—an allusion to the

Figure 12.1. The eighteenth-century façade of the abbey of Ourscamp and detail.

abbey's name in Latin, *Ursicampus*—the field of the bear. Actually, the name had nothing to do with a bear but referred to the original owner of the place, the Gallo-Roman, *Ursus*. These buildings still exist although the one on the left was badly damaged during the Second World War. After the French Revolution, in 1807, a new owner, Radix de Sainte-Foy, who was fond of ruins and English gardens, had the magnificent thirteenth-century church demolished solely because he wanted a beautiful, romantic ruin in his park.

Hubert Robert also enjoyed ruins. He painted scenes of many of them and others he made up. He also amused himself by using his imagination to 'ruin' perfectly intact monuments, as he did for the Grand Gallery of the Louvre, in a painting now in Russia, at the *Palais Alexandre de Tsarskoe-Selo*. This sort of demolition can easily be forgiven.

There are also ruins of pseudo-abbeys. One was built in the beginning of the nineteenth century by an eccentric Englishman who went so far as to name it Font-hill Abbey at the risk of misleading historians and archaeologists. The ruins of this supposed abbey, in which no monk ever set foot, can still be seen in the area around Salisbury.

At La Ferté Abbey, Cîteaux's first foundation in 1114 in the diocese of Chalon-sur-Saône, Abbot Claude Petit (1677–1710) restored the monastery and built an abbatial palace in the style of the day. This abbey has been transformed into a château and is surrounded by gardens which cover the foundations of the former monastery.

In Flanders, at Loos Abbey—now surrounded by a suburb of Lille—Abbot Ignatius Delfosse undertook the reconstruction of his church in 1720. Three monks from the abbey opposed this work and petitioned the governor of Lille to have it stopped. After a visit from the abbot of Clairvaux—the father-abbot of Loos—two master-masons were commissioned to inspect the buildings. They reported that the church was in danger of falling into ruin and should be rebuilt. After that, the three monks were sent off to other monasteries and the work was continued, directed by the architect Girard of Lille. The very thing that happened in building monasteries during the Middle Ages was repeated again. People from all around—who had taken refuge with these monks during the wars—came in droves to help them with their work, building with them and using their wagons to transport the materials needed. This monastery is still intact, although it has been transformed into a detention home. The chapel, stripped of all its splendid ornaments, serves as a chapel for the inmates.

At Igny Abbey, another Clairvaux foundation in Champagne, the monks wanted to rebuild their monastery in the style of the day. Charles-François de Montiers from Meinville, bishop of Chartres and commendatory abbot of Igny (1709–1746), obtained authorization from the king to make an extraordinary cutting in the abbey forests. He began to construct new buildings in 1733. Simultaneously, the former monastery, the church included was demolished and replaced by a small rotunda, which looked more like a manor house chapel, hidden away, in the wing of one of the new buildings, and covered with a small cupola on pendentives. These were the buildings that J. K. Huysmans saw when he visited the abbey where he converted to Catholicism. In his novel *En Route*, he tells us that the little chapel there was 'alarmingly ugly'. This monastery remained intact until the end of the First World War. The Germans blew it up it in August 1918 during their abrupt retreat.

In Champagne during this period, the abbey of Trois Fontaines—Clairvaux's first foundation in 1118—had as its commendatory abbot Pierre de Tencin, the brother of Madame de Tencin. At the height of his career as archbishop of Lyon, cardinal, and Minister of State to Louis IX, and enriched by his participation in the financial affairs of his friend Law, de Tencin decided to rebuild his monastery. He began in 1741 by erecting a monumental portal at the entrance to the monastery. This entryway, incorporating two main buildings, can still be seen. They were linked by a gallery with ten rounded arches. The old church was not demolished but simply 'redressed' in the current style. The transverse arches and ribs were decorated with rosettes; the corbels and cornices were reshaped; capitals with acanthus leaves were fitted to the pillars bearing the grand arcades of the nave; the walls were covered with slabs of marble. Only the west façade was preserved in its original state.

Not far from Paris, near Ermenonville, is the abbey of Chaalis, founded in 1136 by King Louis the Fat in memory of his cousin, Charles the Good, the Count of Flanders basely assassinated in 1127 while he was attending Mass in Saint Donatien Church in Bruges. Louis II of Bourbon-Condé, the commendatory abbot, decided to rebuild the monastery in 1736. The beautiful thirteenth-century church was preserved, but the other buildings were demolished and replaced by new ones on a more grandiose scale. He called on Jean Aubert, the great architect of the Hotel Biron who had also worked on the *Mews* of the *château* of Chantilly. But lack of money delayed things and he died in 1741 before the work had even begun. Work started in 1743, but adequate funding was not available and things dragged on. By 1749 only the north wing had been completed, hardly a third of what had been projected. The abbey borrowed money and went into debt. In 1764 they had to cancel the contract and finally, in 1770, declared bankruptcy. Louis XVI then closed the abbey and in 1785 it was liquidated. By the Revolution, there were no longer any monks at Chaalis. The buildings, including the church, were demolished. The splendid yet lamentable ruins of the north transept still stand in the sun. Only the most recent building was saved. At present it shelters the collections of the Musée Jacquemart André which now belongs to the Institut de France.

THE RENOVATION OF CÎTEAUX AND CLAIRVAUX

The monks of the great burgundian abbey of Cîteaux, the motherhouse of cistercian houses around the world, also decided to renovate their buildings. The plans, which respected the old and venerable church, were entrusted to the architect Nicolas Lenoir—called 'the Roman' because he had studied at the Academy of Rome to distinguish him from Alexander Lenoir, the founder of the Museum of French Monuments.

In 1760 they began by building a large wing parallel to the church, to the left of the façade. In a classical style that was both somber and majestic, this was all that was realized of Lenoir's grandiose project, the designs of which are now kept in the public library of Dijon. This wing still exists and it sheltered the cistercian community that returned to Cîteaux in 1898. Except for a fifteenth-century library building, all the rest has disappeared, including the magnificent twelfth-century church whose very foundations were ripped out.

At Clairvaux, the abbey founded by Saint Bernard, the immense buildings are still intact and were converted into a prison in 1808. These buildings date back to the abbacies of Pierre Mayeul (1740–1761) and François Le Blois (1761–1780). They have a stately appearance with a triangular pediment which at the center of the façade gives it a military look. Demolition of the church built by Saint Bernard and enlarged by an immense chevet with ambulatory and radiating chapels about twenty years after his death began in 1812. There was no trace of it after 1819. And this all took place during the reign of King Louis XVIII.

At Sept-Fons in Bourbonnais, abbot Eustache de Beaufort obtained authorization from King Louis XIV in 1673, through the intervention of Colbert, to cut timber in his forest of Chignon to make some renovations and to do some construction work. He was thus able to replace the simple palisade enclosing the monastery with a solid wall of stone.

He also needed to construct housing for new members, who were arriving in large numbers. Abbot Dom Jalloutz (1757–1788) enlarged the monastic enclosure and erected a cloister wall nearly two miles long, one yard thick, and four yards high. It still exists. At the same time, he began constructing the monastery, with the king's authorization to exploit the forests of his abbey as he wished and according to his need. Work was begun in 1760 on plans drawn up in Paris. First the infirmary was built. Then came the farm buildings, the other out-buildings, the guest house, guest chapel, refectory, chapter and lay brothers' dormitory. In 1774 the church was lengthened and the cloister, the refectory, and the monks' dormitory were built. At this time, monks and lay brothers had separate chapters, refectories, and dormitories. In 1780, the façade of the church was finished as were the two large buildings which framed it, in the current style. In all this work, finished in 1783, the monks worked with 'their whole souls', as the chronicler testifies.

At Royaumont, the royal abbey founded in 1228 by Louis IX, all the thirteenth-century buildings still exist except the church, which the Marquis de Travannel had torn down after he had acquired the property in 1791. The pillars of the nave were sawn almost entirely through. Chains were then passed around them and attached to oxen. As the pillars gave way, the vaulting came crashing down, bringing the roof, tower, and sections of the wall in its wake. Only the north transept was left standing, along with a turret which housed a spiral staircase.

The marquis, formerly Marie-Antoinette's banker, had been identified in 1793 as a suspect and, naturally wanting to save his neck, he lost no time writing this note to the Committee of Public Welfare: 'In the month of May 1791, I purchased the one-time abbey of Royaumont. After I had acquired it, I demolished that infamous church which had been built by one of our former tyrants—whom superstition named Saint Louis. It was also the burial place of his children.' This magnificent proof of his good citizenship saved him from the scaffold.

Always carefully maintained, the monastery did not need to be rebuilt in the seventeenth century. But Abbot de Balivière, confessor to Louis XVI, who had held the abbey *in commendam* at the end of the eighteenth century, had the former abbatial lodge demolished because it was too simple for his taste. In 1785 he had Louis Le Masson replace it with a charming little palace which still exists. It is in the Florentine style inspired by the villas of Palladio. Three façades out of four are provided with terraces and stairways. The vestibule—decorated with Tuscan columns— opens to the right and left into the parlor and a circular dining room. To supply the income for this expenditure, the abbot had to sell the house the abbey had in Paris, near Saint Eustache Church.

Besides these abbatial palaces, other monastic buildings of this period look more like manor houses than monks' dwellings, with their spacious rooms, broad corridors, and monumental stairways. In many instances, with only a few adaptations, they were well-suited to the secular purposes to which they were put after the Revolution. Numberless are the police stations, schools, museums, libraries, and hospitals now in these former monasteries—not to mention the barracks, mental hospitals, and prisons.

CARTHUSIANS AND PREMONSTRATENSIANS

The Carthusians also experienced a period of architectural renewal in the seventeenth and eighteenth centuries. It was during this time that they rebuilt the charterhouses at Bosserville, near Nancy, and of Notre-Dame-des-Prés, at Montreuile-sur-Mer. The Grande Chartreuse was entirely rebuilt after a fire in 1676, by Dom Innocent Le Masson, the Prior General. Those buildings, still standing today, were reclaimed by the Carthusians in 1940. The charterhouse at Vauclaire in Périgord—on a beautiful site on an island at the foot of a wooded hill—suffered greatly in the Religious Wars and was rebuilt in the seventeenth century. The pretty little charterhouse of Reposoir in Savoy, lost in the mountainside above Sallanches, was rebuilt after a fire in 1705. It is presently occupied by a community of Carmelites. The small fourteenth century cloister still stands. The charterhouse at Valsainte in the canton of Fribourg in Switzerland, one of the most flourishing charterhouses, was entirely rebuilt after a fire in 1732.

The Premonstratensians also experienced great architectural activity during this same period. They began with Prémontré Abbey, the cradle of the Order, situated in a valley of the Coucy forest. Three large buildings constructed between 1718 and 1757 still exist with a circular section forming a projecting centerpiece and large pilasters with Ionic capitals, masterpieces of classical architecture.

But it was especially in the Low Countries, where the Premonstratensians were, and still are, very prosperous, that this architectural renewal was obvious. Bonne Espérance

Figure 12.2. The eighteenth-century façade of Prémontré Abbey.

Abbey, near Binche in Hainaut, was rebuilt in the beginning of the seventeenth century. The classic church was finished in 1776 under the direction of the architect Laurent-Benoit Dewez who has already been mentioned. This abbey, still completely intact, is now occupied by the Minor Seminary of the Tournai Diocese. Near Louvain, the two large abbeys of Parc and Averbode, as well as that in Tongerloo in the Province of Antwerp—all three of them still used by the Premonstratensians —were magnificently rebuilt in the seventeenth and eighteenth century. Ninove Abbey in western Flanders, whose beautiful church was built from 1635 to 1723, has become a parish. Heylissem Abbey near Louvain, transformed at the end of the eighteenth century, gives evidence of the work of Dewez, who drew up the plans for the church and abbatial palace.

THE BAROQUE STYLE IN MONASTIC ARCHITECTURE

The term *baroque* comes from the Portuguese *berreuco*, which denotes a steep, pointed cliff or an irregular pearl. This name is given to the elaborate, florid style of architecture which developed in sixteenth-century Italy. Bernini, in the seventeenth century, is one of its best known representatives. At the end of the eighteenth century, this style became more and more elaborated until it reached such a profusion of decoration and intricacy that it was given the name *rococo*, or harsh style.

So fashionable was it that many abbeys were built in that style, with churches in new shapes where everything was in motion; in curved, wavy lines, projecting entablatures, cornices and pediments; in arabesque decor, in tall emphatically gesturing statues whose clothing seemed to be caught in violent winds; in sumptuous ornamentation with colored marbles, gold, silver and bronze; in paintings which covered cupolas, vaults, roofs, and even pillars. The Benedictines built a number of churches in this exaggerated,

Figure 12.3. The benedictine church at Zwiefalten.

theatrical style. This section will be limited to the most famous ones.

First of all there was Einsiedeln Abbey (or Our Lady of the Hermits) in Switzerland, not far from *Lake Zurich*. Founded in the tenth century, and rebuilt in 1704 by Gaspard Moosbrugger, a monk of the abbey, it was finished in 1770 by his successors, Thomas Meyer from Soleure and John Rueff. This abbey has a profusion of statues apparently in motion perched above the cornices so that their legs seem to be dangling in space. The vaulting is painted in *trompe d'oeil,*

Figure 12.4. The side aisle and pulpit at Zwiefalten.

life deception, and on all sides, marbles, bronzes in inexhaustible richness.

Also in Switzerland is the famous Abbey of Saint Gaul, begun in 1756 by Peter Thumb with the help of a lay brother, Gabriel Loser, and finished in 1769 by Jean Michel and Fernand Baer. The interior decoration in this church is very comparable with Einsiedeln.

The masterpiece in this style is the abbey of Melk in Austria. It is perched up on a cliff overlooking the Danube. The church's two large towers and cupola loom above the immense buildings which extend further than the eye can see. This abbey with its grandiose construction, luxuriously decorated with multicolored marble, and pilasters with gold capitals, is the best preserved of all the benedictine buildings of this period. It was the work of Jacob Prandtauer who played a very important role in monastic architecture in Austria.

THE CISTERCIANS ADOPT THE BAROQUE STYLE

In spite of the poverty and simplicity dear to their founders and the principles laid down by Saint Bernard, it would have been difficult for the Cistercians to resist the general infatuation with baroque and rococo styles, particularly in the monasteries of central Europe. Everywhere in southern Germany and Austria, in Hungary and Poland monasteries were being built in the baroque style.

Waldsassen church in the Upper Palatinate, rebuilt between 1681 and 1704, holds its own in every way with the benedictine churches just mentioned. Other cistercian churches in the same style were Furstenfeld in Upper Bavaria, not far from the infamous Dachau, finished in 1730; Furstenzell in Lower Bavaria, near Scarding, built from 1739 to 1745; Raitenhaslach, also in Bavaria and Schönau in Wurttemberg. These were a far cry from the simple lines of the first cistercian churches, such as Fontenay, which had only straight lines bisected by right angles in a somber style stripped of ornamentation.

Along with these churches rebuilt in the baroque style, there were some old ones in which only the interior was changed to suit modern tastes. The abbey church at Ebrach in Franconia typifies this kind of transformation. Built in the thirteenth century on the same plan as its mother-abbey, Morimond, Ebrach's interior was entirely transformed into the baroque style in the eighteenth century. Similarly, the thirteenth-century church at Doberan, in Mecklemburg-Schwerin, with a large ambulatory and radiating chapels added at the end of the fourteenth century, was also

Figure 12.5. The cistercian church at Vierzehnheiligen (Bavaria).

Figure 12.6. Baroque decor at the benedictine church of Ottobeuren (Württemberg).

redecorated in the eighteenth century. Among the new embellishments was an angel with extended wings, suspended from the vault, soaring in the air over one of the tombs, holding a crown in its right hand and a palm branch in the left. On its bosom was a pennant with the following inscription: *'Sey getreüwe bis in den Todt, so will ich dir die Kron des Lebens geben'*, a german translation of the eleventh verse in the second chapter of Revelations: 'Be faithful unto death and I will give you the crown of life.' It is easy to imagine Saint Bernard's reaction to fantasies of this kind.

Of all the german baroque churches built by the Cistercians, none surpasses the lush and luxurious ornamentation

Figure 12.7. Baroque decor at the cistercian priory
of Birnau on Lake Constance.

of two pilgrimage churches: Birnau, on the shore of Lake
Constance, built in 1750, and Vierzehnheiligen (the Fourteen Saints), near Lichtenfeld in Upper Franconia, which
dates back to 1772. In these churches—— dependencies of
Salem and Langheim Abbeys respectively—baroque fantasies are pushed to the extreme.

In Austria, the churches of Rein, not far from Graz,
and Lilienfeld, near Passau, were more or less transformed and interiorly redecorated in the same style. These

churches remain in the care of the Cistercians of the Common Observance. Also worthy of note is Engelszell Church on the Banks of Danube near Engelhartszell, rebuilt around 1760, and still maintained by the Cistercians of the Strict Observance.

The largest of the cistercian churches in the baroque style was once known as Grüssau, but is now called Krzeszow, as it is in Poland, in Silesia, not far from Liegnitz. Built between 1728 and 1734, on a very large plan, it is 336 feet long.

In France the baroque style enjoyed much less success. As far as cistercian churches go, there is only one example in the baroque style. Valloires Abbey church in Ponthieu was rebuilt between 1741–1756 after a fire of 1647 which completely destroyed the abbey. The architect, Raoul Coignart, drew up the plans in 1738 and the cornerstone was laid in 1741. Its decoration was entrusted to an Austrian gentleman named Pfaffenhoffen, better known as Pfaff. Having found refuge at Abbeville after killing an adversary in a duel, he did a lot of work in Picardy. Valloires Abbey managed to escape demolition and is now used as a sanatorium. The church, including all its decorations, statues, wainscotting, and a beautiful wrought-iron grill, is still intact. Above the sanctuary, two enormous angels with extended wings are suspended from the vault.

CARTHUSIAN SIMPLICITY PUT TO THE TEST

If the Cistercians were drawn into constructions contrary to the spirit of their founding fathers, they were not alone among religious families who had originally held to these same principles of poverty and simplicity. As we have seen, the Carthusians were not always successful in convincing their benefactors that only a very simple monastery was appropriate to hermits. In several cases they grudgingly and with misgivings accepted the splendid buildings given them, an architect's pride and joy. This was the case at the charterhouse at Pavia, now the home of a cistercian community.

Many of the charterhouses built in the seventeenth and eighteenth centuries failed by far to conform to the spirit of Saint Bruno. At the charterhouse in Naples, the prior, Dom Severo Turboli, undertook the huge task of enlarging the monastery. In the early seventeenth century he called on famous artists like Guido Reni and Bernini to embellish his church. It was magnificently redecorated. Altars made of marble were adorned with precious stones.

The same was true at the Milan charterhouse where, in 1629, Daniele Crespi painted scenes from the life of Bruno on the walls and on the vault of this sumptuously restored church. At the Charterhouse of Xeres in Spain, the church was magnificently adorned with a sculpted and gilded retable, as well as with paintings by Zurbaran. In 1667 a new façade was superimposed on the original and ornamented with columns and niches containing statues of the saints of the Order.

At the charterhouse in Grenoble, the sacristy was completely decorated between 1727–1764, in the most beautiful 'churrigueresque' style, named after its main representative, José Churriguera. These churches are the exception. The great majority of charterhouses always remained faithful to the spirit of poverty and simplicity of the Order's early fathers.

13

CONCLUSIONS

DESPITE REVOLUTIONS, BLOODY, insidious persecutions and expulsions, monasticism lives on and monks continue to build monasteries.

As if to excuse himself for having gone into some detail on the monastic life, Sainte-Beuve—who was a free-thinker and liked to affirm this by inviting friends to his Good Friday banquets where meat was served—warns his readers at the beginning of his book, *Port-Royal*, that they must 'accept as one of the first conditions of this book that it is the history of a monastery.' And, he adds, 'There will hardly be any more monasteries; very few of them will be re-established.' This was written in 1840 by one of the most educated men in Europe. He could not have been a worse prophet. He reveals his total ignorance of the tide of monastic restoration then in full flood.

To mention only the Cistercian Order—to which Port-Royal belonged—monks and nuns returned to France in 1815, and by 1840 had already revived eight monasteries for men and six for women, all within twenty-eight years.

Figure 13.1. Belfry of the cisterican abbey of Our
Lady of Gedono (Indonesia).

Not bad. In addition, in 1837, Dom Guéranger had gathered
a small group of monks at the old benedictine priory of
Solesmes and by 1837 was able to restore the Benedictine
Order in France. At the same time Lacordaire was setting
about the re-establishment of the Friars Preacher in France.
In the same year, 1840, he gave a very successful lenten
preaching series at Notre Dame, and put on once again the
white robes of a Dominican.

A century and a half have now passed and in that span of time, countless monastic foundations have given a striking denial of Sainte-Beuve's predictions in *Port-Royal*.

In 1990, the Benedictines had two hundred fifty-three monasteries of men divided into twenty-one congregations with a total of 9,096 religious, and three-hundred-fifty-one monasteries of women with 7,932 members and 10,979 sisters in thirty-four congregations.

The Cistercians of the Strict Observance in 1993 have ninety-two monasteries of men, seventeen of them in North America, with a total of 2,693 monks, and sixty-two monasteries of women, six of them in North America, with a total of 1,875 nuns. In the United States, the Cistercians of the Strict Observance have founded nine abbeys since 1944. These are located in the states of Georgia, Utah, Oregon, South Carolina, Virginia, Missouri, California, and Colorado. The nuns have five monasteries, one founded in Massachusetts in 1949, has daughter houses in Iowa, Arizona, and Virginia; and another was founded from Belgium in 1962, north of San Francisco.

The Cistercians of the Common Observance, divided into a number of congregations, have seventy-one monasteries of men with 1,315 monks, and sixty-two monasteries of women with 1,161 nuns. In the United States, they have three houses of monks and one of nuns.

The Carthusians number eighteen monasteries of monks and five of nuns. To secure greater seclusion, several houses have been relocated in recent decades. The house of monks formerly near Düsseldorf, Germany, for example, now occupies a site near Lake Constance. Two houses of carthusian nuns, one in France and the other in Italy, have been built with hermitages and gardens for all the sisters. For the first time in carthusian history, the nuns share the architecture which has always been characteristic of the monasteries of men. Portes, one of the early monasteries of the Order, has

Figure 13.2. Cloister walk at the cistercian Abbey
of New Clairvaux (Vina, California).

recently been reopened, and three new houses have been
established: a nuns' house in Spain, and two for monks
in the new world: one in Vermont, in the United States,
and another, more recently, in southern Brazil. Both are
flourishing and attracting vocations.

The Order of Hieronymites is being re-established in Spain
where three monasteries are already active, among them
is the famous monastery of Yuste. For about twenty years
or more, numerous foundations have been made by the

Benedictines and Cistercians all over the world, notably in Canada, the United States, Venezuela, Columbia, the Congo, Transvaal, Tanganyika, Morocco, Cameroon, Brazil, Argentina, India, Viet-Nam and Japan. A monk of Solesmes, Dom Paul Bellot, who died in 1944, was well known for his architectural talent. After directing the new buildings at his own abbey, he built such monasteries as: Quarr on the Isle of Wight, Oosterhout in Holland, and Saint Paul near Wisques. Often it is the monks themselves who not only draw up the plans for the buildings, but become masons, carpenters, roofers, joiners, and electricians so that the entire monastery is the work of their own hands.

Among the recent and most daring examples of monastic architecture is the church at the Benedictine Abbey of Collegeville in Minnesota, consecrated on 24 August 1961. The problem there was not easy to resolve. First of all, the community numbered nearly four hundred monks—in

Figure 13.3. The church of the benedictine Abbey of Saint John (Collegeville, Minnesota).

itself, a record. At the time they had to provide a choir for the monks who chanted the Office in Latin, and for the lay brothers who said it in English. They also had to provide ample space for the twelve hundred university students, some five hundred high school students, and about twelve hundred lay persons belonging to the local parish whose church it was as well. This arrangement was soon changed, in 1964, when all monks began chanting the office together, in English, in the upper church, which terminates in an amphitheater arrangement. The parish church and one of the students' choirs are now in the crypt. The altar is in the center, easily visible to everyone. In the crypt, on either side of the chapel, are two large passageways which open onto thirty-four small chapels for private Masses.

The façade of the church has an immense stained-glass window sectioned like cells in a honeycomb. In front of the façade, at a height of over a hundred feet, stands a unique concrete bell-portico. It rests on four feet that spread out at the base, forming four mini-vaults bearing an enormous concrete slab, ninety feet high, two feet thick. On the upper portion of this slab, a large vertical rectangle is cut out. From it, standing out in relief, is a large oak and concrete cross over eight yards high. The five bells from the old church were placed in a large horizontal opening in the slab, under the cross. This large bell-portico can seem astonishing at first sight. It reveals great attention to detail and accomplishes the task of bringing the church to everyone's attention.

Of about the same period is the dominican house of studies at Arbresle, near Éveux, entrusted to Le Corbusier. This architect's work—such as the chapel at Ronchamp and the radiant house in Marseille—is already so well known that it is quite unnecessary to elaborate on his theories or style. The challenge at Arbresle was to build a convent for over a hundred students and professors, along with a chapel, chapter house, library, classrooms, and over a hundred cells, not

Figure 13.4. Belfry of the dominican convent at
Arbresle by Le Corbusier.

to mention the refectory, the kitchen, and all the rest. Then,
too, the problem was to do this as economically as possible.
The construction took three years, from 1956–1959. Many
elements in this architectural composition surprise us: the
roof shaped as an off-center pyramid, walls leaning to the
exterior and interior, the openings strewn here and there
in no apparent order, the light shafts and sunbreakers. But
the building has been designed in such a way that all the

cells have doors leading onto an open-fronted loggia which replaces the cloister 'in the open air and deep silence', and all of it with a starkness and simplicity perfectly in accord with the Order's early rules.

In recent years, the monks of Saint Benoît-sur-Loire have been building their monastery in the shadow of the magnificent romanesque church. The monks at Landevennace in Brittany and those at Tournay, not far from Tarbes, have also made plans.

All this shows that monasticism has a great deal of life, and that while it keeps to its essential traditions, it is not afraid to modify certain nonessentials. There will always be monks and nuns, men and women who wish to leave the world to retire into solitude and give themselves completely to God, while calling down blessings on the world.

In conclusion, allow me to quote this beautiful passage from the great christian scholar, Pierre Termier, whom I had the honor of meeting in my youth. This page is found at the end of the chapter on the antiquity of man in his wonderful book, *La joie de connaître* (*The Joy of Knowing*). After discussing the Patriarchs who transmitted the Wisdom and Prophets from one generation to another from the fall of Adam to the election of the People of God, the author adds:

> As the earth makes billions of revolutions
> around the sun, many crimes are committed on
> its surface, many bestial clamors, many cries
> of pain and despair, many blasphemies rise
> from this planet to strange destinies, to
> frightening firmaments. But the sacred
> voice of the solitudes where a few good and
> simple men are praying, easily hides these
> clamors and blasphemies. And the smoke of
> a few sacrifices, the blue, slender thread
> rising in the calm morning air, exudes a
> perfume so powerful that it obliterates
> the odor of crime.

GLOSSARY OF MONASTIC ARCHITECTURE

by Carole Hutchinson

ABACUS	The top member of a capital.
ABUTMENT	A pier or wall of solid masonry erected to counter the thrust of an arch or vault.
AISLE	The lateral division of part of a church parallel to the main span and separated from it by an arcade of piers or columns, less frequently by a solid screen wall.
AMBULATORY	A semi-circular occasionally polygonal aisle or walkway which encircles an apse. Originally it was intended as a processional way.
APSE	The vaulted semi-circular or polygonal termination of the east end of a church beyond the sanctuary.
AQUEDUCT	An artificial channel, often an elevated masonry structure for

carrying water from its source to its destination.

ARCADE

A row of arches supported on columns or piers. They may be either free-standing or blind i.e., attached to a wall solely for decorative purposes.

ARCH

A curved structure of wedge-shaped blocks designed to span an opening and supported only at the sides. See: CORBELLED, DIAPHRAGM, HALF ARCH, HORSESHOE, LANCET, OGEE, POINTED ARCH, RELIEVING ARCH, ROUND, SEGMENTAL, SQUINCH, STILTED, TREFOIL.

ARCHITRAVE

1. The lowest of the three parts of an ENTABLATURE.

2. The molded frame surrounding a door or window.

ARMADIUM

A cupboard fashioned into the thickness of the wall of a sanctuary to the left of the altar and used for storing the sacred vessels and books. Also found in cloister galleries. Synonymous with AUMBRY.

ASHLAR

Large blocks of worked stone used for building.

AUMBRY

See ARMADIUM.

BALDACCHINO

A canopy over an altar, throne or tomb, either supported on columns or suspended from the ceiling.

BAROQUE

The style of architecture which flourished in the 17th and part of the 18th centuries. It is characterized by flamboyant decoration, huge curvaceous forms and a sense of mass and solidarity.

BARREL VAULT	A continuous vault either semi-circular or lightly pointed, also called a TUNNEL VAULT.
BAY	The structural division of a building emphasized by columns or piers and the vaulting.
BLIND ARCADE	An arcade attached to a wall purely for decorative purposes.
BOSS	A projecting ornament—usually circular—masking the intersection of a vault.
BUTTRESS	A masonry support positioned against the exterior of a wall to resist the outward thrust of an arch or vault. ANGLE BUTTRESS—two buttresses meeting at the corner of a building. CLASPING BUTTRESS—formed when a solid pier of masonry encloses a corner. DIAGONAL BUTTRESS—one placed at the corner of a building and equidistant from both walls. FLYING BUTTRESS—an arch or half arch springing from a detached pier and abutting a wall to counteract the thrust of the vault. SETBACK BUTTRESS—two buttresses set back from a corner of a building.
CAEN STONE	Oolitic, fine grained and very hard limestone originating from the area around Caen in Normandy and widely used in the building of romanesque abbeys.
CALDARIUM	The warming room in a monastery. Synonymous with CALEFACTORY.
CALEFACTORY	See CALDARIUM.
CAMBERED	Slightly arched.

CAPELLA AD PORTAS — Gate chapel. A special feature of cistercian abbeys where lay persons were strictly excluded from the monastic enclosure but permitted to worship in a chapel close by the main entrance.

CAPITAL — The head or crowning feature of a column or pilaster.

CAPITULUM — Latin term for a chapter of the *Rule of Saint Benedict* and hence for the daily assembly of a monastic community in the CHAPTER HOUSE where a chapter of the Rule was read aloud.

CARRELS — Divisions of a room or cloister gallery into individual study areas with desks.

CELL — 1. A small monastic house legally dependent on its motherhouse.

2. The private room of a monk or nun.

3. A hermit's dwelling.

CELLAR — The part of a monastery used for storage purposes, usually the ground floor of the west range.

CELLARER — The monk responsible for the general provisioning of a monastery.

CHAMFERED — A bevelled or mitred angle without a molding.

CHANTRY CHAPEL — A small chapel within a cathedral or abbey church endowed for the celebration of masses for the soul of the donor.

CHANCEL — The eastern arm or sector of a church containing the high altar. Synonymous with sanctuary and presbytery.

CHAPTER HOUSE — The hall in the east cloister range

of a monastery, adjacent to the church where a daily assembly of the community took place. Sometimes called Chapter Room. See also CAPITULUM.

CHARNAL HOUSE	See OSSUARIUM.
CHEVET	The french term for the east termination of a church consisting of a semi-circular or polygonal apse and ambulatory with or without radiating chapels.
CHOIR	In the strict sense the screened area of the church between the nave and the sanctuary which contains the stalls reserved for the monks or clergy. In architecture the term is often used to denote the entire eastern arm of the church, including the sanctuary. In the latter case, the area containing the monks' stalls is distinguished from it by the term RITUAL CHOIR.
CHOIR SCREEN	A partition of wood or stone usually elaborately carved and decorated which separates the monks' choir from the nave. See also ROOD SCREEN and PULPITUM.
CINQUEFOIL	A five-leaved shape incorporated in a circle or arch.
CLASSICAL ORDERS	See CORINTHIAN, DORIC, and IONIC.
CLERESTORY	CLEARSTORY. Alternative spelling: CLERESTOREY. The upper section of the nave, choir and transepts containing a range or series of windows.
CLOACA	The main sewer outlet.
CLOISTER	A covered arcade around a courtyard

	connecting the church with the domestic buildings of the monastery.
CLOISTER VAULT	See DOMICAL VAULT.
COLONADE	A row of columns bearing an entablature or arches.
COLLAR BEAM	A horizontal beam tying a pair of rafters together above the level of the wall-top.
COLUMN	A vertical, cylindrical support, normally consisting of base, shaft and capital. In classical architecture it is part of an ORDER.
COMPOSITE	A Roman addition to the CLASSICAL ORDERS. The capital combines the volutes of the IONIC capital with the acanthus leaves of the CORINTHIAN. Often featured in 18th century neo-classical abbeys.
CONFESSIO	A chamber forming part of the crypt of a church either directly under or close to the foundations of the high altar and intended for the monastery's relic or relics.
CONVENTUALS	The domestic buildings of a monastery.
CORBEL	A stone bracket projecting from a wall in support of a roof, vault, parapet, shaft, or other feature. Usually they are decorated with carving.
CORBELLED ARCH	A false arch consisting of blocks of masonry each laid so as to overlap the one beneath until the gap is bridged by a single slab.
CORBELLED VAULT	Built on the same principle as a corbelled arch.
CORINTHIAN	The third of the CLASSICAL ORDERS. A high base, sometimes a pedestal,

slim, fluted column shaft with fillets, bell-shaped capital with acanthus leaf ornament.

CORNICE

1. In classical architecture the top projecting section of an ENTABLATURE.

2. Any projecting ornamental molding along the top of a building, wall, arch, etc.

COURSE

A continuous level range of masonry.

CROCKETS

In gothic architecture, ornaments, usually in the form of buds or curled leaves, placed at regular intervals on the sloping sides of spires, gables, canopies or pinnacles.

CRENELLATION

The appearance of real or decorative fortifications in the form of battlements and turrets often found in monastic gatehouses. They served a real defence purpose in the houses of the Knights Templars and other military orders.

CROSSING

The space at the intersection of the NAVE, SANCTUARY and TRANSEPTS in a cruciform church.

CRYPT

Cellar or vault beneath the floor of a church but not necessarily underground and usually containing graves or re-interred relics.

CUPOLA

A dome, especially a miniature dome with a lantern top.

CUSPS

1. In gothic arches or tracery, the projecting points between the lobes or foils.

2. A projecting point on the underside of an arch or window dividing it into foils or leaves.

DAY STAIR	The stairway mounting from the cloister to the dormitory.
DECORATED ARCHITECTURE	Style which appeared in the latter part of the thirteenth and lasted until the middle of the fourteenth century. It is characterized mainly by the OGEE, a double or S shaped curve which occurs mainly in arches and in the tracery of windows. As the name implies it also reveals a lavish decoration which covers surfaces and encrusts arches, gables, etc. Leaves are highly stylized.
DIAPHRAGM ARCH	A stone arch spanning the nave of a church with no roof vault.
DOMICAL VAULT	A dome rising directly on a circular or polygonal base. Also called a CLOISTER VAULT.
DONJON	A castle keep or inner stronghold of a castle equipped with living quarters. Characteristic of the PRECEPTORIES, that is, the houses of the Knights Templars and other military orders.
DORIC	The first and simplest of the CLASSICAL ORDERS. Doric columns have no base and their shafts, which are relatively short, are surmounted by a square abacus.
DORMER WINDOW	A small gabled window projecting from a sloping roof.
DORMITORY	Communal sleeping quarters of the monks. Synonymous with DORTER.
DORTER	See DORMITORY.
DRUM	The circular or polygonal wall supporting a dome.

EARLY ENGLISH
ARCHITECTURE

Term applied to the style of GOTHIC which characterizes English buildings for most of the thirteenth century. Towards the close of this century it began to give way to the DECORATED style.

EARLY GOTHIC

See GOTHIC.

ENGAGED SHAFT
or COLUMN

A shaft or column partially set in to a pier or wall.

ENTABLATURE

The upper part of a CLASSICAL ORDER between columns and pediment consisting of architrave, frieze and cornice.

EQUILATERAL ARCH

See POINTED ARCH.

EUCHARISTIC OVEN

Usually located in the sacristy and used for the baking of communion wafers; they are a rare feature of monastic remains.

FAÇADE

The exterior of a building; a term usually reserved for one of its principal sides generally containing an entrance.

FAN VAULT

A form of rib vault in which the bay division and vaulting compartments are ignored and the ribs radiate from wall shafts in a fan-like pattern.

FARMERY

See INFIRMARY.

FERETORY

A shrine for relics designed to be carried in processions.

FILLET

1. A narrow band between moldings.

2. A narrow, flat, raised band running down a shaft between the flutes in a column.

3. The uppermost part of a CORNICE.

FLUTING

Shallow, concave grooves running

	vertically on the SHAFT of a COLUMN, or PILASTER, separated by FILLETS.
FRATER	See REFECTORY.
FRIEZE	1. The middle division of an ENTABLATURE between the ARCHITRAVE and the CORNICE normally decorated but may be plain.
	2. The decorated band running along the upper part of a wall immediately below the CORNICE.
GABLE	The triangular, upper section of a wall at the end of a pitched roof.
GALILEE	A french term synonymous with NARTHEX; this refers to the porch or vestibule at the west end of an abbey church. So called because the abbot led feastday processions into church through this entrance and was said to represent Christ leading his disciples into Galilee.
GARTH	The open central space enclosed by the cloister galleries.
GATEHOUSE	The building at the main entrance to a monastery.
GOTHIC ARCHITECTURE	General term used to describe the style which flourished in western Europe from the twelfth to the sixteenth century. It developed in three distinct stages: EARLY (thirteenth century) DECORATED (fourteenth century) buildings became more ornate and tracery more naturalistic. PERPENDICULAR (fifteenth century) the full flowering of what the French term, FLAMBOYANT.

GRANGE — Originally a barn. The term came to designate monastic farms at a distance from the monastery. These included a chapel and living quarters for the accommodation of lay brothers working there.

GROIN VAULT — Formed by the intersection of two barrel vaults at right angles, the compartments thus formed meeting at a groin.

HALF ARCH — As its name implies, an arch from the springing line to the apex only. Also called a QUADRANT.

HOODMOULD — A dripstone to protect the head of a door or window from the elements.

HORSESHOE ARCH — Shaped like a round or pointed horseshoe.

IMPOST — The projecting member on which an arch rests.

INFIRMARY — The part of the monastery which housed the sick and infirm. It was usually sited to the east of the main complex and provided with its own chapel and dormitory. Synonymous with FARMERY.

JAMB — The side of a door or window frame.

KAISERSAAL — Literally an 'imperial hall' it formed a feature of the baroque abbeys of Germany and Austria.

LANCET WINDOW — A narrow, lance-like, window terminating in a sharp point, its span is shorter than its radii. Characteristic of the EARLY GOTHIC period.

LANTERN TOWER — A small, windowed tower or turret crowning a CUPOLA or DOME.

LAVABO	A fountain supplied with running water where the monks washed before entering the refectory for meals. Synonymous with LAVATORIUM, LAVATORY and LAVER.
LAVATORIUM	See LAVABO.
LAVATORY	See LAVABO.
LAVER	See LAVABO.
LIERNE RIBS	Short, subsidiary vaulting ribs serving a purely decorative function and characteristic of the later DECORATED and PERPENDICULAR periods.
LIERNE VAULT	A vault in which LIERNES (tertiary ribs) which do not spring from wall supports are added to link the main ribs and tiercerons (secondary ribs).
LIGHTS	The glazed areas between the uprights of a window.
LOGGIA	A gallery open on one or more sides sometimes columned.
LOOPHOLE WINDOW	A small, narrow, often unglazed window.
LUNETTE	A semi-circular window or solid panel in a dome, arch, or vault.
MACHICOLATION	A projecting parapet on a castle wall with holes in the floor through which missiles could be dropped on attackers. Associated with the establishments of the Knights Templars and other military orders.
MARTYRIUM	A building erected on the site of a martyrdom or, in a church, containing the tomb or relics of a martyr.
MENSA	1. Latin for 'table', the term used for

that part of the monastic lands farmed for the direct benefit of the monastery and supplying its table.

2. The surface of an altar.

MISERICORD

1. A bracket on the underside of a hinged wooden seat in a choir stall which afforded the monks support during long periods of standing.

2. A small dining room, often located in the infirmary building where special food, including meat, was served.

MOLDINGS

The varieties of contour given to piers, arches, etc.

MULLION

A stone bar dividing a window vertically.

NARTHEX

A covered porch or vestibule stretching across the west end of a church. See also GALILEE.

NAVE

The whole area of a church west of the crossing; more specifically the central space bounded by aisles.

NEWEL STAIRS

Spiral stairs.

NIGHT STAIRS

The stairway leading from the dormitory down into a transept which allowed the monks direct access to the church for the celebration of the night office.

NORMAN ARCHITECTURE

The english term for the ROMANESQUE, circa 1050–1200. It is not particularly associated with Normandy except in having been introduced into England by William the Conqueror in 1066.

OCULUS

A round window or opening.

OGEE	A curve of two arcs, one convex, the other concave; an arch consisting of two such curves.
OGIVE	The french term for a pointed arch.
ORDERS	Designs of columns and their entablatures. The Greeks developed the DORIC, IONIC and CORINTHIAN ORDERS to which the Romans added TUSCAN and COMPOSITE. In the classical revival of the eighteenth century there was strict adherence to greek and roman originals.
ORIEL	A bay window supported on corbels.
OSSUARIUM	A repository for bones. In monasteries where burial grounds were limited and graves had to be reused, bones from earlier burials were stacked in a building designed for the purpose. Synonymous with CHARNEL HOUSE and OSSUARY.
PARAPET	A low wall, sometimes battlemented, placed as a protection where there is a sudden drop.
PARCLOSE	A screen enclosing a chapel or shrine and separating it from the main area of the church to afford privacy to worshippers.
PARLOUR	A room in which conversation was permitted.
PAVILION	A projecting sub-division of a building usually forming a central feature of a main façade.
PEDIMENT	A triangular gable above an entablature in classical architecture. A similar feature over any window or door.

PENDENTIVES	Inverted triangular, concave segments upon which a circular dome is supported above a square or polygonal compartment.
PENTICE	A passage or corridor running along the side of a building, its single pitch (pent) roof being carried on corbels set into the wall of the building. Alternative spelling: PENTISE.
PENTROOF	Or PENTICE ROOF: the sloping roof of a pentice or lean-to building.
PIER	A solid masonry support as distinct from a column. Piers can be simple— round, square or rectangular—or compound, composite, multiform, i.e., of a more complex profile achieved by applying moldings, engaged shafts, etc.
PILASTER	A rectangular column projecting from a wall and used merely for decorative purposes, but conforming to the ORDERS.
PILLAR	A detached, upright support which deviates in slope and proportion from the ORDERS.
PINNACLE	A small turret-like termination crowning spires, buttresses, the angles of parapets, etc.; usually pyramidal or conical in shape.
PISCINA	A stone basin with a drain, intended for washing the sacred vessels. It is normally set into a niche on the righthand side of an altar; more rarely it is mounted on a pedestal.
PERPENDICULAR ARCHITECTURE	Originally popularized in London in the 1330s, the style was a

reversal of the DECORATED style and is characterized by a stress on straight, vertical and horizontal lines, by slender, vertically subdivided supports and large windows.

PLINTH Projecting masonry at the base of a wall or pillar.

POINTED ARCH An arch with two curves meeting at an acute angle. Also called EQUILATERAL not to be confused with LANCET.

PORTICO A colonnaded entrance to a building.

PRECEPTORY A house of the Knights Templars.

PRESBYTERY The area of a major church east of the monks' choir. There the high altar is situated and the priests (presbyters) celebrate the Eucharist. Synonymous with SANCTUARY.

PULPITUM The solid screen that closed off the monks' choir from the remainder of the nave, usually one bay east of the ROOD SCREEN.

PURLIN A horizontal timber beam supporting the rafters.

QUADRANT ARCH See HALF ARCH.

QUADRIPARTITE Divided into four sections. A QUADRIPARTITE VAULT is divided by transverse, diagonal and wall ribs into four compartments of equal size.

QUATREFOIL Four lobed or leafed design.

QUOINS Large, dressed corner stones forming the external angles of buildings.

RABBET A channel or groove usually made to receive a door or frame.

RAIL A horizontal member in a timber framework.

RANGES	The monastic buildings which are grouped—ranged—around a cloister.
REFECTORY	The dining hall of the monks. Synonymous with FRATER.
RELIEVING ARCH	An arch built into the wall above a true arch to relieve it of some of its load.
RELIQUARY	A richly ornamented container to hold the relic(s) of a saint.
REREDORTER	The building containing the latrines, so called because it is normally situated at the rear or far end of the dormitory (dorter).
REREDOS	A decorated screen or hanging behind an altar.
RESPOND	A half column where an arch or line of arches joins a wall.
RETABLE	A raised shelf or ledge above and behind the altar, used for candles, flowers etc.
RETROCHOIR	The part of a church which lies east of the sanctuary behind the high altar, often the location of a shrine.
RIB	A projecting band either structural or decorative, separating the cells of a vault.
RIBBED VAULT	A development of the GROIN VAULT in which groins are replaced by arched ribs constructed across the sides and diagonals of the vaulted bay to form a support for the infill of stones. This can be quadripartite, sexpartite, or have any number of compartments.
RITUAL CHOIR	See CHOIR.
ROCOCO	Not a style in its own right but the

final phase of the BAROQUE when lightness and color began to supercede the weightiness and solidity of earlier buildings. The new decoration was asymmetrical and curvaceous with shell-like coral forms.

ROMANESQUE ARCHITECTURE

The style prevalent in western Europe until the advent of Gothic. Some experts place its origins in the seventh century, others in the tenth at the time of the rising of the Order of Cluny in France. It is characterized by the round arches. See also NORMAN ARCHITECTURE.

ROOD

A large crucifix displayed over a high altar or screen.

ROOD SCREEN

A screen placed originally one bay west of the pulpitum and usually of wood; so called because it was normally surmounted by a rood (crucifix).

ROSE WINDOW

A circular window with mullions radiating like the spokes of a wheel.

ROUND ARCH

The simplest type of arch, composed of a semi-circle of voussoirs and characteristic of ROMANESQUE architecture.

SACRISTY

A room attached to the church where the sacred vessels and vestments are kept.

SANCTUARY

The part of a church containing the high altar. Synonymous with PRESBYTERY and CHANCEL.

SCRIPTORIUM

The room where writing was done and manuscripts copied.

SEDILIA

Seats, usually three, in the sanctuary

for the officiating clergy, usually a celebrant, a deacon and a sub-deacon.

SEGMENTAL ARCH
A segment of a circle drawn from a centre below the springing line. See SPRINGER.

SEGMENTAL VAULT
A vault whose section is a segmental arch.

SEXPARTITE VAULT
A quadripartite vault into which an additional transverse rib has been introduced, thus dividing it into six unequal compartments instead of four.

SHAFT
1. The trunk of a column between the base and the capital.

2. In medieval architecture one of several slender columns clustered against or around a pillar, pier door jamb, or window surround.

SLYPE
A narrow passageway through a cloister range.

SOFFIT
The underside of an arch or lintel.

SPANDREL
The triangular surface or space between two arches or between an arch and a wall.

SPRINGER
The lowest stone of an arch or vaulting rib.

SQUINCH ARCH
An arch constructed diagonally across the interior angle of a rectangular or square space. A series of squinches convert the square or rectangle into a circle or octagon.

STELLAR VAULT
A vault with ribs, secondary ribs (TIERCERONS) and tertiary ribs (LIERNES) arranged so as to form a star-shaped pattern.

STILE	A vertical member in a timber framework.
STILTED ARCH	An arch that springs from a point above its imposts so that the sides seem vertical at the base.
STRING COURSE	A molding or narrow projecting COURSE running horizontally along the face of a wall.
TIERCERON RIBS	Pairs of ribs which spring from the same point as the principal ribs but which meet at oblique angles instead of being carried from one side of the vault to the other in a continuous line.
TRACERY	The intersecting, ornamental ribwork holding the glass in gothic windows. Also found in walls, screens and vaults. PLATE TRACERY, the earliest and simplest type consists of openings pierced through solid stone. BAR TRACERY (tracery proper) uses stone ribs arranged in complicated patterns. CURVILINEAR TRACERY as its name implies involves sinuous lines and curves. FLAMBOYANT TRACERY, literally flame shaped stone work.
TRANSEPT	The transverse part of a cruciform church set at right angles to the main axis.
TRANSEPTS	Alternative way of expressing TRANSEPT as the two arms of a cross-shaped church. It is thus possible to be more specific and refer to a night stair or chapel located in the north or south transept.
TRANSOM	A stone bar dividing a window horizontally.

TRANSVERSE	A term applied to vaulting ribs or arches set at right angles to the axis of the building.
TREFOIL	A three-lobed or leaved ornament in a circle or arch.
TRILOBE ARCH	An arch divided by two cusps into three lobes or leaf shapes.
TRUSS	Roof timbers framed together to bridge a space.
TUNNEL VAULT	See BARREL VAULT.
TYMPANUM	The triangular area between the lintel of a doorway and the arch above it; often they are beautifully carved.
UNDERCROFT	A chamber, usually vaulted, supporting a principal chamber above.
VAULT	An arched stone ceiling. See: BARREL, TUNNEL, CORBEL, GROIN, DOMICAL, FAN, LIERNE, QUADRIPARTITE, RIB, SEGMENTAL, STELLAR.
VOLUTES	A spiral or scroll-like conformation atop an IONIC column.
VOUSSOIRS	The wedge-shaped stones used for forming an arch.
WAGON ROOF	A curved, wooden rafter roof resembling the covering of a wagon.
WAINSCOT	Timber panelling on walls.
WALL-PLATE	A timber laid lengthwise on a wall top to receive the rafters.
WATER-HOLDING BASE	A base of a column pier, etc. with a hollow molding.
WATER-LEAF DESIGN	A leaf shape used in twelfth century capitals. The water-leaf is very simple, broad, and unribbed and curves

outward towards the angle of the abacus where it turns inward.

WATTLE and DAUB   A method of wall construction consisting of branches or laths (wattles) fixed between the vertical beams of timber-framed buildings and plastered over with clay (daub).

CISTERCIAN PUBLICATIONS, INC.

TITLES LISTING

—CISTERCIAN TEXTS—

BERNARD OF CLAIRVAUX

Apologia to Abbot William
Bernard of Clairvaux, Letters of
Five Books on Consideration: Advice to a Pope
Homilies in Praise of the Blessed Virgin Mary
Life and Death of Saint Malachy the Irishman
Love without Measure: Extracts from the
    Writings of St Bernard (Paul Dimier)
On Grace and Free Choice
On Loving God (Analysis by Emero Stiegman)
Parables and Sentences (Michael Casey)
Sermons for the Summer Season
Sermons on Conversion
Sermons on the Song of Songs I-IV
The Steps of Humility and Pride

WILLIAM OF SAINT THIERRY

The Enigma of Faith
Exposition on the Epistle to the Romans
Exposition on the Song of Songs
The Golden Epistle
The Mirror of Faith
The Nature and Dignity of Love
On Contemplating God: Prayer & Meditations

AELRED OF RIEVAULX

Dialogue on the Soul
Liturgical Sermons, I
Mirror of Charity
Spiritual Friendship
Treatises I: On Jesus at the Age of Twelve,
    Rule for a Recluse, The Pastoral Prayer
Walter Daniel: The Life of Aelred of Rievaulx

JOHN OF FORD

Sermons on the Final Verses of the
    Songs of Songs I-VII

GILBERT OF HOYLAND

Sermons on the Songs of Songs I-III
Treatises, Sermons and Epistles

OTHER EARLY CISTERCIAN WRITERS

Adam of Perseigne, Letters of
Alan of Lille: The Art of Preaching
Amadeus of Lausanne: Homilies in Praise of
    Blessed Mary
Baldwin of Ford: Spiritual Tractates I-II
Gertrud the Great: Spiritual Exercises
Gertrud the Great: The Herald of God's
    Loving-Kindness
Guerric of Igny: Liturgical Sermons I-[II]
Helinand of Froidmont: Verses on Death

Idung of Prüfening: Cistercians and Cluniacs:
    The Case for Cîteaux
Isaac of Stella: Sermons on the Christian Year,
    I-[II]
The Life of Beatrice of Nazareth
Serlo of Wilton & Serlo of Savigny: Seven
    Unpublished Works
Stephen of Lexington: Letters from Ireland
Stephen of Sawley: Treatises

—MONASTIC TEXTS—

EASTERN CHRISTIAN TRADITION

Besa: The Life of Shenoute
Cyril of Scythopolis: Lives of the Monks of
    Palestine
Dorotheos of Gaza: Discourses and Sayings
Evagrius Ponticus: Praktikos and Chapters on
    Prayer
Handmaids of the Lord: Lives of Holy Women
    in Late Antiquity & Early Middle Ages
    (Joan Petersen)
Harlots of the Desert (Benedicta Ward)
John Moschos: The Spiritual Meadow
Lives of the Desert Fathers
Lives of Simeon Stylites (Robert Doran)
Luminous Eye (Sebastian Brock)
Mena of Nikiou: Isaac of Alexandria & St
    Macrobius
Pachomian Koinonia I-III (Armand Veilleux)
Paphnutius: Histories/Monks of Upper Egypt
Sayings of the Desert Fathers
    (Benedicta Ward)
Spiritual Direction in the Early Christian East
    (Irénée Hausherr)
Spiritually Beneficial Tales of Paul, Bishop of
    Monembasia (John Wortley)
Symeon the New Theologian: The Theological
    and Practical Treatises & The Three
    Theological Discourses (Paul McGuckin)
Theodoret of Cyrrhus: A History of the
    Monks of Syria
The Syriac Fathers on Prayer and the Spiritual
    Life (Sebastian Brock)

WESTERN CHRISTIAN TRADITION

Anselm of Canterbury: Letters I-III
    (Walter Fröhlich)
Bede: Commentary...Acts of the Apostles
Bede: Commentary...Seven Catholic Epistles
Bede: Homilies on the Gospels III
The Celtic Monk (U. Ó Maidín)
Gregory the Great: Forty Gospel Homilies
Life of the Jura Fathers
Maxims of Stephen of Muret

CISTERCIAN PUBLICATIONS, INC.

TITLES LISTING

Meditations of Guigo I, Prior of the
Charterhouse (A. Gordon Mursall)
Peter of Celle: Selected Works
Letters of Rancé I–II
Rule of the Master
Rule of Saint Augustine
Wound of Love: A Carthusian Miscellany

CHRISTIAN SPIRITUALITY

Cloud of Witnesses: The Development of
Christian Doctrine (David N. Bell)
Call of Wild Geese (Matthew Kelty)
Cistercian Way (André Louf)
The Contemplative Path
Drinking From the Hidden Fountain
(Thomas Špidlík)
Eros and Allegory: Medieval Exegesis of the
Song of Songs (Denys Turner)
Fathers Talking (Aelred Squire)
Friendship and Community (Brian McGuire)
From Cloister to Classroom
Life of St Mary Magdalene and of Her Sister
St Martha (David Mycoff)
Many Mansions (David N. Bell)
Mercy in Weakness (André Louf)
Name of Jesus (Irénée Hausherr)
No Moment Too Small (Norvene Vest)
Penthos: The Doctrine of Compunction in the
Christian East (Irénée Hausherr)
Rancé and the Trappist Legacy
(A.J. Krailsheimer)
Russian Mystics (Sergius Bolshakoff)
Sermons in a Monastery (Matthew Kelty)
Silent Herald of Unity: The Life of
Maria Gabrielle Sagheddu (Martha
Driscoll)
Spirituality of the Christian East
(Thomas Špidlík)
Spirituality of the Medieval West
(André Vauchez)
Tuning In To Grace (André Louf)
Wholly Animals: A Book of Beastly Tales
(David N. Bell)

—MONASTIC STUDIES—

Community and Abbot in the Rule of
St Benedict I–II (Adalbert de Vogüé)
Finances of the Cistercian Order in the
Fourteenth Century (Peter King)
Fountains Abbey and Its Benefactors
(Joan Wardrop)
The Hermit Monks of Grandmont
(Carole A. Hutchison)
In the Unity of the Holy Spirit
(Sighard Kleiner)
Joy of Learning & the Love of God:
Essays in Honor of Jean Leclercq
Monastic Odyssey (Marie Kervingant)

Monastic Practices (Charles Cummings)
Occupation of Celtic Sites in Ireland
(Geraldine Carville)
Reading St Benedict (Adalbert de Vogüé)
Rule of St Benedict: A Doctrinal and Spiritual
Commentary (Adalbert de Vogüé)
Rule of St Benedict (Br. Pinocchio)
St Hugh of Lincoln (David H. Farmer)
Stones Laid Before the Lord (Anselme Dimier)
Venerable Bede (Benedicta Ward)
What Nuns Read (David N. Bell)
With Greater Liberty: A Short History of
Christian Monasticism & Religious
Orders (Karl Frank)

—CISTERCIAN STUDIES—

Aelred of Rievaulx: A Study (Aelred Squire)
Athirst for God: Spiritual Desire in Bernard of
Clairvaux's Sermons on the Song of
Songs (Michael Casey)
Beatrice of Nazareth in Her Context
(Roger De Ganck)
Bernard of Clairvaux: Man, Monk, Mystic
(Michael Casey) [tapes and readings]
Bernardus Magister (Nonacentenary)
Catalogue of Manuscripts in the Obrecht
Collection of the Institute of Cistercian
Studies (Anna Kirkwood)
Christ the Way: The Christology of Guerric of
Igny (John Morson)
Cistercian Abbeys of Britain
Cistercians in Denmark (Brian McGuire)
Cistercians in Medieval Art (James France)
Cistercians in Scandinavia (James France)
A Difficult Saint (Brian McGuire)
Dore Abbey (Shoesmith & Richardson)
A Gathering of Friends: Learning & Spirituality
in John of Forde (Costello and
Holdsworth)
Image and Likeness: The Augustinian
Spirituality of William of St Thierry
(David Bell)
Index of Authors & Works in Cistercian
Libraries in Great Britain I (David Bell)
Index of Cistercian Authors and Works in
Medieval Library Catalogues in Great
Britian (David Bell)
Mystical Theology of St Bernard
(Étienne Gilson)
The New Monastery: Texts & Studies on the
Earliest Cistercians
Nicolas Cotheret's Annals of Cîteaux
(Louis J. Lekai)
Pater Bernhardus (Franz Posset)
A Second Look at Saint Bernard
(Jean Leclercq)
The Spiritual Teachings of St Bernard of
Clairvaux (John R. Sommerfeldt)

CISTERCIAN PUBLICATIONS, INC.
TITLES LISTING

Studies in Medieval Cistercian History (various)
Studiosorum Speculum (Louis J. Lekai)
Three Founders of Cîteaux
  (Jean-Baptiste Van Damme)
Towards Unification with God (Beatrice of
  Nazareth in Her Context, 2)
William, Abbot of St Thierry
Women and St Bernard of Clairvaux
  (Jean Leclercq)

MEDIEVAL RELIGIOUS
—WOMEN—

Lillian Thomas Shank and John A. Nichols, editors
Distant Echoes
Hidden Springs: Cistercian Monastic Women
  (2 volumes)
Peace Weavers

—CARTHUSIAN—
TRADITION

Call of Silent Love (A Carthusian)
Freedom of Obedience (A Carthusian)
Guigo II: The Ladder of Monks & Twelve
  Meditations (Colledge & Walsh)
Interior Prayer (A Carthusian)
Meditations of Guigo II (A. Gordon Mursall)
Prayer of Love and Silence (A Carthusian)
Way of Silent Love (A Carthusian Miscellany)
Wound of Love (A Carthusian Miscellany)
They Speak by Silences (A Carthusian)
Where Silence is Praise (A Carthusian)

-STUDIES IN CISTERCIAN-
ART & ARCHITECTURE

Meredith Parsons Lillich, editor
Volumes II–V are now available

—THOMAS MERTON—

Climate of Monastic Prayer (T. Merton)
Legacy of Thomas Merton (P. Hart)
Message of Thomas Merton (P. Hart)
Monastic Journey of Thomas Merton (P. Hart)
Thomas Merton/Monk (P. Hart)
Thomas Merton on St Bernard
Toward an Integrated Humanity
  (M. Basil Pennington, ed.)

CISTERCIAN LITURGICAL
—DOCUMENTS SERIES—

Chrysogonus Waddell, ocso, editor
Hymn Collection of the...Paraclete
Institutiones nostrae: The Paraclete Statutes
Molesme Summer-Season Breviary (4 volumes)
Old French Ordinary & Breviary of the Abbey
  of the Paraclete (2 volumes)

Twelfth-century Cistercian Hymnal
  (2 volumes)
The Twelfth-century Cistercian Psalter
Two Early Cistercian *Libelli Missarum*

-STUDIA PATRISTICA XVIII-

Volumes 1, 2 and 3

❖ ❖ ❖ ❖ ❖ ❖ ❖ ❖ ❖ ❖ ❖ ❖

Editorial queries & advance book
information should be directed to the
Editorial Offices:

Cistercian Publications
1201 Oliver Street
Western Michigan University
Kalamazoo, Michigan 49008
Tel: (616) 387-8920 • Fax: (616) 387-8921

• • •

Customers may order
these books through booksellers
or directly by contacting the warehouse
at the address below:

Cistercian Publications
Saint Joseph's Abbey
167 North Spencer Road
Spencer, Massachusetts 01562-1233
Tel: (508) 885-8730 • Fax: (508) 885-4687
email: cistpub@spencerabbey.org

• • •

Canadian Orders:
Novalis
49 Front Street East, Second Floor
Toronto, Ontario M5E 1B3
Telephone: 416-363-3303 1-800-387-7164
Fax: 416-363-9409

• • •

British & European Orders:
Cistercian Publications
Mount Saint Bernard Abbey
Coalville, Leicester LE67 5UL
Fax: [44] (1530) 81.46.08

• • •

*Cistercian Publications is a non-profit
corporation. Its publishing program is
restricted to monastic texts in translation
and books on the monastic tradition.*

*A complete catalogue of texts in
translation and studies on early,
medieval, and modern monasticism is
available, free of charge, by contacting
any of the addresses above.*